Iceland Wharf
Old Ford Station
Old Ford Goods & Coal Station
Bow Goods Sta.
Wharf
Towing Path
B.Ss
Crown Works
Saw Mills
Timber Yard
OLD FORD ROAD
COOKS ROAD
BOW BACK RIVER
Bow Bridge
Lime Works
Wharf
Tramway Depot
WREXHAM ROAD
RIDGDALE STREET
BALDOCK
GROVE HALL PARK
Convent
BOW AND BROMLEY
DIVISION
MALMESBURY ROAD
TREDEGAR ROAD
MORVILLE STREET
MORVILLE ST.
FAIRFIELD ROAD
LACEY ST.
MOSTYN GROVE
APPIAN ROAD
LEFEVRE ROAD
PARNELL ROAD
USHER ROAD
ARMAGH ROAD
LIBRA ROAD
SUTHERLAND ROAD
SAXON ROAD
VERNON ROAD
CARDIGAN ROAD
Bow Rd. Sta.
Bow Station
BOW ROAD
Tredegar House
LANDSEER RD.
BENWORTH ST.
HARLEY GROVE
COBORN STREET
HIGH STREET
Grave Yard
Ch.
Foundry
Wharf
PRIORY ST.
FRANKLIN ST.
WASHINGTON ST.
JEFFERSON ST.
ARROW ROAD
BRUCE ROAD
GRACE STREET
DEVONS ROAD
Starch Factory
R.A. Inst.
Bromley Station
ST. LEONARD'S STREET
NORRIS RD.
REEVES ROAD
TIBBATT'S ROAD
DONALD ST.
BEVAS STREET
LINGEN ST.
MARNER STREET
EMPSON ST.
COLIN ST.
CAMPBELL ROAD
ROUNTON ROAD
FAIRFOOT ROAD
CHILTERN ROAD
WELLINGTON ROAD
ARCHIBALD ST.
QUICKETT STREET
IRETON ST.
BRITISH STREET
MERCHANT STREET
BROKESLEY STREET
SOUTHERN GROVE
CEMETERY RD.
Hospital
Mortnary Chapel
(Nonoo formist)
TOWER HAMLETS CEMETERY
Mortnary Chapel
(Ch. of Eng.)
Schs.

I0812302

NIGEL HENDERSON'S

STREETS

PHOTOGRAPHS OF LONDON'S EAST END 1949–53

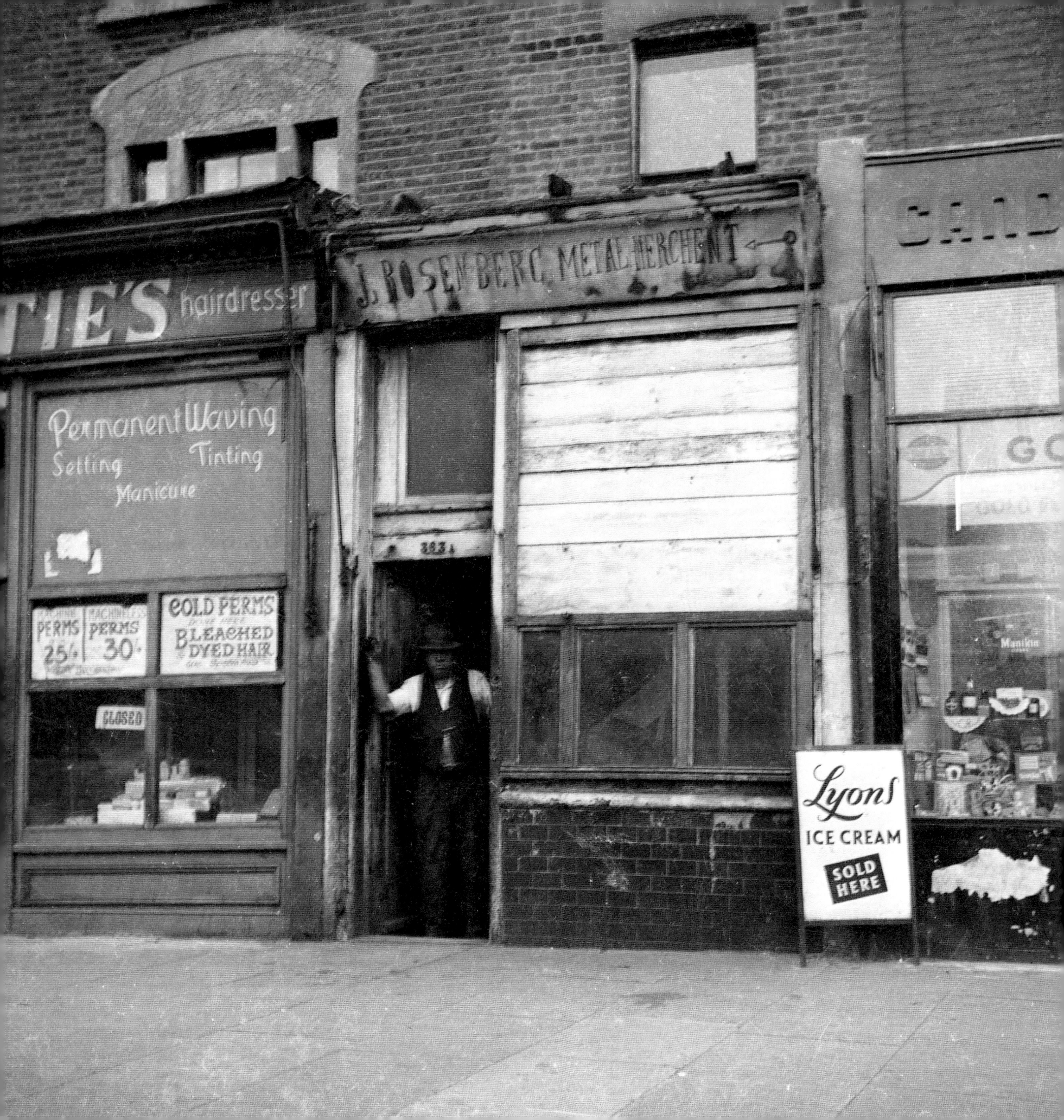
TIE'S hairdresser
J. ROSENBERG METAL MERCHENT
Permanent Waving
Setting Tinting
Manicure
MACHINE PERMS 25/-
MACHINELESS PERMS 30/-
COLD PERMS
DONE HERE
BLEACHED & DYED HAIR
CLOSED
363
Lyons
ICE CREAM
SOLD HERE

NIGEL HENDERSON'S

STREETS

PHOTOGRAPHS OF LONDON'S EAST END 1949–53

EDITED BY CLIVE COWARD

TATE PUBLISHING

First published 2017 by order of the Tate Trustees
by Tate Publishing, a division of Tate Enterprises Ltd,
Millbank, London SW1P 4RG
www.tate.org.uk/publishing

© Tate Enterprises Ltd 2017
Images © Nigel Henderson Estate / Tate Archive, unless otherwise stated

All rights reserved. No part of this book may be reprinted or reproduced or utilised in any form or by any electronic, mechanical or other means, now known or hereafter invented, including photocopying and recording, or in any information storage or retrieval system, without permission in writing from the publishers or a licence from the Copyright Licensing Agency Ltd, www.cla.co.uk

A catalogue record for this book is available from the British Library

ISBN 978 1 84976 499 5

Distributed in the United States and Canada by ABRAMS, New York
Library of Congress Control Number: applied for

Designed by Peter Dawson, gradedesign.com
Colour reproduction by DL Imaging, London
Printed and bound by Graphicom SRL, Italy

FRONT COVER Boys playing on the street
BACK COVER (from top) Texture study of a wall; people walking past shops; chimney sweep, Zeland Road, Bow E3
ENDPAPERS Ordnance Survey map 1951. London Metropolitan Archives, City of London
FRONTISPIECE J. Rosenberg, metal merchant, 363 Commercial Road, Stepney E1
PAGE 6 Boy, possibly Jimmie Deachey, on Chisenhale Road, Bow E3 1951
PAGE 8 Woman in a wheelchair

Measurements of artworks are given in centimetres, height before width. Nigel Henderson's images have been scanned from 5.5-cm square negatives, unless otherwise stated.

MIX
Paper from responsible sources
FSC® C013123

CONTENTS

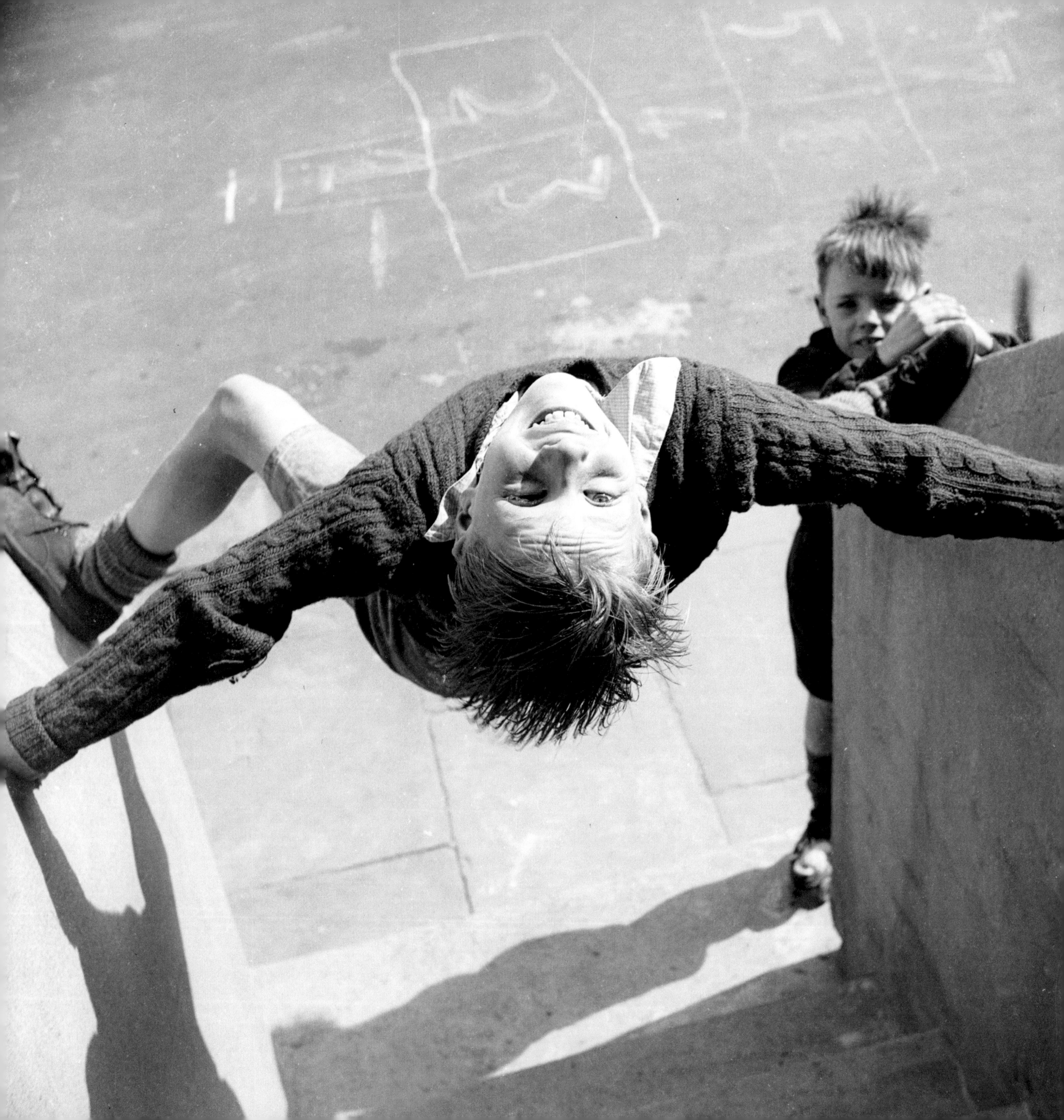

LONDON, cathedral of black bones where iron is masticated: where meek nags mouth winter oats by granite drinking troughs: where bright flags twitter against the river, leaden and thick like the cells of a disused battery.

Where the chaff of light flays Goods Yards and School Yard, and where disjointed voices leap black walls, perky as small advancing fires, fresh as new Union Jacks.

Where green smells punctuate the nostrils like acid drops the mouth, and the indifferent, gesticulatory, cur squirts his tart pizzle on scrubbed steps.

Where the air sighs with displacement as cyclist lunges past with fugitive resonance of rusty bell.

Where the bracketed barge conspires to pass, sliding between blinkered houses.

Where streets glint, grudgingly, like shabby coins and, much pummelled, the body's putty sags.

Where the unsticking of day from night is marked by the archaic rooster's yearning, the spasm of his weird Kazoo.

Where, on misty allotments beneath sheltering trees, the clustered brassicas receive these silver bells – those gas corroded droplets.

'MEMORIES OF LONDON 1949' (FOR EDUARDO PAOLOZZI)

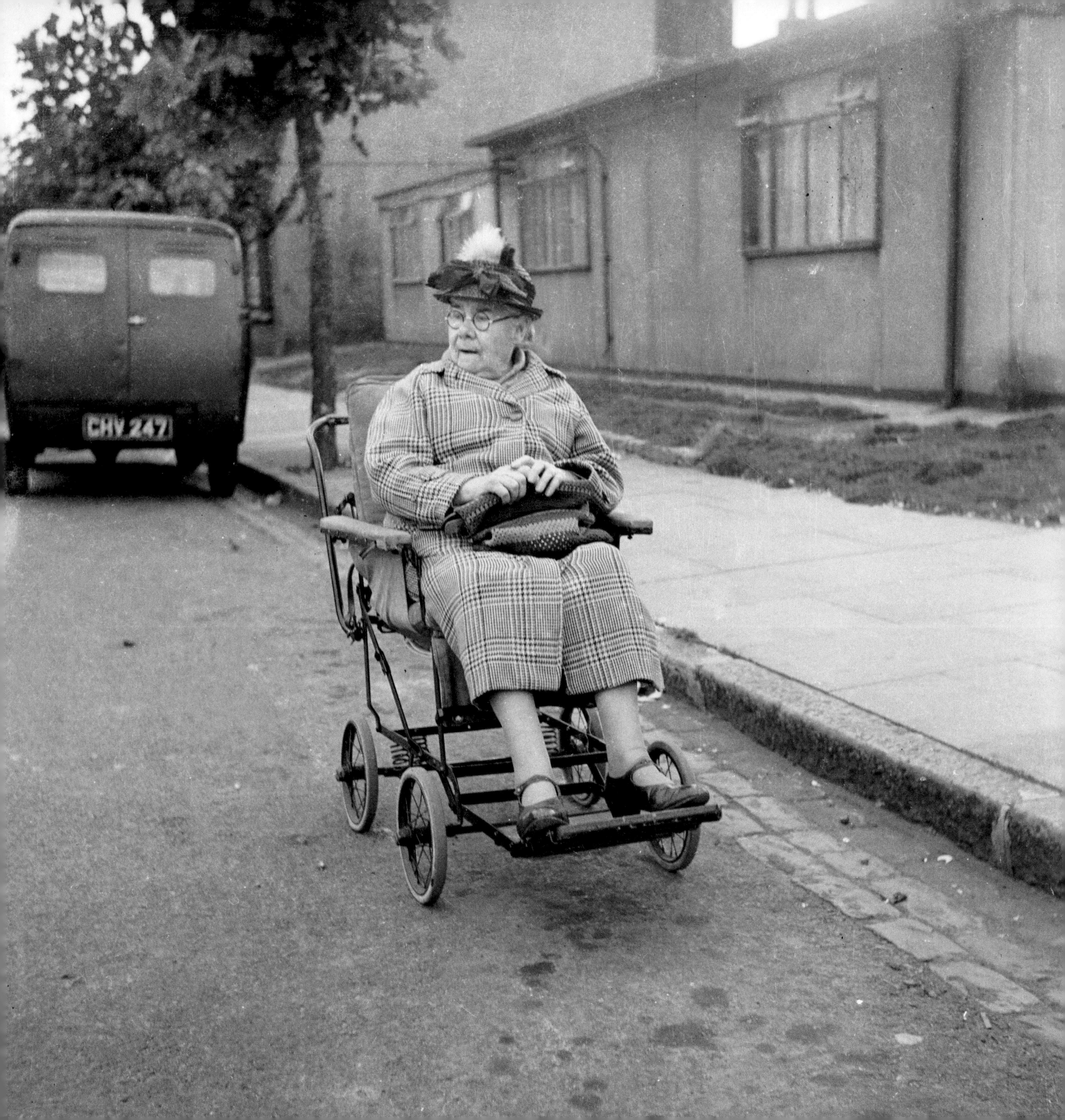
CHV 247

A NOTE FROM THE EDITOR

Nigel Henderson started to take photographs in 1947 when he borrowed a Leica camera from Mr Humphrey Swingler to document the Slade School of Art. His mother-in-law offered to buy him a camera so he bought his own, purchasing a Rolleicord II (2¼ inch-plate) camera and a 5 x 4 plate camera. It was the Rolleicord that Henderson used to document the East End, producing small square negatives from which the photographs in this book have been reproduced.

Very few of the photographs in this book were published during Henderson's lifetime. Photos of children playing on Chisenhale Road appeared first in a publication by Alison and Peter Smithson to accompany their presentation at CIAM (the Congrès Internationaux d'Architecture Moderne) in 1953. It wasn't until 1978 however, and the Midland Group exhibition *Nigel Henderson Photographs of Bethnal Green 1949–1952* that more would be published.

Henderson did produce prints from these negatives, the first being 'stressed images' in 1949 of boys playing on bicycles, ranging in size from 8¼ x 17¾ inches to 15¾ x 19¾ inches. Later on he would sell more conventional 8 x 10 inch prints of the East End during solo exhibitions, such as those at Anthony d'Offay Gallery in 1977, and at Serpentine Gallery in 1983.

Titling his photographs was not a priority for Henderson. The individual negatives are not captioned, and while some of the contact sheets have headings such as 'Railings', 'Children', 'Markets', 'Wall: textures', not all of the images relate to the label or category provided. Photographic prints were given titles, some being quite generic, for instance *Street Games 1949–52*, *Shop 1949–52* and *Street 1949–52*, while others were allocated specific titles identifiable to certain negatives: *Phil's 1952*, *Bag-Wash* and *Wall, McCullum Road.* In keeping with Henderson's practice, we have kept captioning in this book to a minimum.

The captions included have come from either the Midland Group exhibition catalogue, where photographs were captioned and published during Henderson's lifetime (these appear in *italics*) or, where locations are identifiable, additional information has been sourced from Kelley's Post Office Directories of London from the 1950s. All of the images in this book date from between 1949 and 1953 and are therefore not identified as such in the captions. Where a more specific date is known, it has been provided.

Quotes from Henderson are peppered throughout the book and provide further insight into his thoughts, practice and environment. Information relating to the sources of these quotes can be found on page 113.

Nigel Henderson's collection was generously presented to Tate Archive in two parts – firstly in 1992 by Henderson's second wife, Janet and the Henderson family, and the remainder in 2010 by Jo, Ned and Stephen Henderson and the Henderson families.

An Archives & Access project, made possible through a £1.9 million grant from the Heritage Lottery Fund, provided Tate with the opportunity to digitise all 3,000 negatives in the Henderson collection (roughly 2000 of which are of the East End) and make them available online at www.tate.org.uk. A selection of prints from the publication are available from the Tate shop.

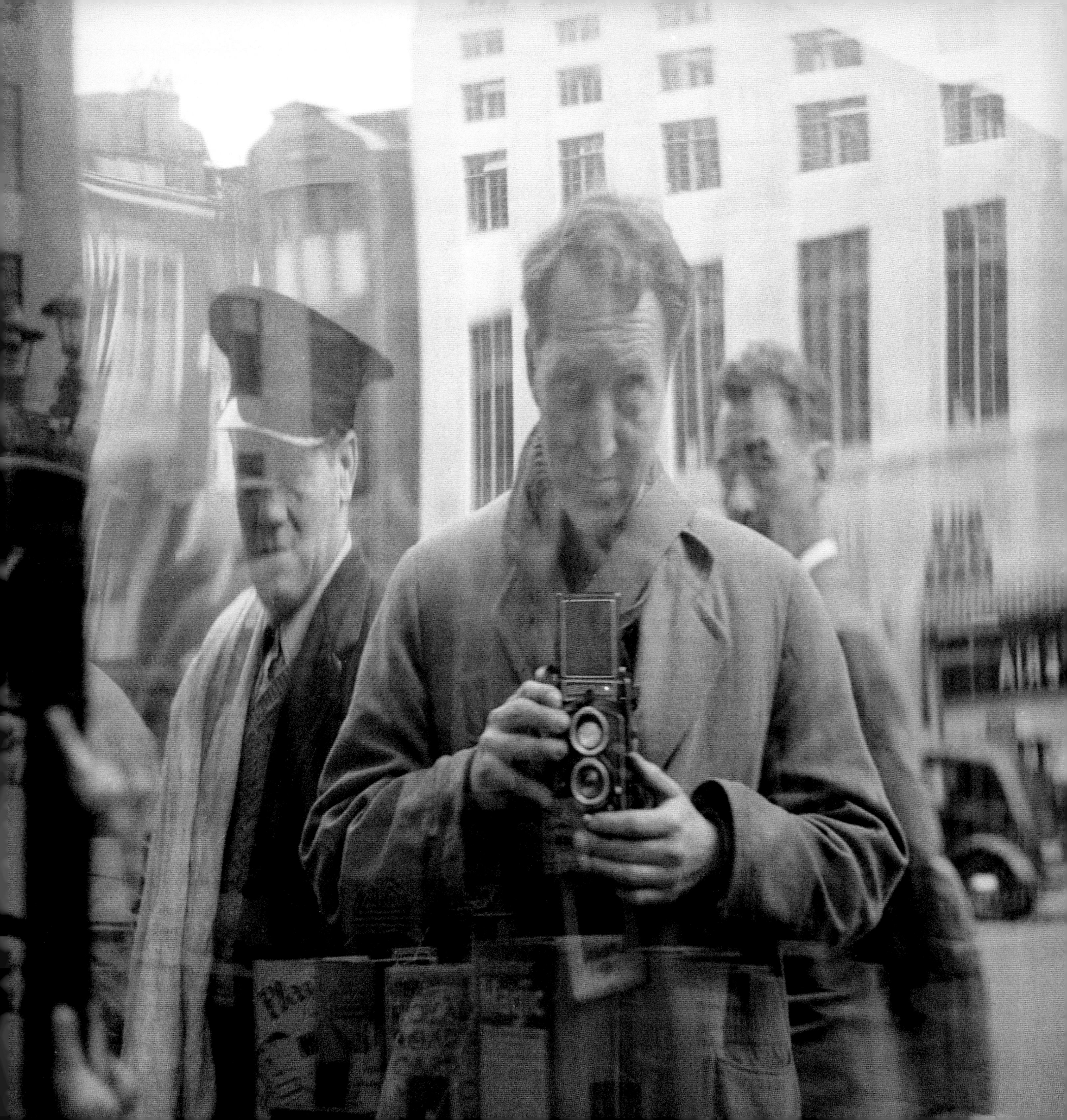

INTRODUCTION

'... for walking around – always taking streets unfamiliar to me had become a soothing experience for a restless and anxious mind.'

OPPOSITE Nigel Henderson reflected in a window c.1950. Black and white negative, 5.5 x 5.5. Tate

In 1954, Nigel Henderson (1917–85) held his first solo exhibition at the Institute of Contemporary Arts in London. Entitled *Photo-Images*, the exhibition was a result of his time in London's East End and his new working interest in photography. From the moment Henderson purchased a camera in 1947 to the time of the exhibition he had been experimenting – not only by taking numerous images of the East End streets, but also with the printing process, utilising his photographic enlarger to produce photograms (photographs made without a camera in the darkroom by directly exposing objects onto photosensitive paper) or 'Hendograms', as he would call them. He began by making photograms of different materials and textures – from glass bottle fragments to textiles – and then by slanting, pleating or crumpling the paper under the enlarger. *Photo-Images* showcased these images – stressed or stretched prints of bathers on a beach, and boys playing on bicycles on the street where Henderson and his family lived (p.12). It is the later images, those showing the streets of the East End of London that are illustrated here. These images capture the essence of working-class life in the post-war East End, but they are also a visual record of Henderson's artistic eye and working practices.

By the time of *Photo-Images*, Henderson had been a central figure of the Independent Group – the godfathers of British pop art – which included his friends Eduardo Paolozzi (1924–2005) and Richard Hamilton (1922–2011), the architects of New Brutalism, Alison and Peter Smithson (1928–93 and 1923–2003), and the historians and critics Peter Reyner Banham (1922–88) and Lawrence Alloway (1926–90). For the Independent Group, the 'image' was key – 'multi-evocative' and 'non-hierarchical' – reflective of a visual plenitude encompassing what Alloway later termed 'The Long Front of Culture'[1]: 'high' and 'low' – fine art and mass culture mixed together and offered for reading and critique rather than detached aesthetic judgement.

Henderson's photographs inhabit this world – a post-war landscape of austerity but also a world where a deference for the old order was starting to be dismantled. We begin with the texture of the street – details of brick, mortar, cobblestone and tar – before pulling back to see the layers of life and association that played out in the varied environment of post-war London in the years between 1949 and 1953. The textures are scarred and pock-marked, blistered and scratched, and they speak not of decay but of the vulnerabilities of life and the sense of time passing and moving on. Layering, shifts from blurred to focused, work together to create a web of connections within each image, made up of a play of different kinds of surface – both material and photographic. Above all, however, these images have the directness born of the connection between Henderson and his subject.

Henderson had been steeped in a culture of engaged, inquiring looking. His mother Wyn Henderson had been an associate of the writer, heiress and political activist, Nancy Cunard, managing her private press The Hour's Press in France, and of the art collector Peggy

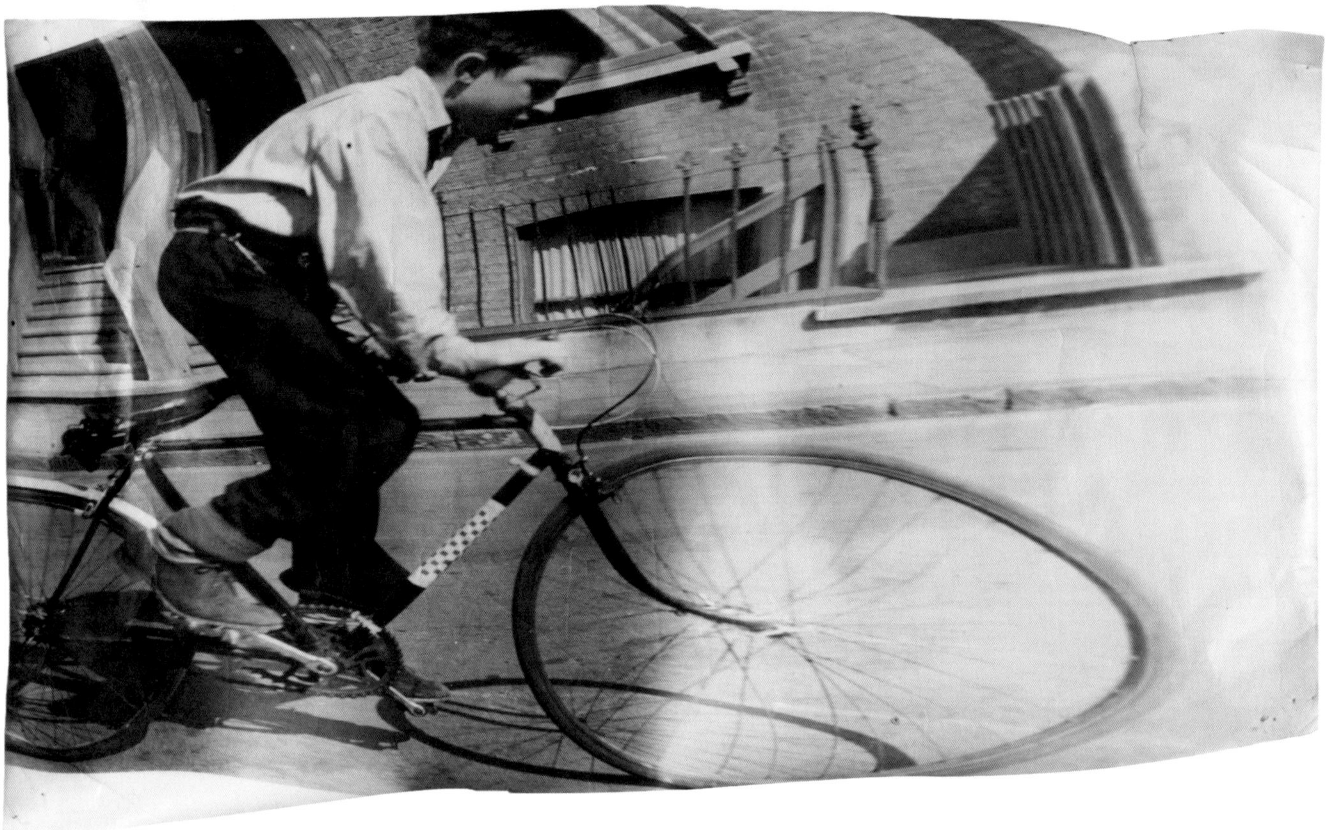

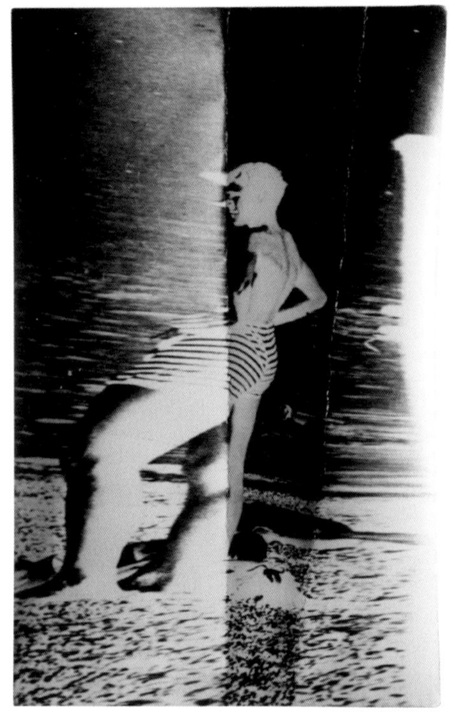

Guggenheim for whom, from 1938, she managed the gallery Guggenheim Jeune in London. The world that Nigel Henderson grew into was that of the surrealist and bohemian non-conformist. As well as frequenting the company of the Bloomsbury Group who his mother had met while living in Gordon Square, he counted Max Ernst (1891–1976) and Marcel Duchamp (1887–1968) as family friends. While helping to install the opening exhibition at Guggenheim Jeune in 1938, Duchamp had encouraged Henderson in his dream of flying, to look from above, as much as continuing his interest in science (Henderson had briefly studied biology at Chelsea Polytechnic). These interests opened up his eyes to the world in markedly different ways – the all-encompassing view from above contrasting with the microscope homing in on essential detail. He had an easy familiarity with the biologist, unpeeling the layers of a dissection or discovering new structures under the microscope; their talismanic power revolved around recognition of the image as an entity and also of its associative qualities. The poetries of the chance encounter that could be found in the street beloved of the surrealists determined the nature of Henderson's photographs. Wandering the streets of London, photographing what his eye was drawn to was itself also a form of collage in motion. We might concentrate on a single image, but to really see the images is to draw the connections between them.

The photographs illustrated here cover not just the immediate surroundings of Henderson's home in Bethnal Green where he lived between 1945 and 1954 with his wife Judith Stephen and two daughters in a house on Chisenhale Road, but also streetscapes of the neighbouring boroughs of Poplar, Hackney, Bow and Stepney. Henderson and Stephen (daughter of Adrian Stephen, brother of Vanessa Bell and Virginia Woolf) had married in 1943 and moved to London's East End in 1945 as a result of Stephen's anthropological work on a course entitled 'Discover your Neighbour'. Run by the sociologist J.L. Peterson in Bethnal Green, it was intended to gather information on the behavioural habits of the local community that would be useful to professionals such as doctors, priests and probation officers, without which understanding it was felt they would not be able to do their work adequately. At the same time, Henderson, discharged from wartime service as a pilot in Coastal Command because of mental fatigue, enrolled for four years at

ABOVE LEFT Nigel Henderson *Stressed Photograph c.*1950. Black and white photographic print 30.5 x 50.7. Tate. Purchased 2007

ABOVE RIGHT Nigel Henderson *Stressed Photograph of a Bather c.*1950. Black and white photographic print 13.8 x 7.7. Tate. Purchased 2007

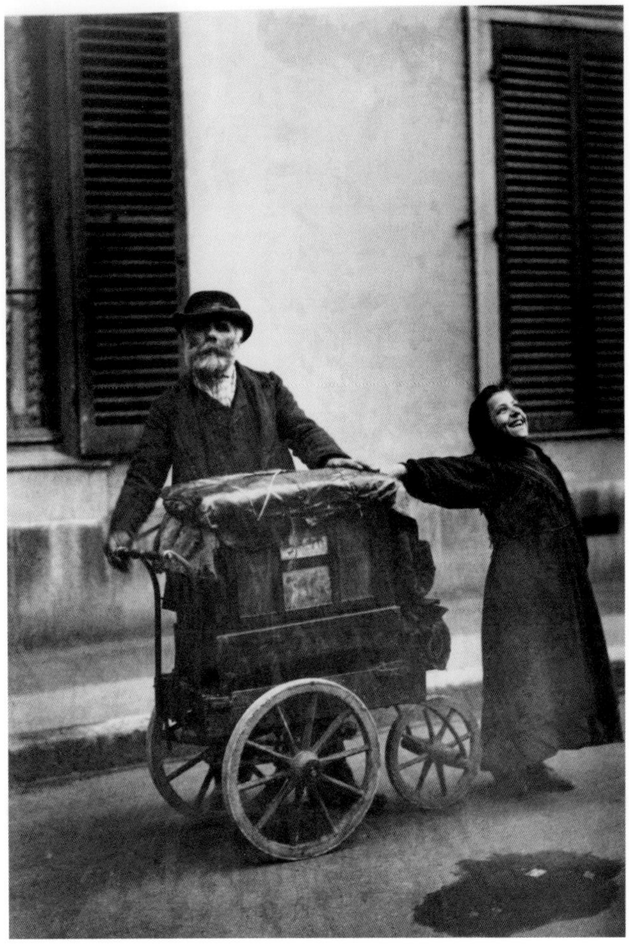

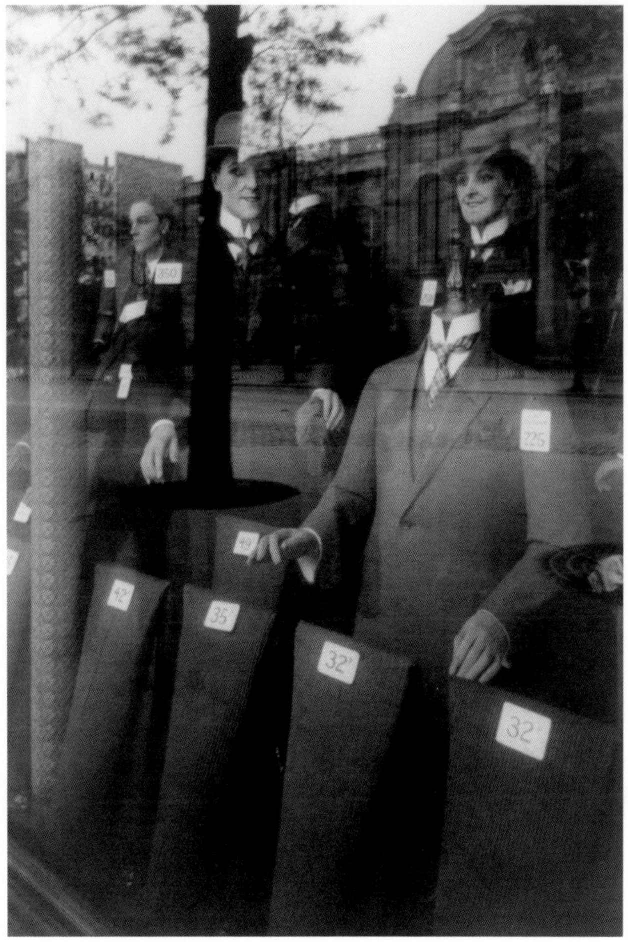

ABOVE LEFT Eugène Atget 1857–1927, *Street Musicians*, taken between 1898 and 1927, printed in 1956. Gelatin silver photographic print. Library of Congress Prints and Photographs Division, Washington D.C., USA

ABOVE RIGHT Eugène Atget 1857–1927, *Men's Fashions*, taken between 1898 and 1927, printed in 1956. Black and white photographic print. Library of Congress Prints and Photographs Division, Washington D.C., USA

the Slade School of Art and started experimenting with photography. Although the purpose of Judith Stephen's work provided a very particular opportunity for Henderson's photographs it would be wrong to overemphasise such a link. Henderson himself recorded very little about the subjects of these photographs – not the place, not the time, nor even identifying many of the people he pictured. For him, these are first and foremost 'images' and he alighted on them with the eye of the collagist.

At the Slade, Henderson painted hardly at all, drew a lot – for which he recognized he had little facility – and with his new friend Eduardo Paolozzi tended to attend lectures and seminars in other disciplines within the University of London, rather than at the Slade. The rest of the time he walked endlessly around Bethnal Green, looking. He later recalled how 'I confined my activity in Bethnal Green to wandering about looking at things… I borrowed a camera and took a few shots… it occurred to me to take the Leica around with me on my compulsive walks about the East End; for walking around – always taking streets unfamiliar to me had become a soothing experience for a restless and anxious mind.'[2]

On a visit to London in 1951 Henderson guided Henri Cartier-Bresson (1908–2004) around the streets of Bethnal Green and the following year Cartier-Bresson's collection *The Decisive Moment* was published. The original French title of the book, *Images à la sauvette*, can be loosely translated as 'images on the run' or 'stolen images', and typifies a key theme of much street photography of the time. However, though this term can be applied to some of Henderson's work (see for example p.38), his photographs are not in any way 'stolen' or taken 'on the run' in the way that the title of Cartier-Bresson's book suggests, nor are they the record of a single moment. While Henderson's photographs may appear similar to Cartier-Bresson's, and to those of Walker Evans (1903–1975) and Eugène Atget (1857–1927) (see above), any similarities are surface deep.

Photographs of scarred, rusted, wounded surfaces (for example those on pp.24, 27, 29 bottom right) are suggestive of an equivalence with the troubled surfaces of paintings by Jean Dubuffet (1901–1985) or Jean Fautrier (1898–1964) (p.14) that evoke what the French art critic Michel Tapié (1909–1987) identified as *Un Art Autre* – an 'other' art – or what

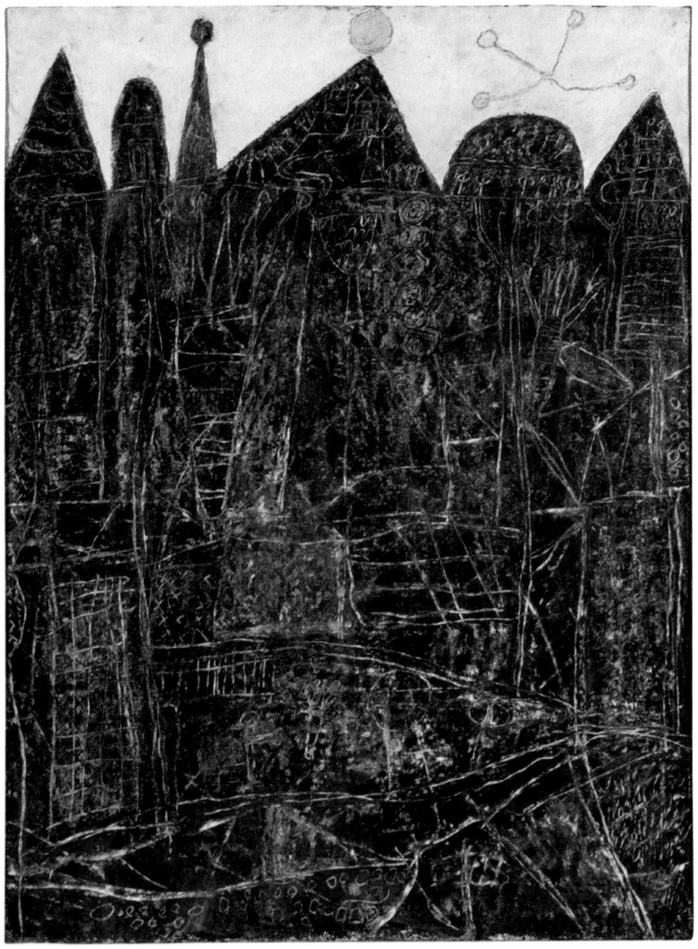

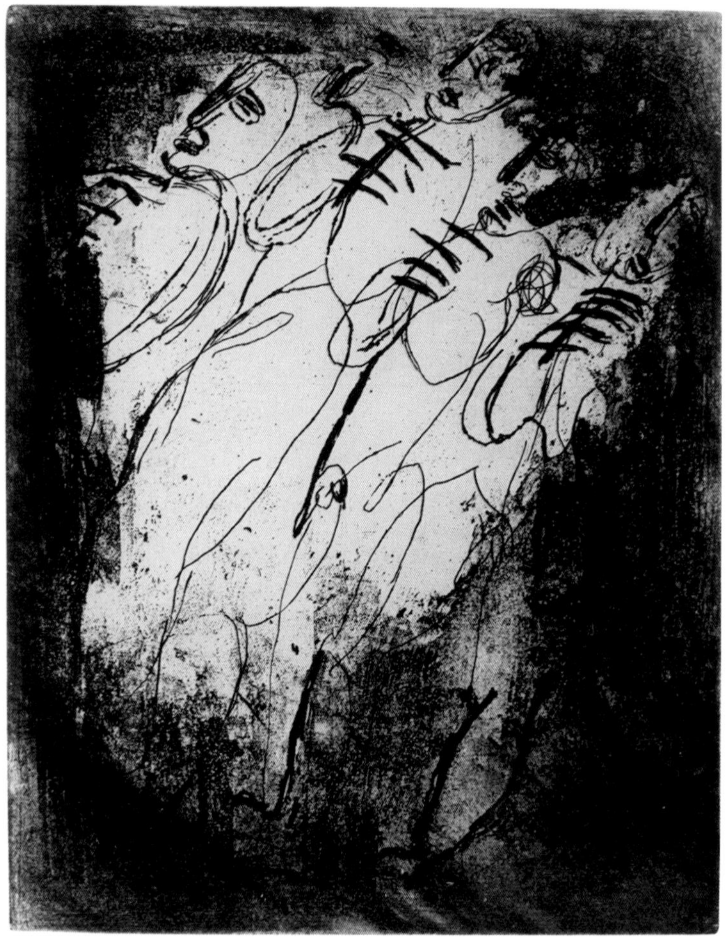

Dubuffet understood as an *Art Brut*, a brutalism that revelled in an authentic directness of approach. More specifically, other photographs (such as those on p.28 top right and p.74) show how close Henderson was to both Dubuffet and Fautrier (see above), but also to Brassai (1899–1984) and especially his photographs of graffiti, which in cataloguing an aspect of the unconscious were lodestars for the surrealists in the 1930s (the key difference being that with Henderson we more often than not see the graffiti in context with the street and the people – mainly children – who made them). However, although tempting to categorise Henderson's photos as *Art Brut*, his 'photo-images' directly defined the 'New Brutalism', a term coined by the Smithsons and by Banham. The term identified a particular approach to architecture, but an architecture founded in an understanding of what Banham termed 'imageability' – the 'visually valuable'. Henderson's photographs defined what this might mean.

The same year that Henderson wandered around London's East End with Cartier-Bresson, he took a sequence of photographs of children playing in the street – playing hopscotch (within lines chalked on the road), skipping, noodling on bicycles (pp.78–80). Starting with the texture of the street, its constituent materials, we might then think of it – backed by houses and shops – as Henderson did, as a form of theatre and collage of community life. For the Smithsons – fellow tutors alongside Henderson, Paolozzi and Hamilton at the Central School – these photographs illustrated an active community. They demonstrated the bond between street, home and hearth, revealing the significance of these social structures in a way that enabled the Smithsons to rethink the relationship between architecture and the lived urban fabric. These photographs were an integral part of the Smithsons' manifesto-like presentation to CIAM (the Congrès Internationaux d'Architecture Moderne) in 1953 at Aix-en Provence, and were reproduced in the 1961 issue of *Uppercase* magazine devoted both to their and Henderson's work (p.15). For the Smithsons, the 'street is not only a means of access but also an arena for social expression ... (of joy, time passing, faith, play-teaching)',[3] and this was bound up with their revaluation of the identity of the individual – of the social networks and associations that Henderson's photographs of the street revealed and that many post-war developments were in danger of erasing.

ABOVE LEFT Jean Dubuffet 1901–1985, *Large Black Landscape* 1946. Oil paint on hardboard 155.1 x 118.6. Tate. Accepted by HM Government in lieu of tax and allocated to the Tate Gallery 1996

ABOVE RIGHT Jean Fautrier 1898–1964, *The Executed* c.1945, published c.1960–4. Photo-etching on paper 33.5 x 26.9. Tate. Purchased 1986

The reaction of the Smithsons both to Henderson's photographs of children playing in a Bethnal Green street and to the experience of accompanying him on walks around the East End, reveal much of what looking meant to Henderson. Peter Smithson later observed that 'a walk with Nigel is to see the inanimate as animate, and this weird business of opening … other people's eyes to see – to have an affection between objects and people.'[4] This lies at the heart of Nigel Henderson's photographs; he saw in his images a kind of grammatical structure that revealed a 'pattern of association': 'Word – Brick; Wall – Sentence; Room – Paragraph; House – Concept, and the totality of the relationship of house to houses and to environment'.[5] His photographs are framed by time and life – not the instant of Cartier-Bresson's snatched image. Henderson explained this by using the analogy of a boot. In thinking of a boot and the traces of its life as a layering of time, he wrote of a boot's 'layers arching under uneven strain like geological strata; their leather the rind of fruit, pithy, the cobbler's tacks eager to be out and off, like seed pips. A new boot is a fine monument to man – an artifact. A worn-out boot traces his images with a heroic pathos … Time works like an analytical chemist with its tinctures and titrations. It gives us intimations of the reality of things.'[6] The boot here becomes a key to a wider view of the world. His photographs of shop windows and stalls in street markets perform in a similar way, coalescing a range of layered signs, the experience of passages of time, in a single image (for example, see especially photographs on pp.30–1, 35, 53 and 67).

When he made the photographs of London streets, Henderson and the Independent Group were forming a new understanding of the image, which was characterised in terms of architecture by the formulation of a New Brutalism. The image was something that was 'visually valuable' for what it reveals about the 'thing itself, in its totality, and with all its overtones of human association.'[7] In defining New Brutalism, Banham was not only describing imageability – the telling image that exists outside of any traditional framework of aesthetic judgement – but also offering a meaning to Henderson's work. Banham describes the significance for New Brutalist architecture of a formal legibility, a clear expression of structure and a valuation of materials for their own sake. The architectural 'image' was a coherent, visually

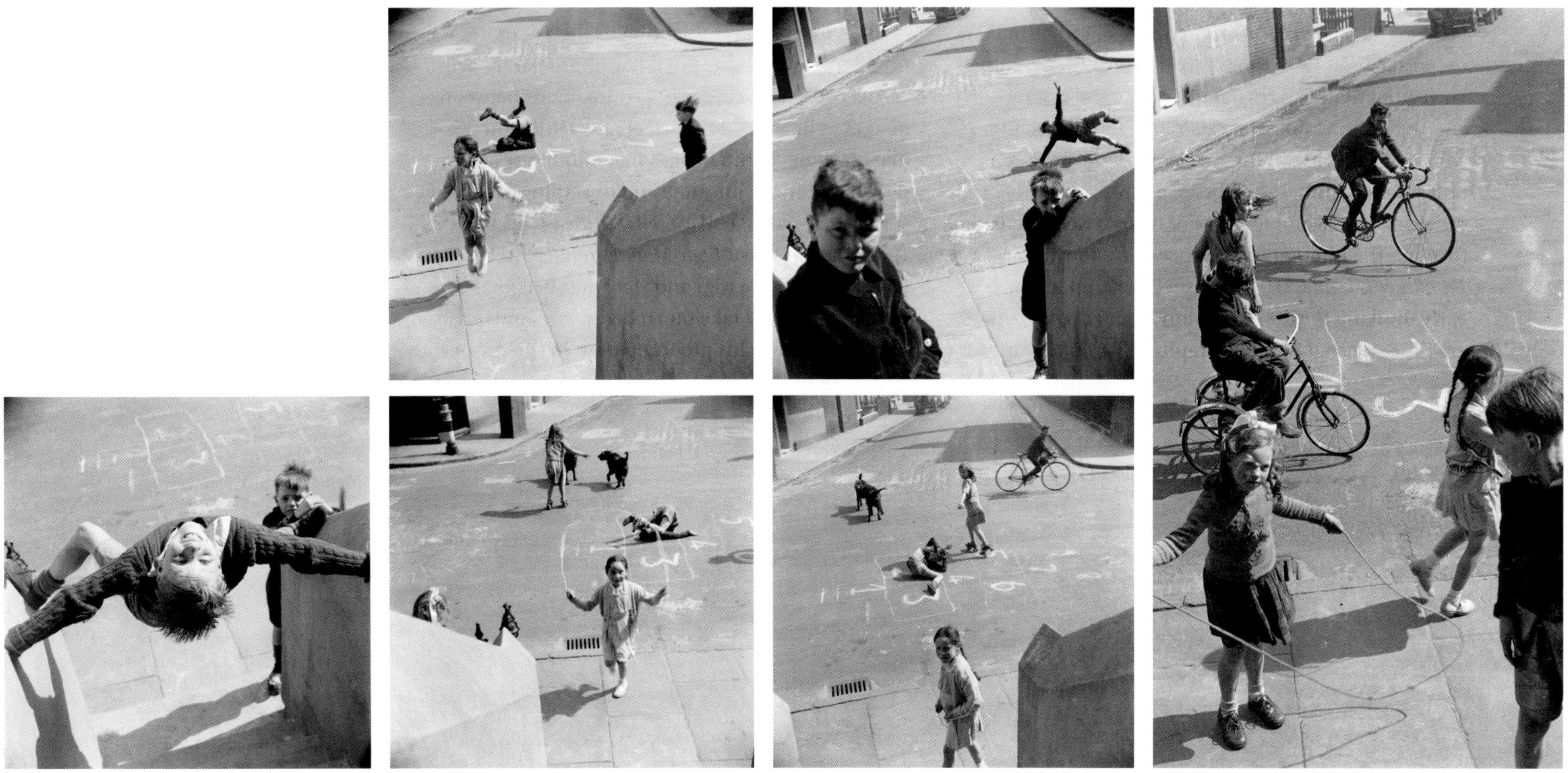

BELOW Henderson's images of children playing on Chisenhale Road, as reproduced in *Uppercase* magazine, 1961

understandable entity that was both memorable in its own terms, and also took part within a pattern of association, which was set beside the degree to which the street was such an important tool for the Smithsons' architecture. The street – as revealed in Henderson's images – announced the Smithsons' architecture of connectivity, of topology rather than geometry, where circulation, and the relationship between the inside and outside was given priority.

The Smithsons recognised how Henderson's images – that describe the existence of such relationships in the environment outside his home in Chisenhale Road – directly corresponded with the basis of their own ideas for a new kind of social architecture. These ideas were first publicly manifested in 1953 in the exhibition *Parallel of Life and Art* at the Institute of Contemporary Arts (see opposite). Conceived by Henderson, Paolozzi and the Smithsons, the exhibition placed photography at its heart. Devised as a kind of enlarged form of tack board in which different types of often re-scaled images jostled for attention, suggesting links between the images of very different kinds of subject, and suggesting that each image could be 'multi-evocative', it provided an object lesson in how to read images. The catalogue arranged this collage of photographs according to thematic categories – such as anatomy, architecture, art, calligraphy, landscape, movement, nature, scale of man, stress, etc – whereas the installation itself took the form of a fairly random environment of images hanging from the ceiling and the walls. Unlike the catalogue, the installation's collage denied hierarchy, and boundaries between different disciplines were broken down; all the different orders and textures of images were mediated through the photographic process. *Untitled (Study for Parallel of Life and Art)* 1952 (p.18) exemplifies the early thinking for the exhibition as a dialogue between art (here figured by photographs of Paolozzi's brutalist plaster and terracotta reliefs) and life (figured through an array of Henderson's photographs and photograms. Although the images produced by Henderson for the installation did not include his photographs of the East End – his experience of gathering his collage images of street life was necessary for his understanding of the workings of 'imageability'.

In notes for a lecture given alongside *Parallel of Life and Art*, Henderson makes this clear in his explanation of the origins of his use of the camera: 'having camera . started using on own environment. Wife sociologist . Bethnal Green – homogenous Streets People Signs Walls Faces ... exciting – a sense of reality began to develop ... I picked up courage & continued to respond to the obvious stimuli that were around me everywhere.'[8] Furthermore, in a prose poem that he sent to Paolozzi, Henderson described one aspect of his response to these stimuli: 'One shop front crowds another in that bizarre interplay of trade and sign that contributes to the complex texture of the city.'[9] Henderson's frieze-like photographs record the collage nature of such signs in a manner akin to photographers Walker Evans and Eugène Atget, yet the suggestion of such references to other photographers is misleading: although he was known in the art world, Henderson was isolated as a photographer, and despite acting as a catalyst for many artists younger than him in the 1950s, he was for a long time under the radar himself as an artist.

His collagist eye, drawing connections between images as he walked the street also settled on juxtaposition within images that emphasises a penchant for the uncanny and unsettling aspect of surrealism – such as *Wig Stall, Petticoat Lane* 1952 (p.62) and *Petticoat Lane Market* 1952 (p.60 bottom left), in which the wigs and stockings become disembodied and take on ambiguous characteristics. Allied to this was his preoccupation in the properties

RIGHT Nigel Henderson, installation view of *Parallel of Life and Art* exhibition at the Institute of Contemporary Arts, London 1953. Black and white photographic print 22.5 x 20. Tate

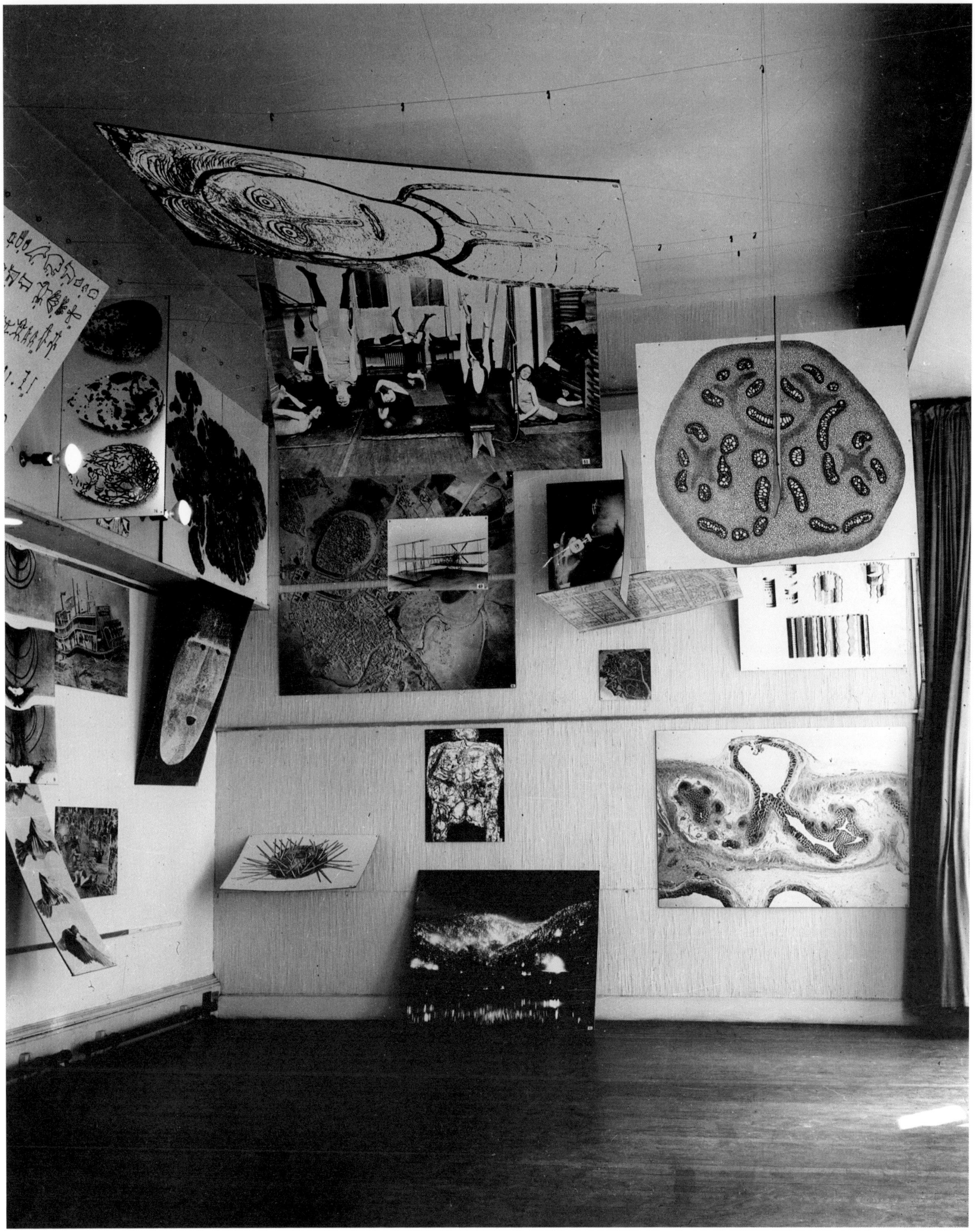

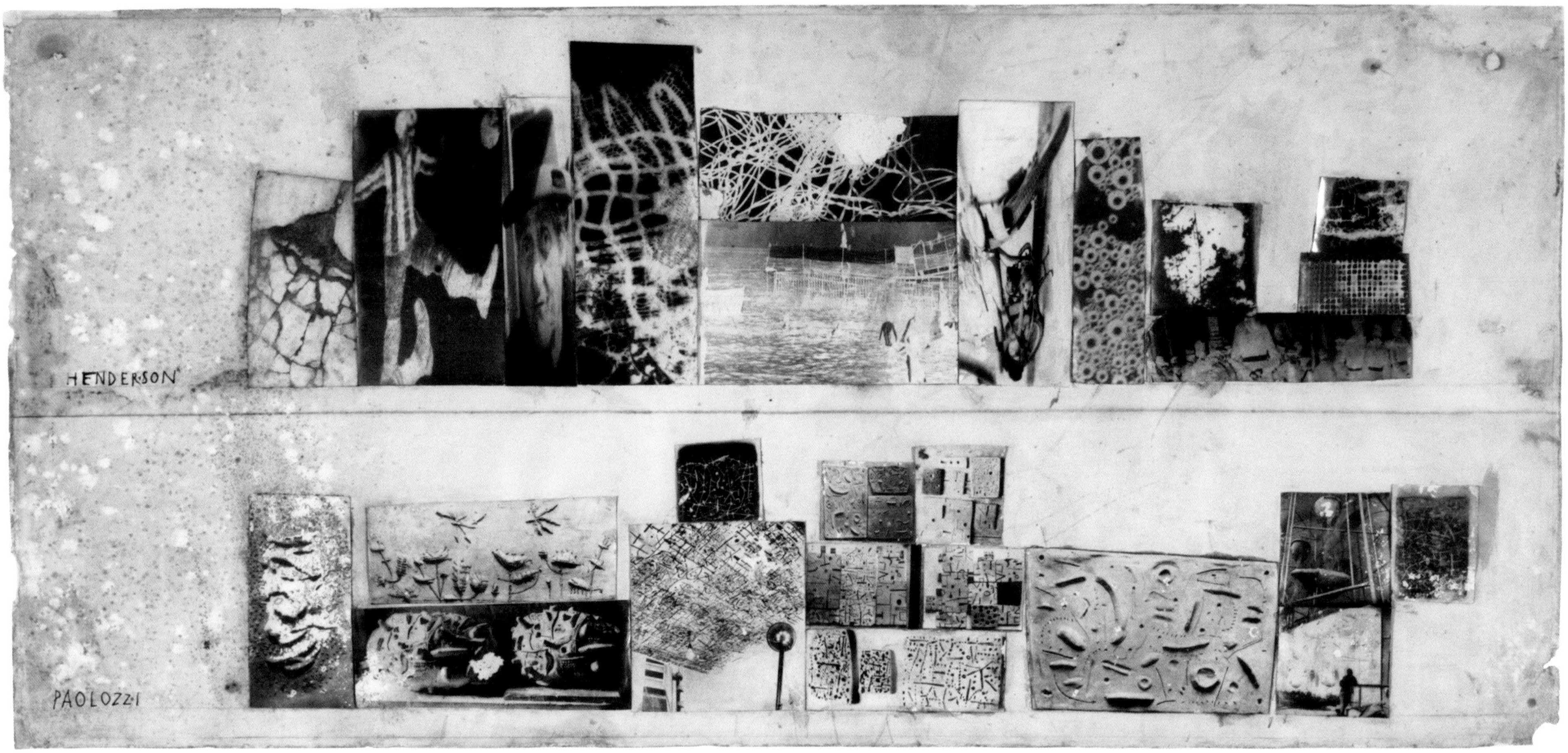

of windows, screens and reflections – as, for example, with *Heads Seen through Pub Window, East End* 1949–53 (p.98 top left) – that reveal, hide or distort. Other photographs, such as *The Bagwash* 1949–53 (p.59 bottom), record the complexities of signage that shaped the local landscape he was documenting – 'the bizarre interplay of trade and sign' – and also allowed not only for a reading of felicitous juxtaposition and association, but also his attention to a distressed quality of Brutalist surface found in such places.

The order of distortion that Henderson captured in *Heads Seen through Pub Window, East End* also formed the basis for much of his experimentation within photographic printing. Thinking back to the series of *Stressed Photographs* from 1950 (p.12), which shows children 'doodling' on bicycles, Henderson later recalled how, with this series, he could form 'an "expressionistic" image giving a slightly "intoxicated" version which suggested to me a certain delirium in which a boy may fantasize and divert himself with a bike for hours on end… I got very interested in the amount of "extraction" one could get out of certain negatives, shifting elements of the "given" around, almost as if one was rephotographing them.'[10]

What Henderson describes here is not only a way of formulating his images through a broad understanding of collage (an 'intoxicated' 'shifting' of elements) but also how these images might be read as an act of 'extraction', of the associative, 'visually-valuable', qualities within them. Henderson's quest for this type of 'imageability' is embodied in these photographs of the street, facing up to the life they record. To use Alison and Peter Smithson's 1957 description of New Brutalism, these images 'drag a rough poetry out of the confused and powerful forces which are at work. Up to now Brutalism has been discussed stylistically, whereas its essence is ethical.'[11]

ABOVE Nigel Henderson and Eduardo Paolozzi *Untitled (Study for Parallel of Life and Art)* 1952. Black and white photographs and pen and graphite on paper 35.8 x 77.9. Tate. Purchased 2007

1 Lawrence Alloway, 'The Long Front of Culture', *Cambridge Opinion*, no. 17, 1959 (reprinted in Edward Leffingwell (ed.), *Modern Dreams, The Rise and Fall of Pop*, MIT Press, London 1988, pp.30–3).

2 Nigel Henderson, 'Autobiographical Sketch' (first published in *Nigel Henderson, Photographs of Bethnal Green 1949–1952*, exh. cat., Midland Group, Nottingham 1978), reprinted in Claude Lichtenstein and Thomas Schregenberger (eds.), *As Found: The Discovery of the Ordinary*, Zürich 2001, p.93.

3 Alison and Peter Smithson, 'Patterns of Association', *Uppercase*, no.3, 1961, unpaginated.

4 Peter Smithson, from transcripts of an interview with Alison and Peter Smithson by Reyner Banham for the Arts Council film *Fathers of Pop*, 1979, quoted in Victoria Walsh, *Nigel Henderson: Parallel of Life and Art*, London 2001, p.54.

5 Nigel Henderson, untitled text, *Uppercase*, no.3, 1961, unpaginated.

6 Ibid.

7 Reyner Banham, 'The New Brutalism' (first published *Architectural Review*, December 1955), reprinted in Claude Lichtenstein and Thomas Schregenberger (eds.), *As Found: The Discovery of the Ordinary*, Zürich 2001, p.132.

8 Nigel Henderson, 'Parallel of Life and Art', manuscript notes for a lecture, Nigel Henderson Collection, Tate Archive (TGA 9211.5.1.7).

9 Nigel Henderson, 'London', typescript, Nigel Henderson Collection, Tate Archive (TGA 9211.4.3 p.2).

10 Nigel Henderson, 'Autobiographical Sketch' (first published in *Nigel Henderson, Photographs of Bethnal Green 1949–1952*, exh. cat., Midland Group, Nottingham 1978), reprinted in Claude Lichtenstein and Thomas Schregenberger (eds.), *As Found: The Discovery of the Ordinary*, Zürich 2001, p.95.

11 Alison and Peter Smithson, 'The New Brutalism', (first published *Architectural Design*, April 1957), reprinted in David Robbins (ed.), *The Independent Group: Postwar Britain and the Aesthetics of Plenty*, Cambridge, Massachusetts and London 1990, p.186.

‘In a street, I feel like a naturalist in a jungle. There is the spoor of people (Boars Head tobacco wrappers, bus tickets, milk bottle tops like medallions; the tree trunks – battered cylinders of dustbins, the lianas of wall crack, the undergrowth of eroded pavement-slabs slicked with crusty lines of cement, blotched with damp). You walk on tiger skin from Devon. You come upon doors annihilated by paper like the mossy encrustations of trees in the bayou, and padded lichenated walls.’

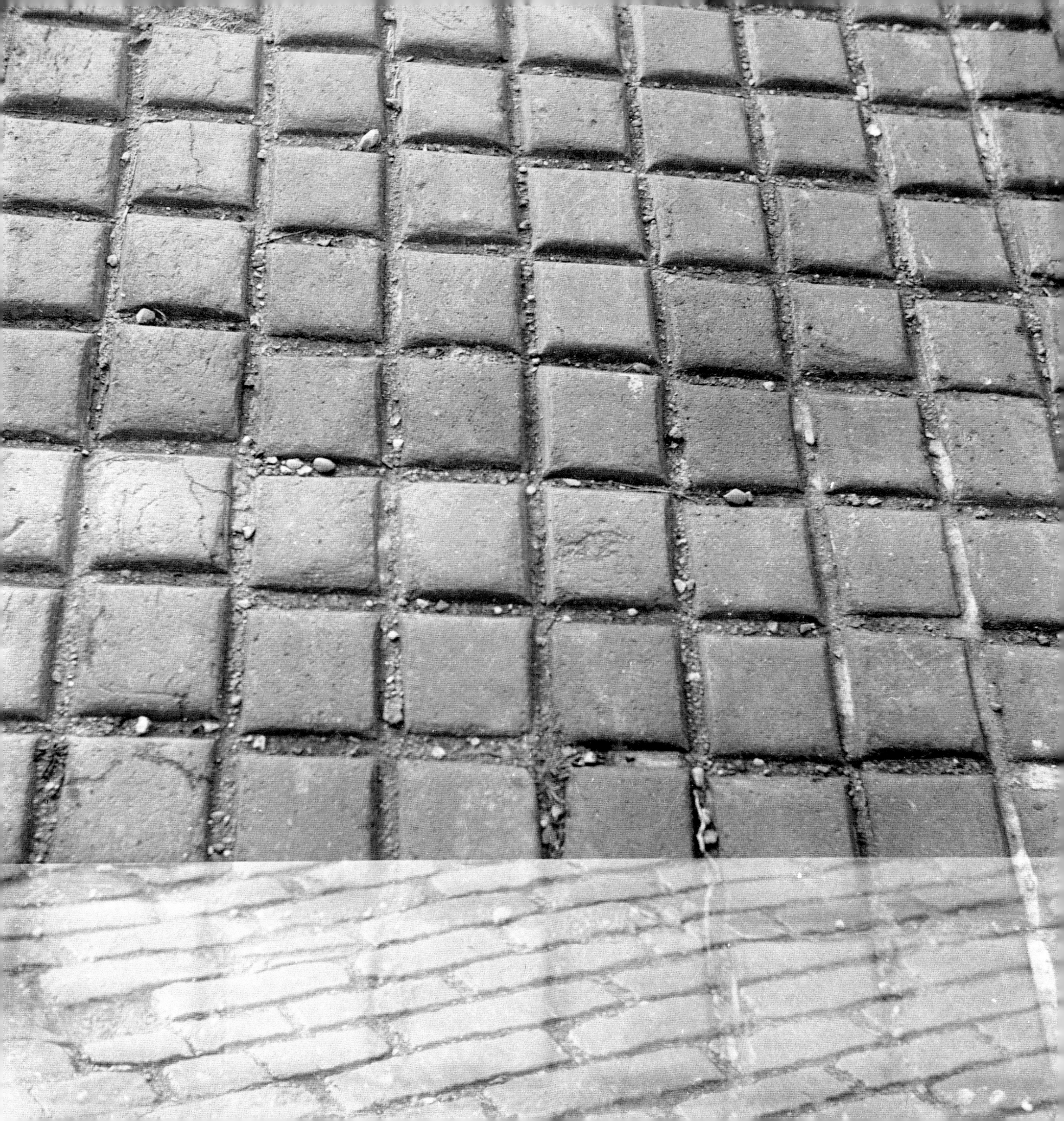

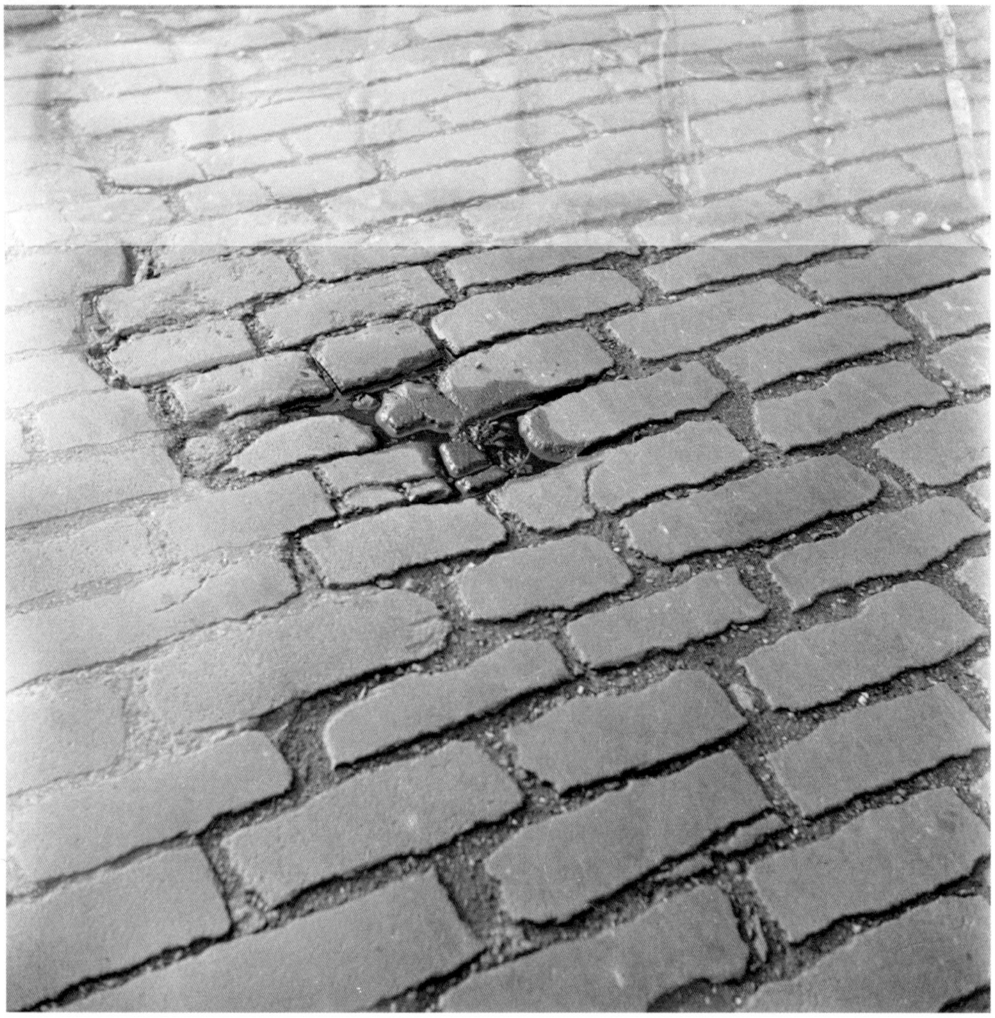

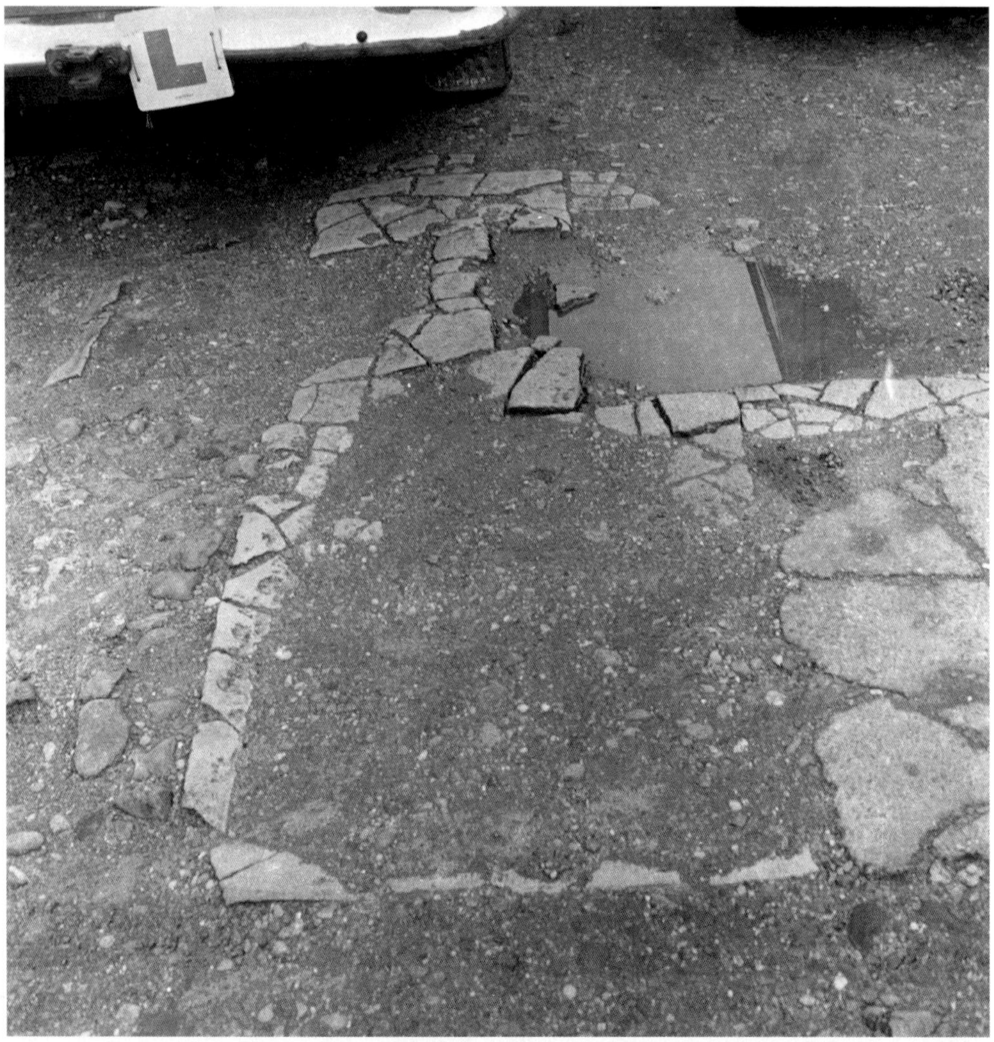

PREVIOUS PAGE AND HERE Texture studies of road surfaces

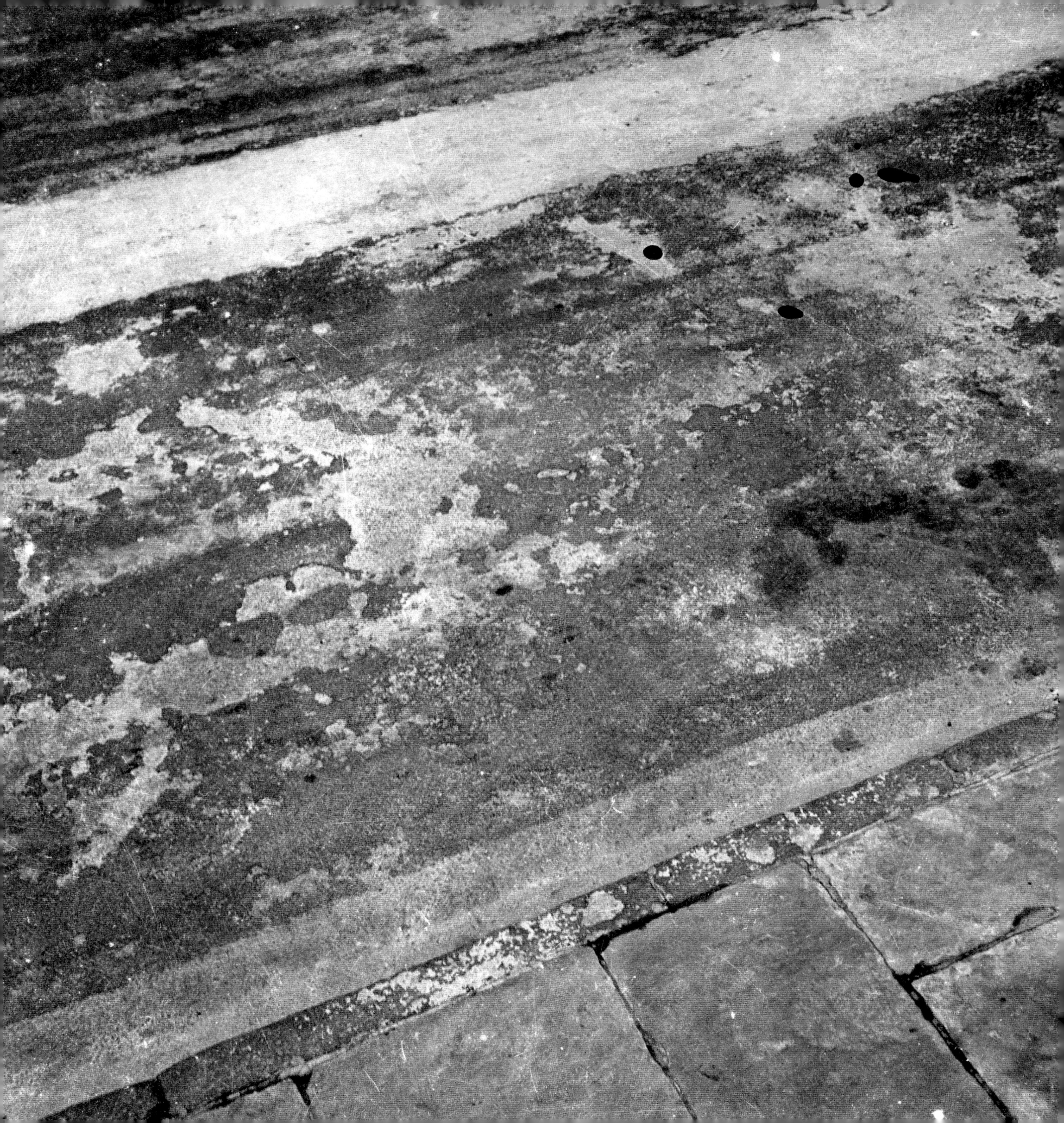

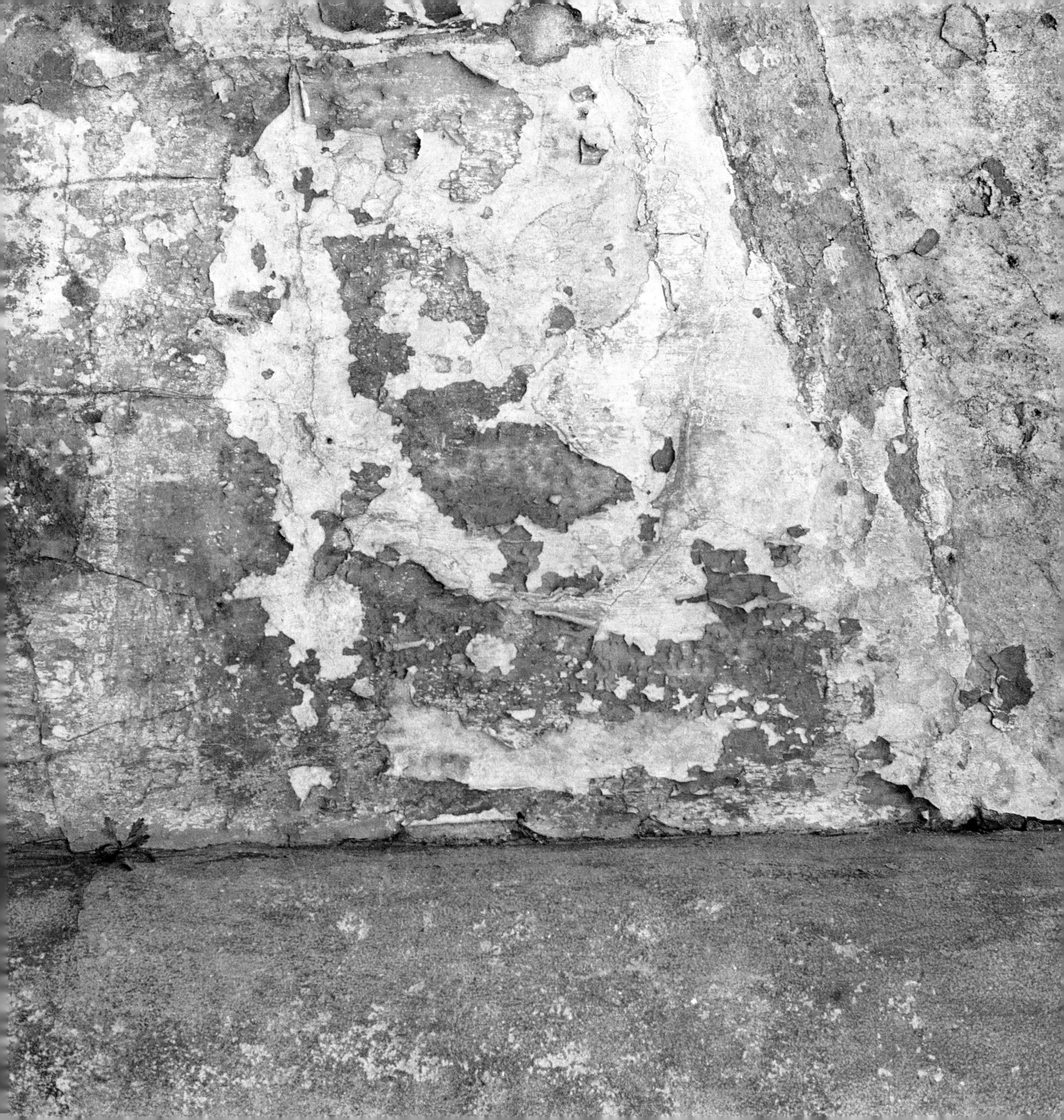

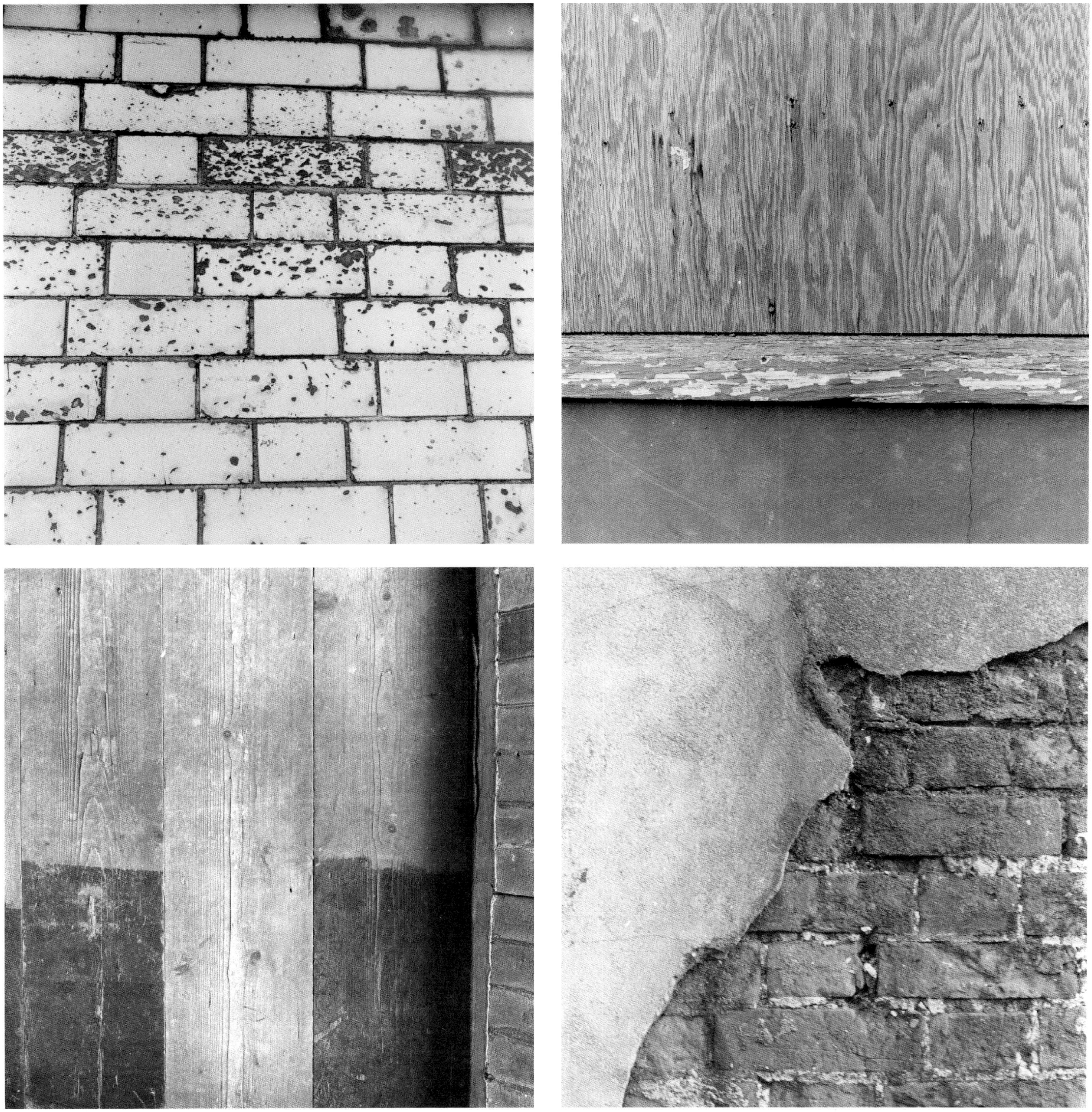

Texture studies of wall surfaces

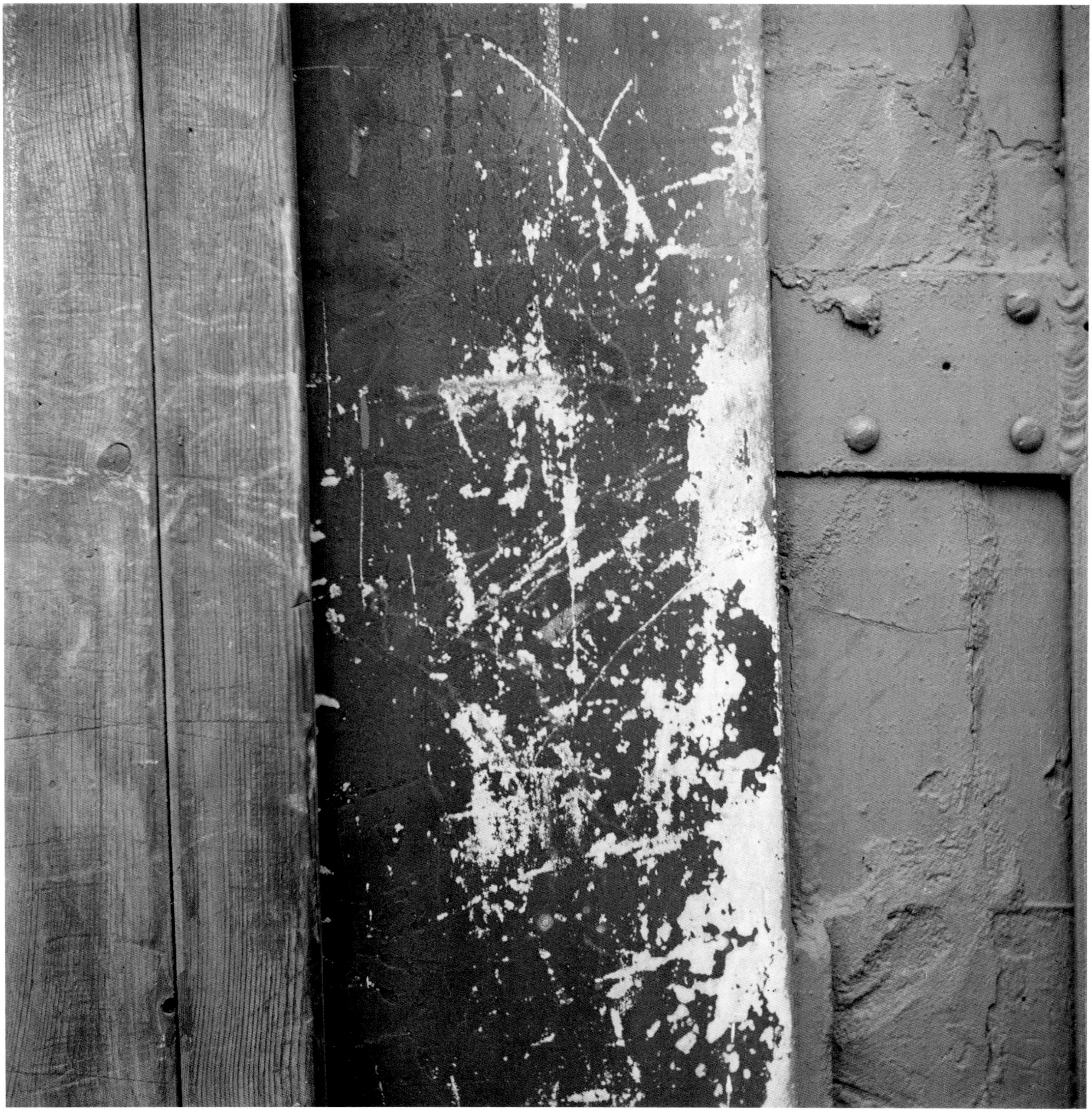

Texture studies of wall surfaces

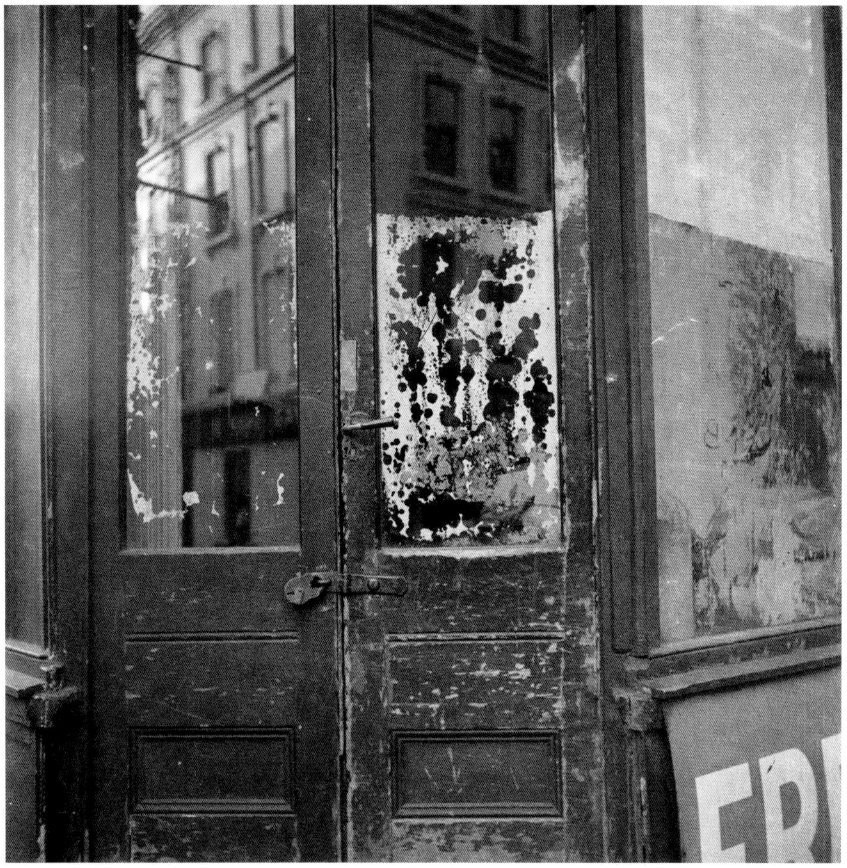
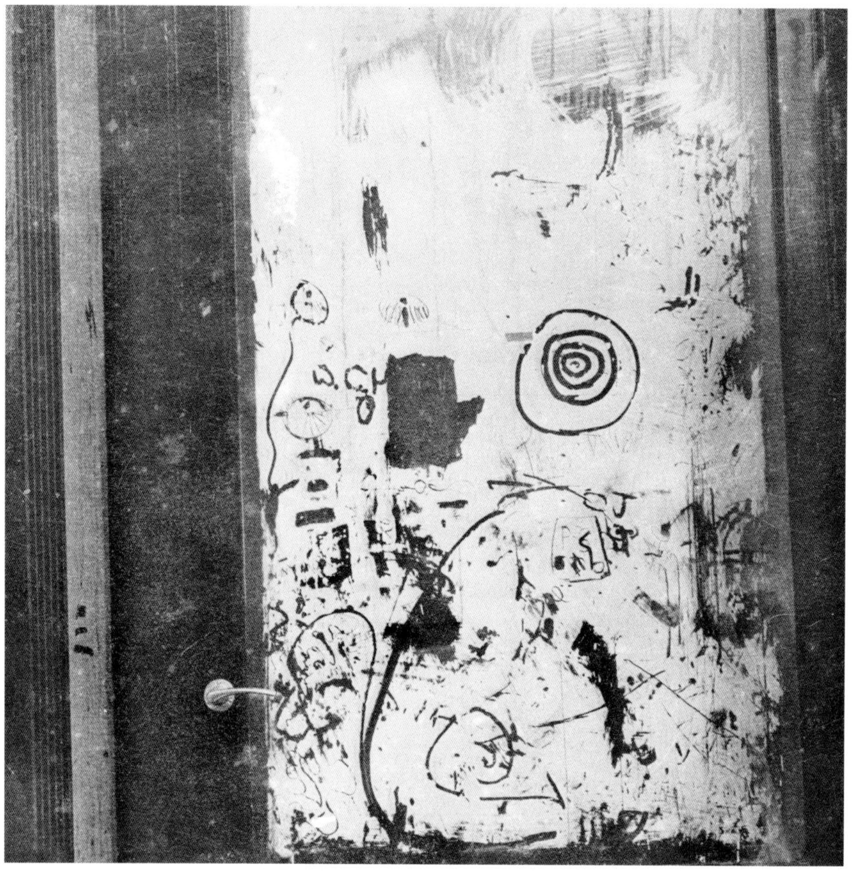
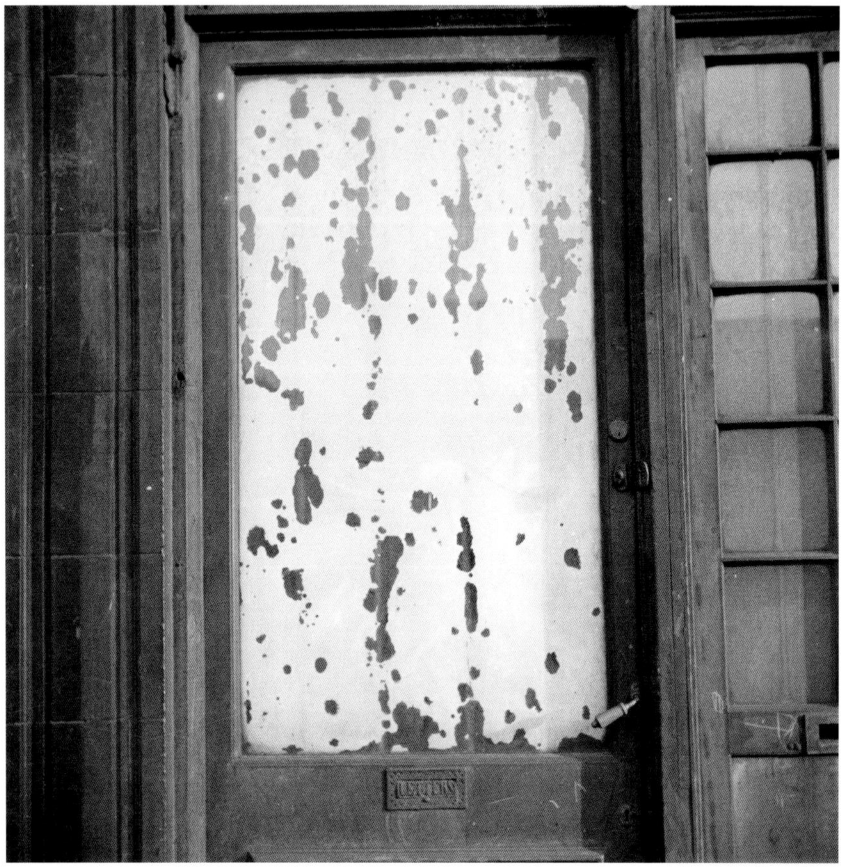
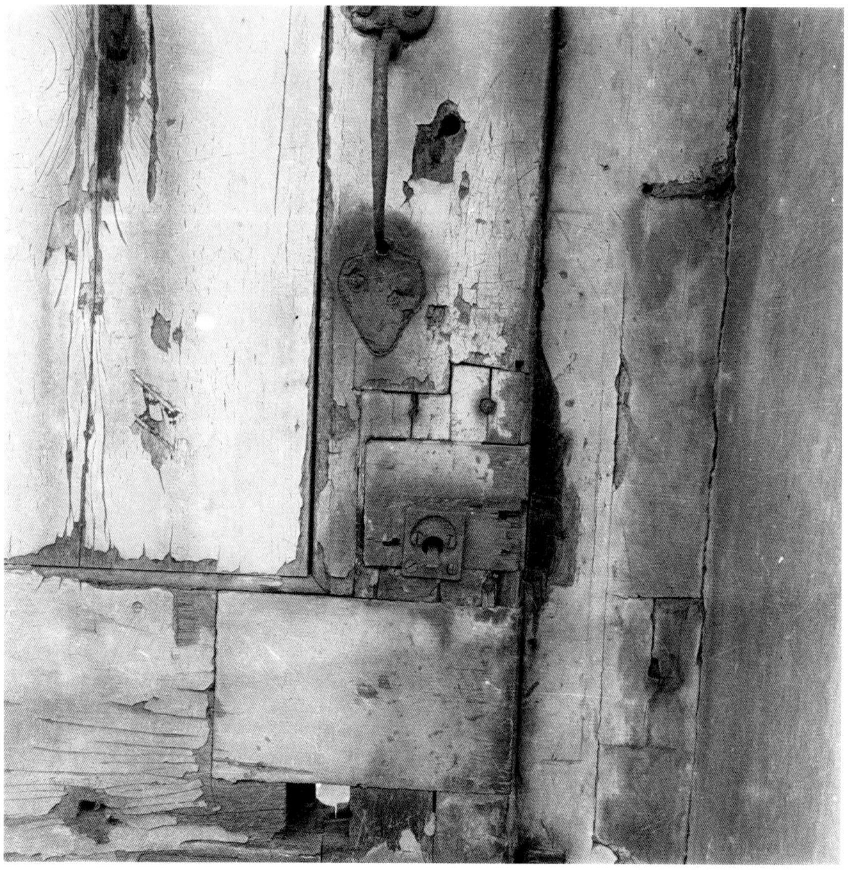

Texture studies of doors

TOP RIGHT *Popular Art*

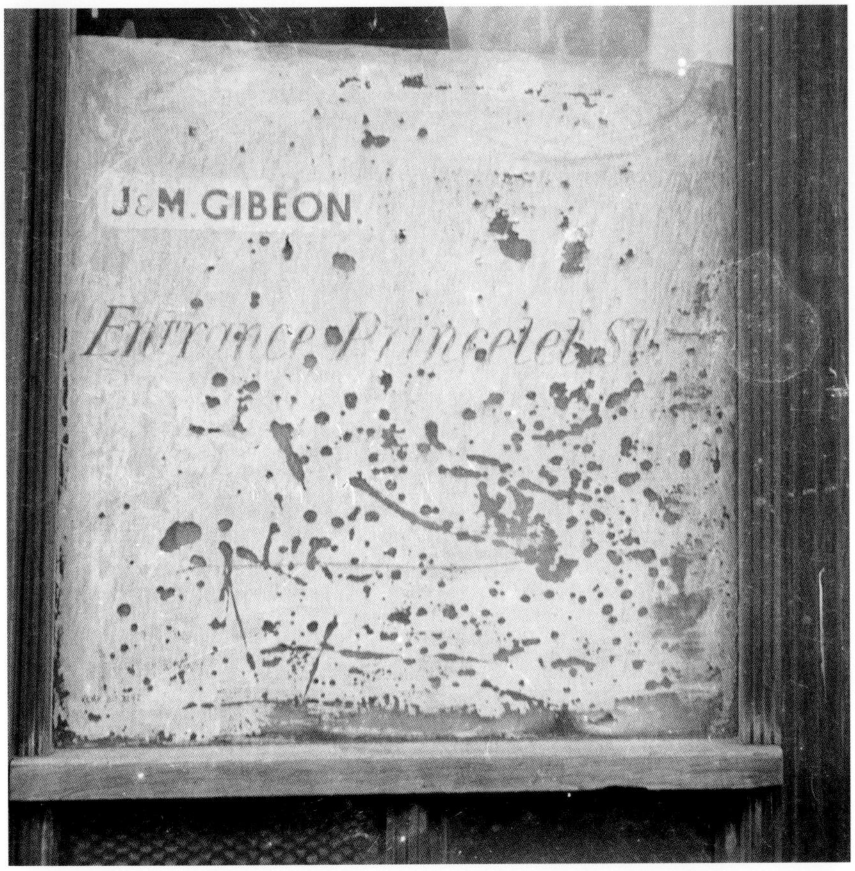

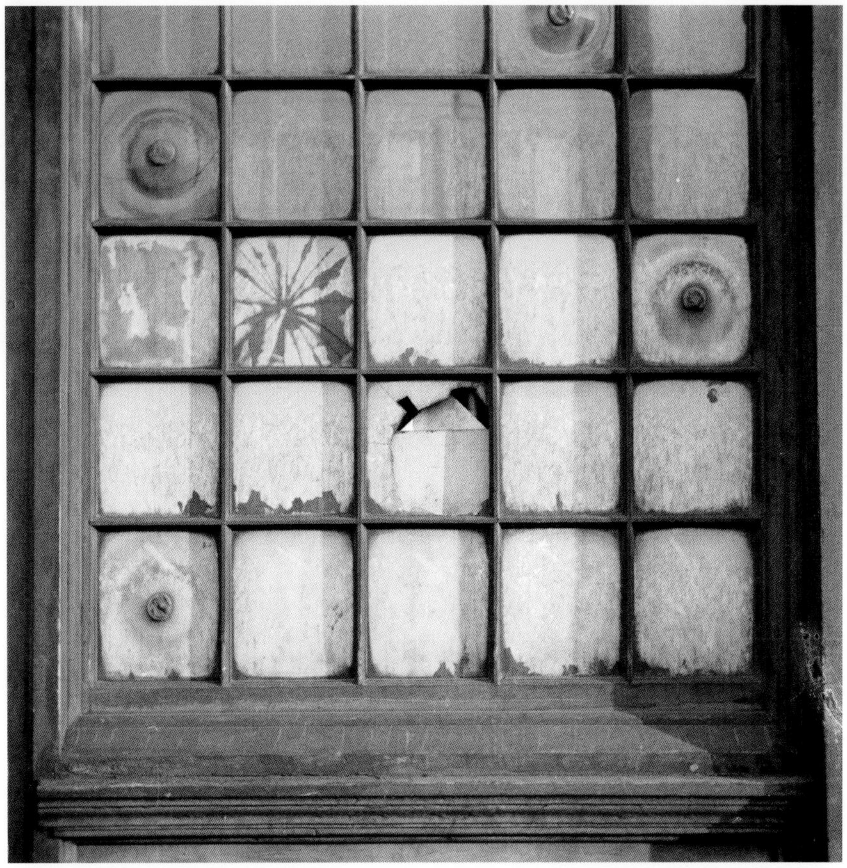

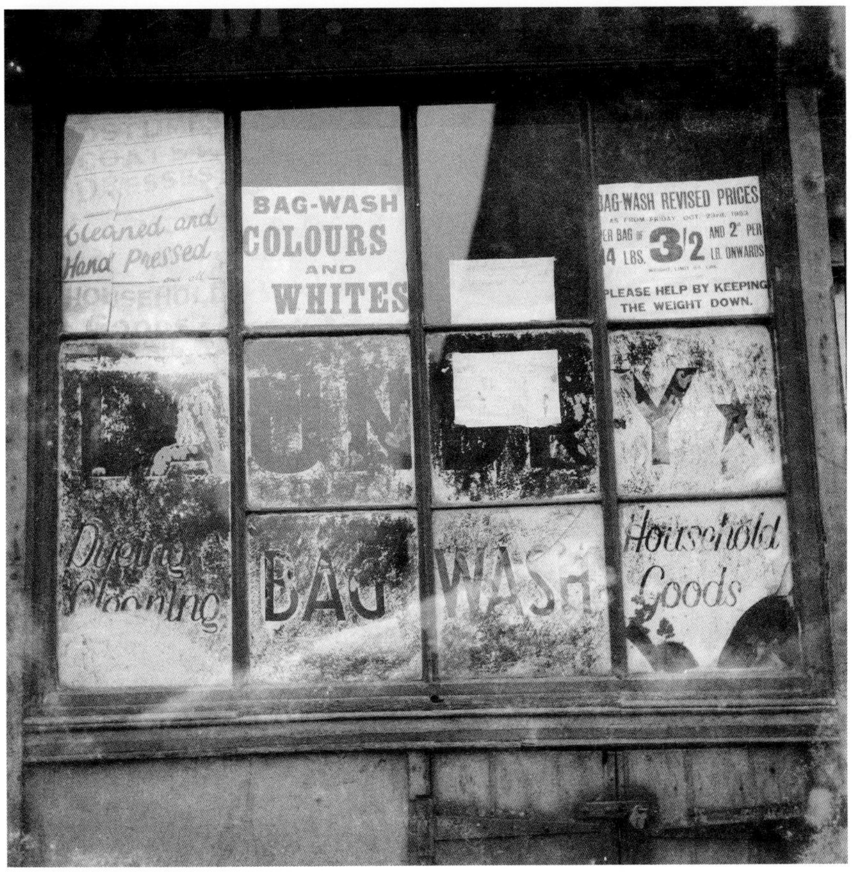

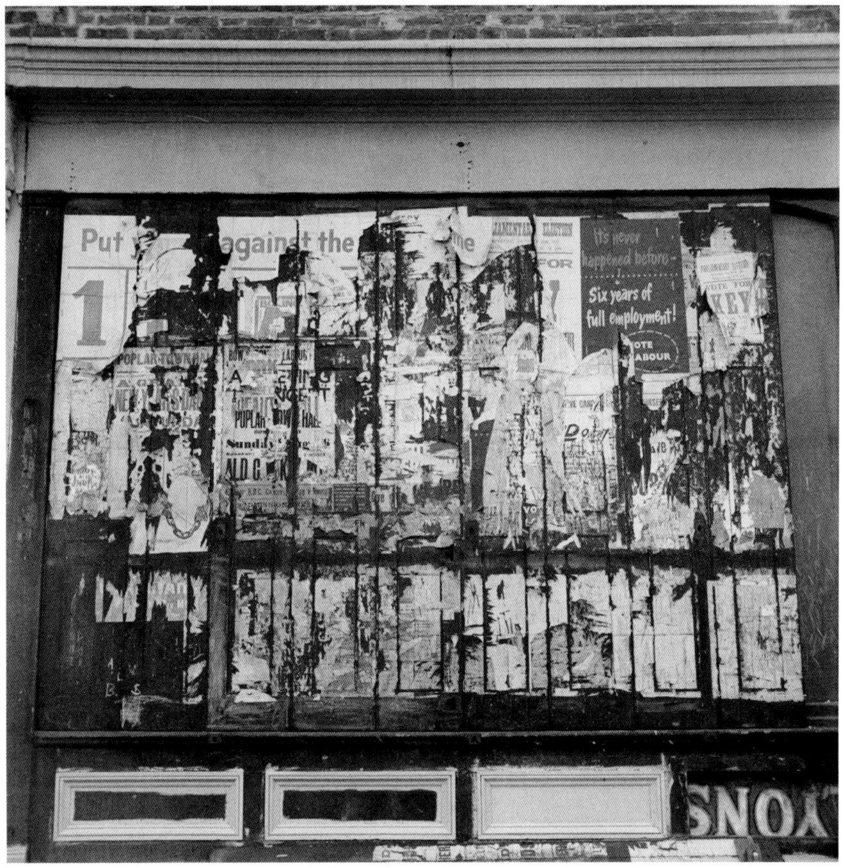

Texture studies of windows

TOP LEFT J. & M. Gibeon, 63A Brick Lane, Spitalfields E1. A gown-maker's window

BOTTOM LEFT *Bag-wash*

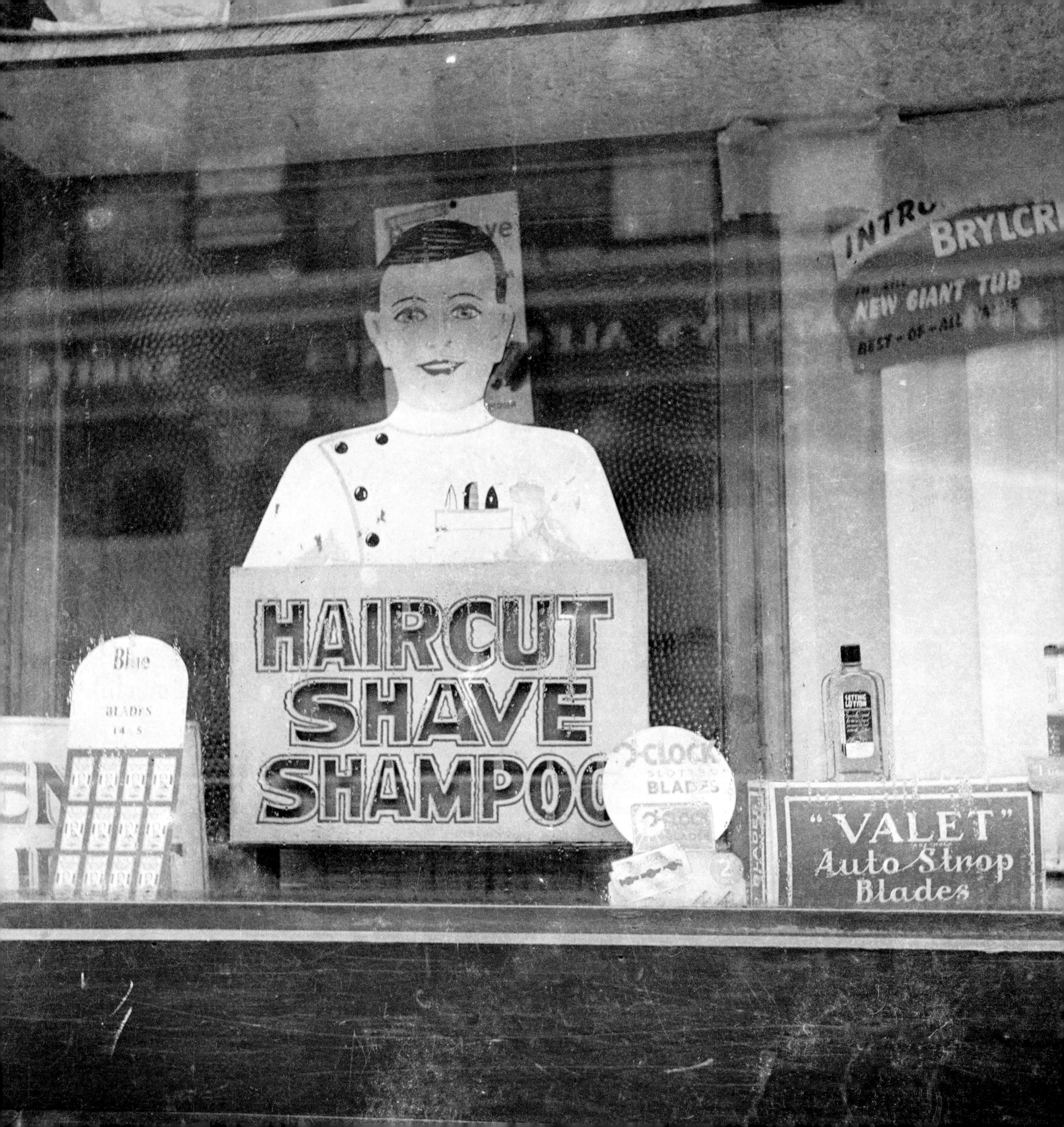
HAIRCUT
SHAVE
NEW GIANT TUB
Blue
BLADES
CLOCK
BLADES
"VALET"
Auto Strop
Blades

Shop windows

RIGHT 1952

BELOW *Barber's Shop Window*

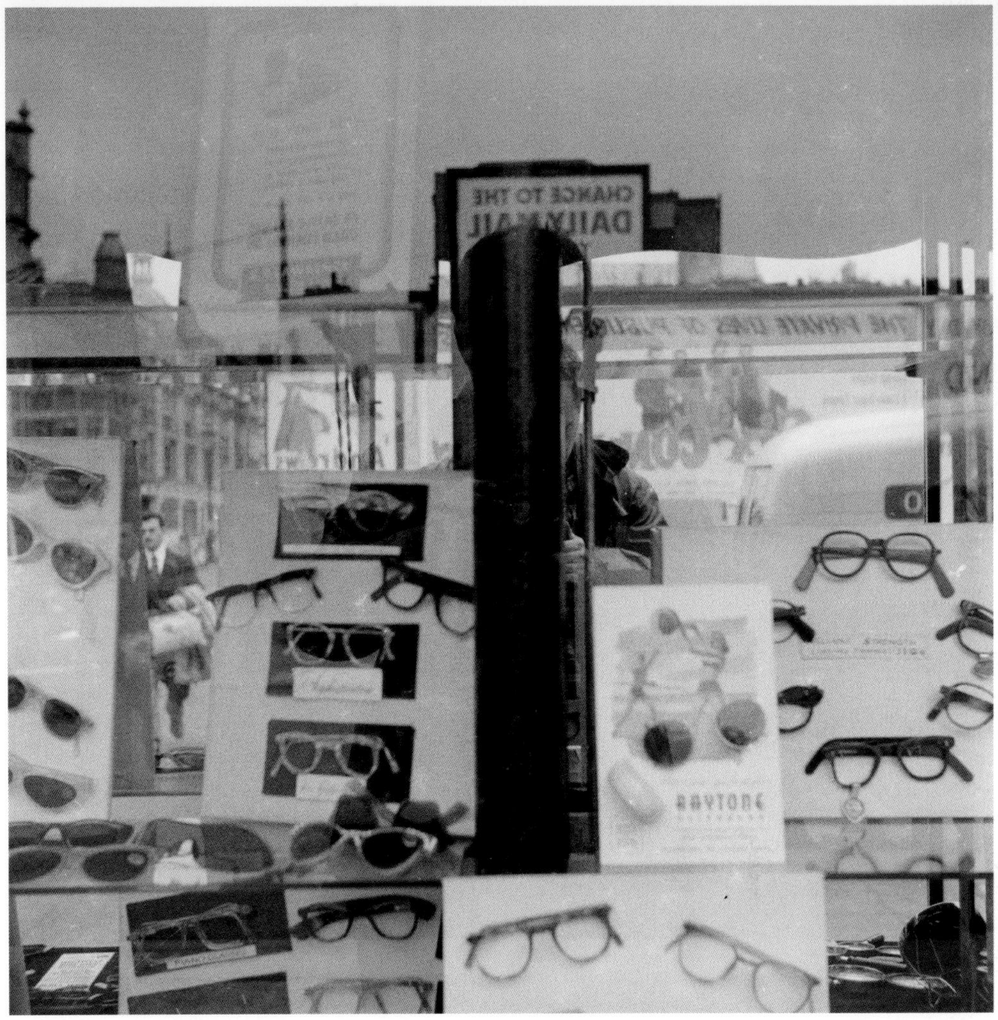

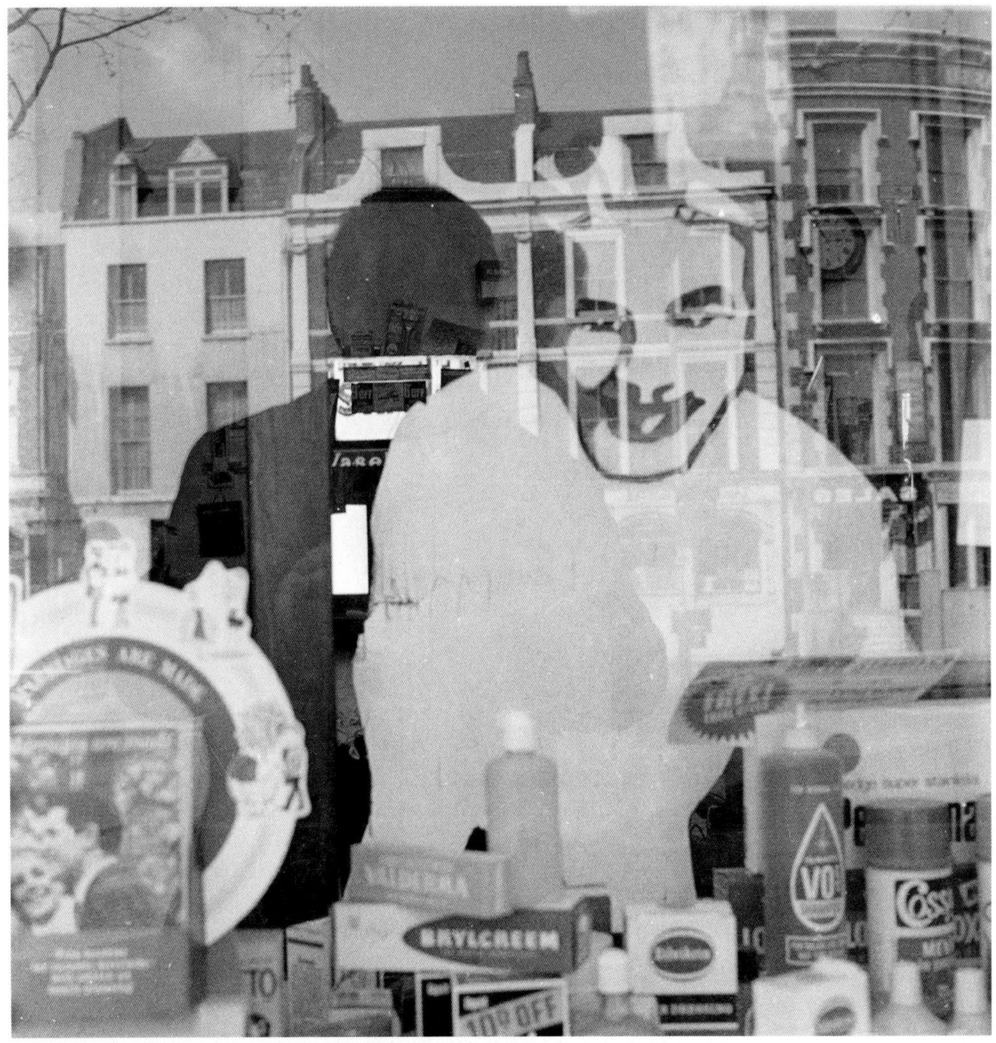

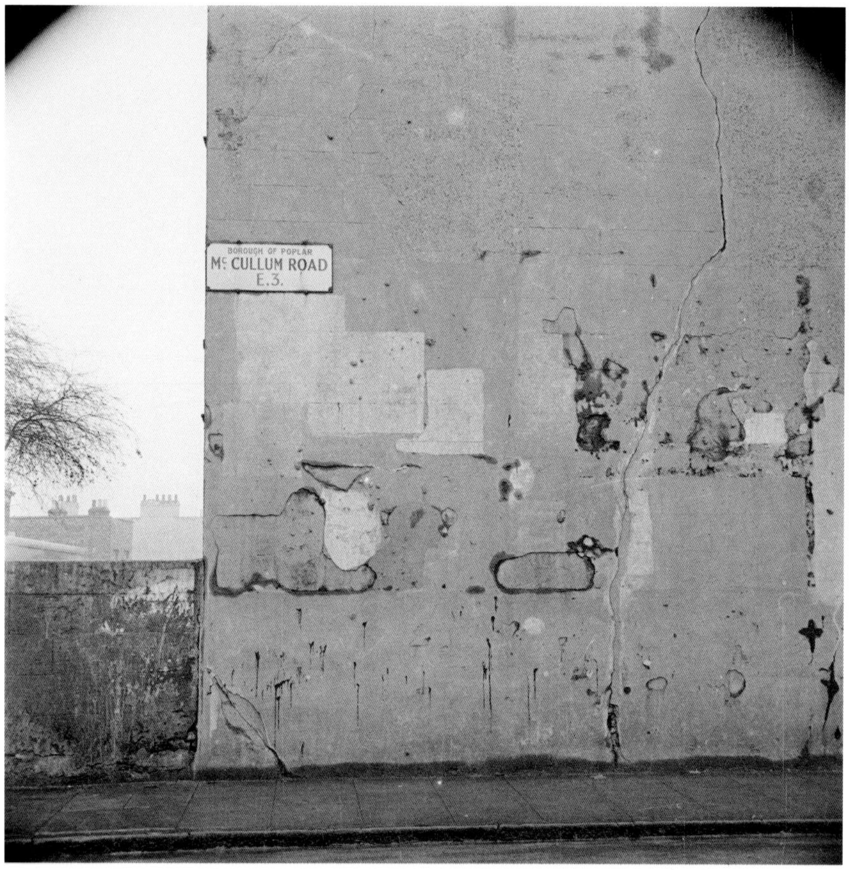

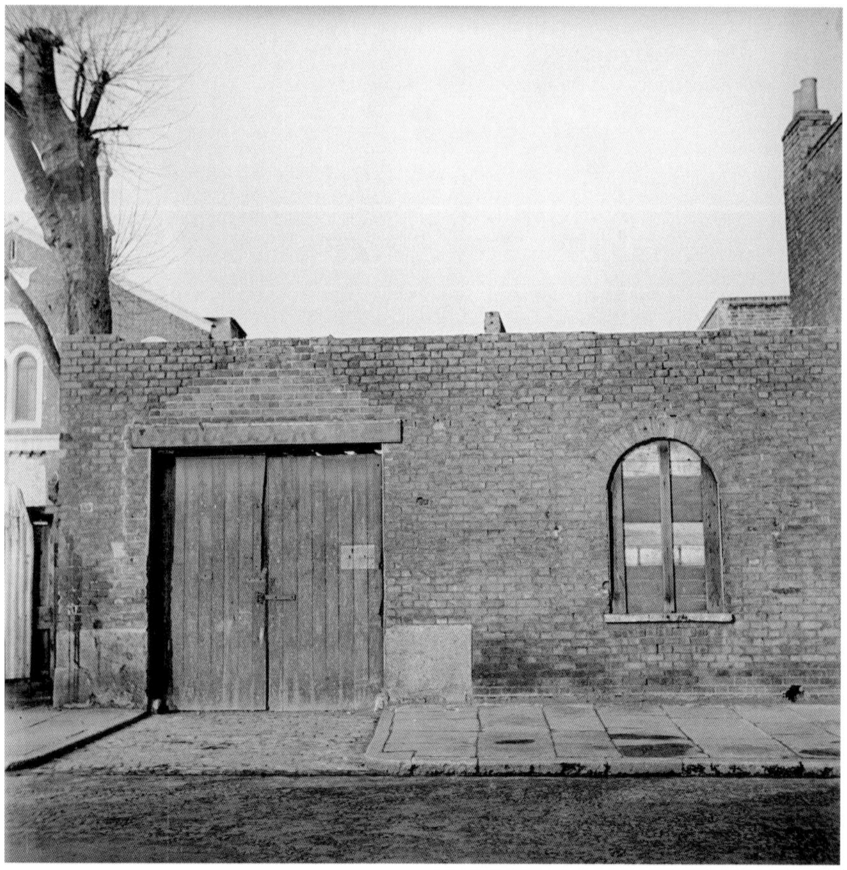

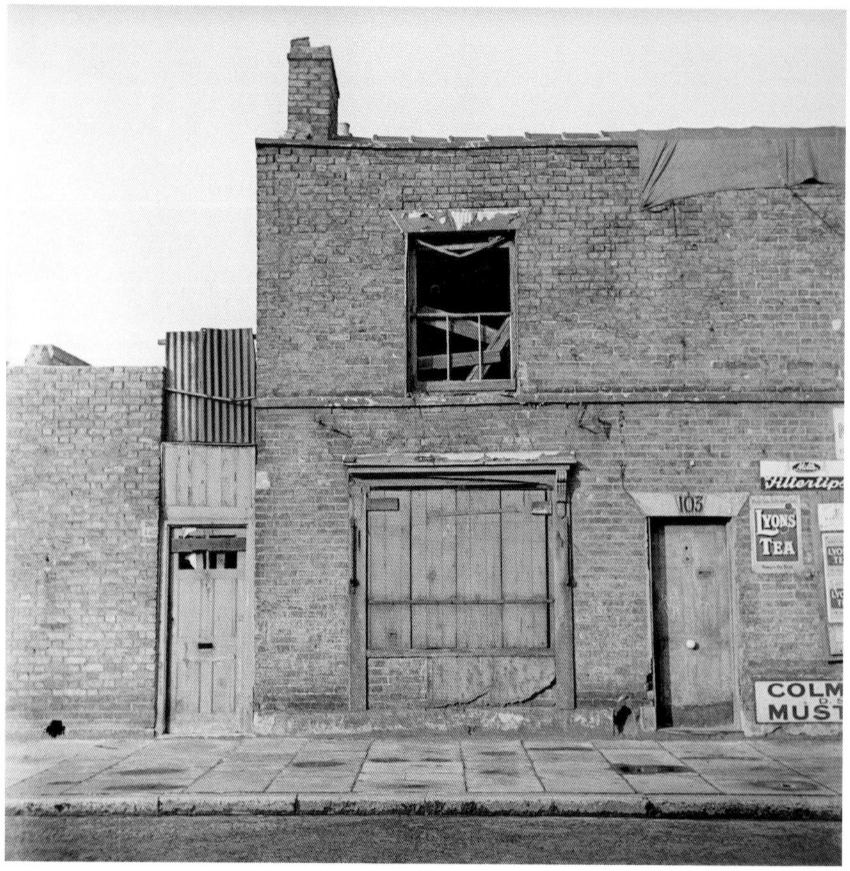

Texture studies of walls

TOP *Wall, McCullum Road*

BOTTOM LEFT AND RIGHT 103 Cephas Street, Bethnal Green E1

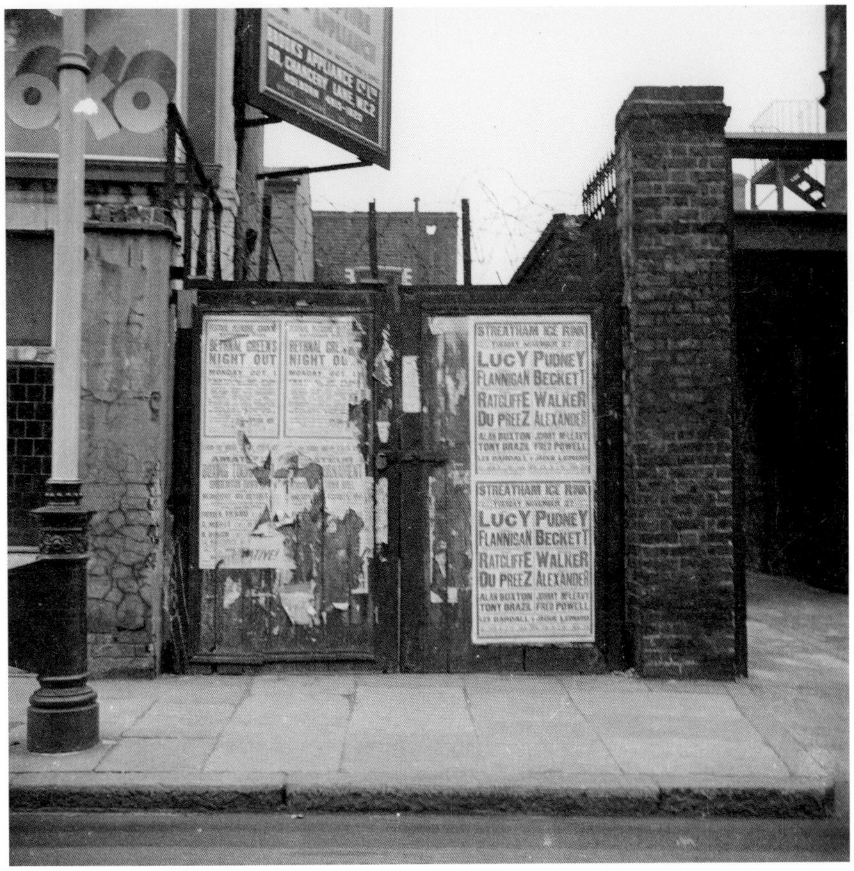

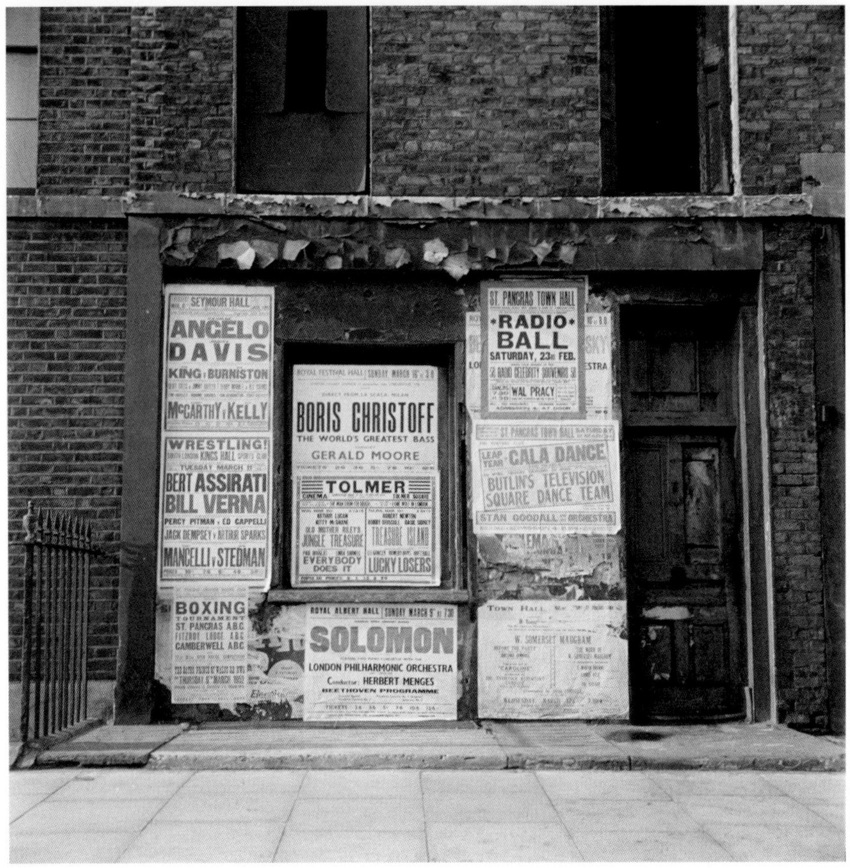

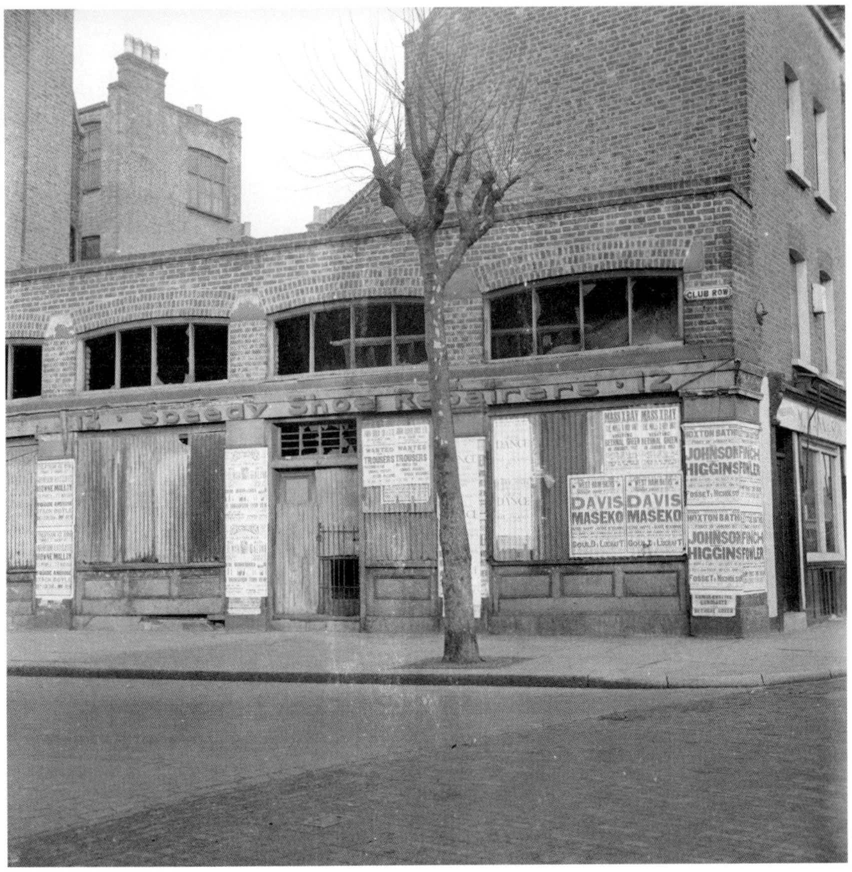

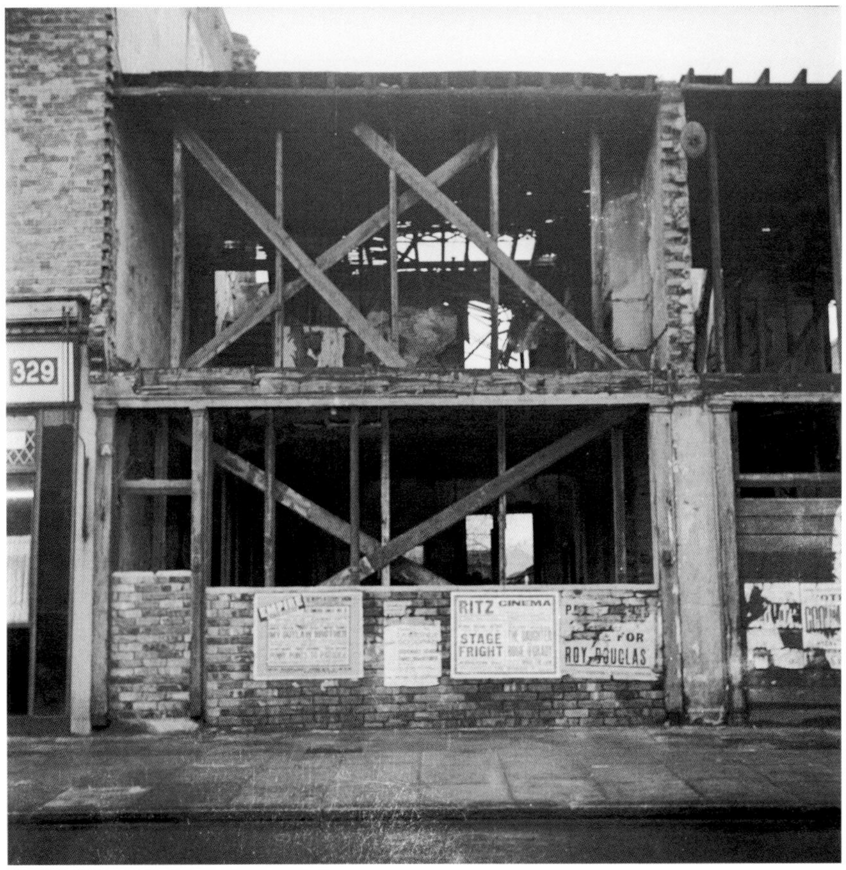

Billboard posters *c.*1951–2

BOTTOM LEFT Speedy Shoe Repairs, 12 Club Row, Spitalfields E1 1952

'My wife and I knew we would experience alienation in the working class environment. Perhaps this feeling intensified the feeling I had that I was watching a theatre... like an audience of one in a public theatre of All. My neighbours appeared to be living out their lives to some pre-determined script. These rituals were formal, very strong and coercive to me [and] because of their unfamiliarity exotic... I found this true of life around me recognizing a poetic homogeneity in the patient tired faces of people and houses and pavements: a savage humility begotten of limited means, I thought.'

'Compote Capades', Roman Road. Corner of Harold Street, Globe Town E2 1952

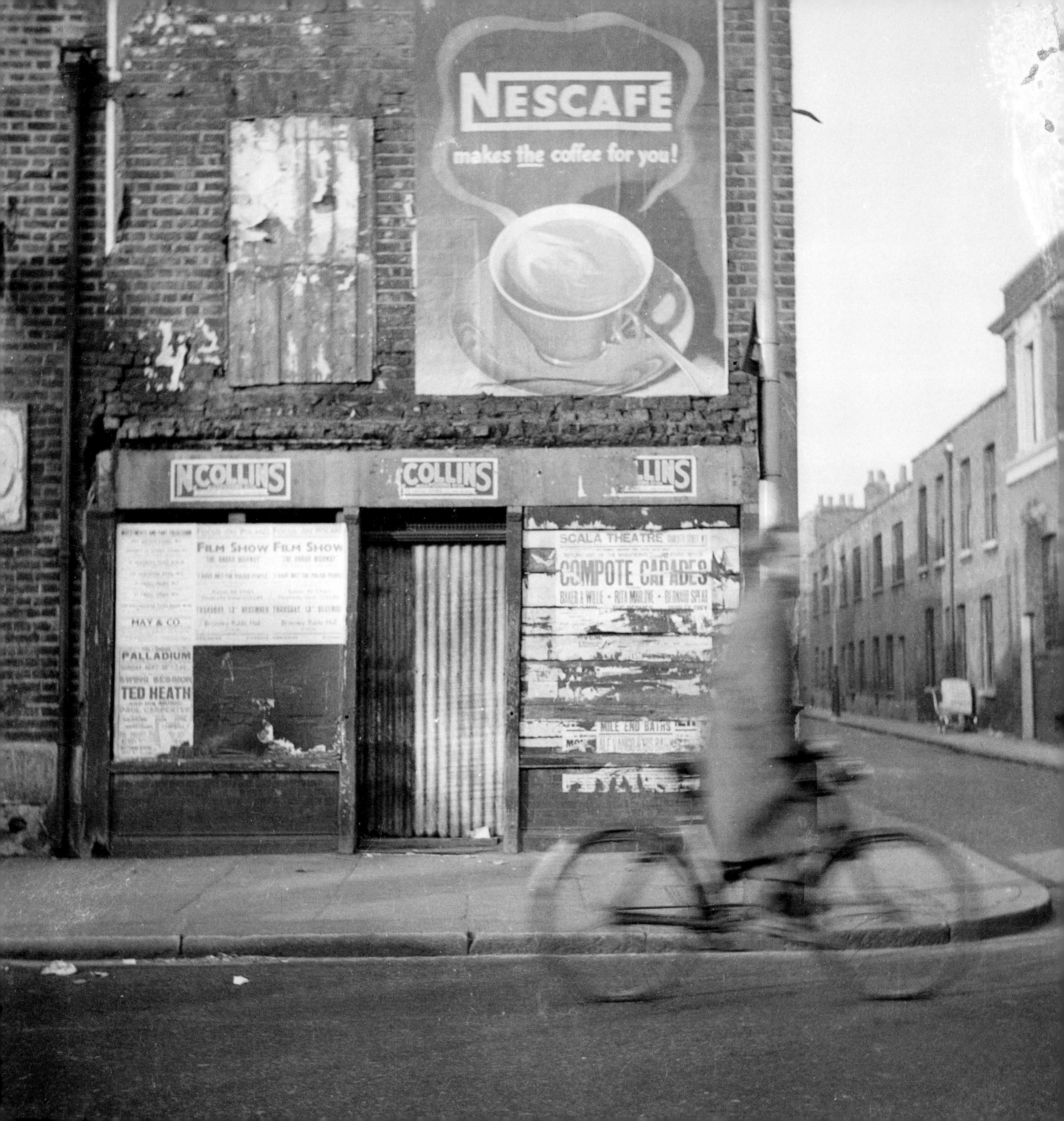
NESCAFÉ
makes the coffee for you!
N. COLLINS
COLLINS
FILM SHOW FILM SHOW
MAY & CO.
PALLADIUM
TED HEATH
SCALA THEATRE
COMPOTE CAPADES
MILE END BATHS

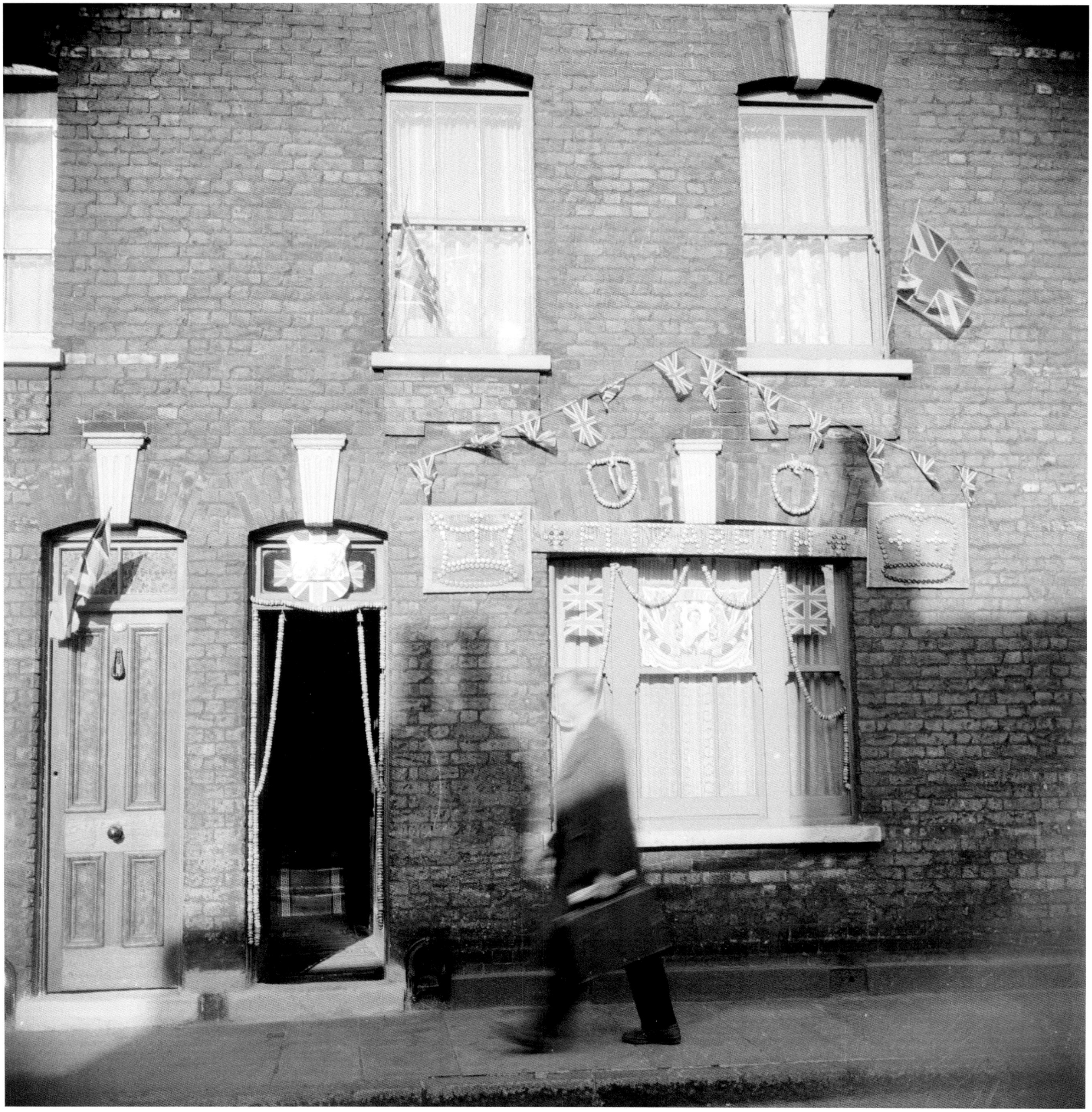

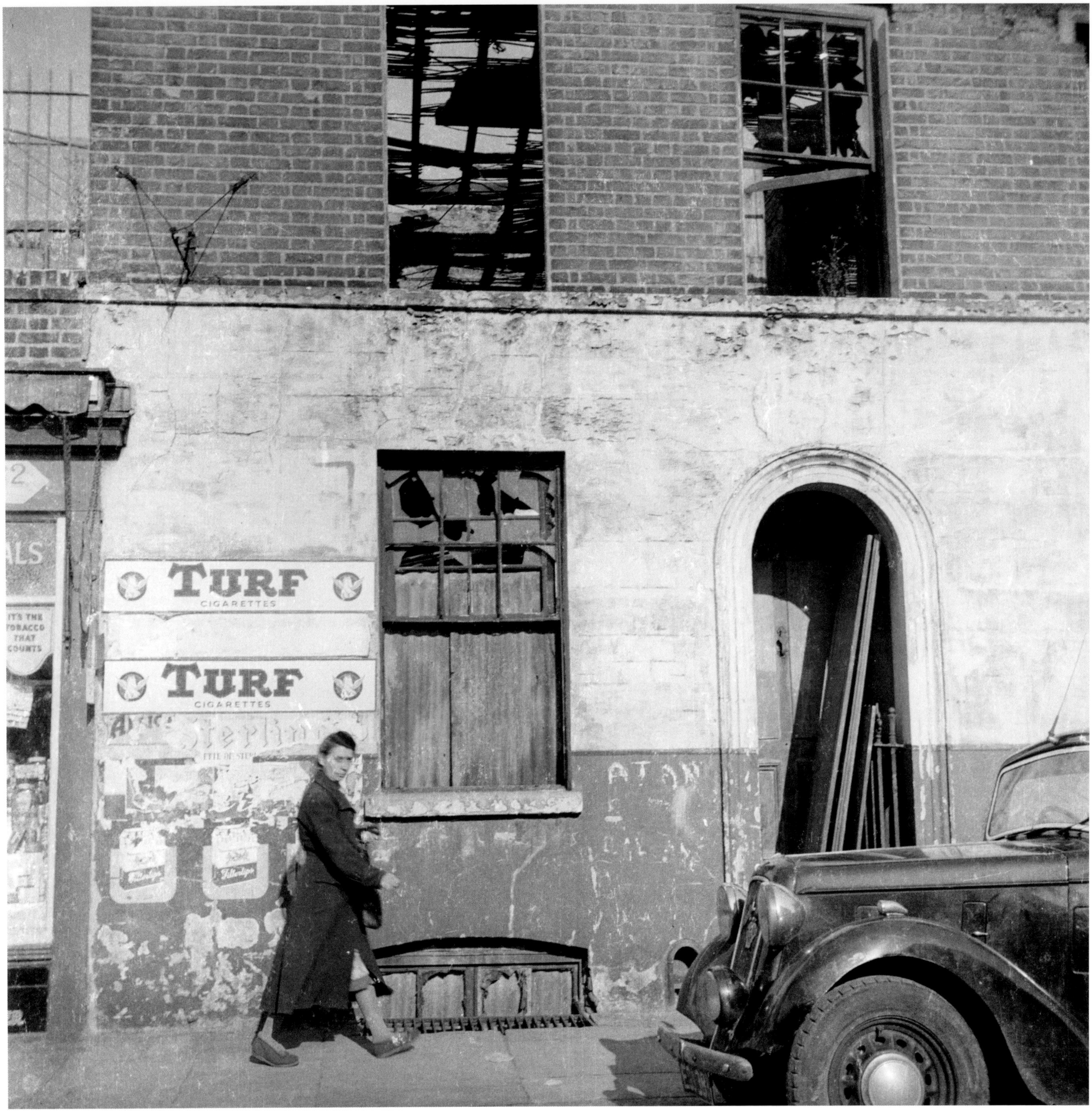

Bombed Side Street House in East End

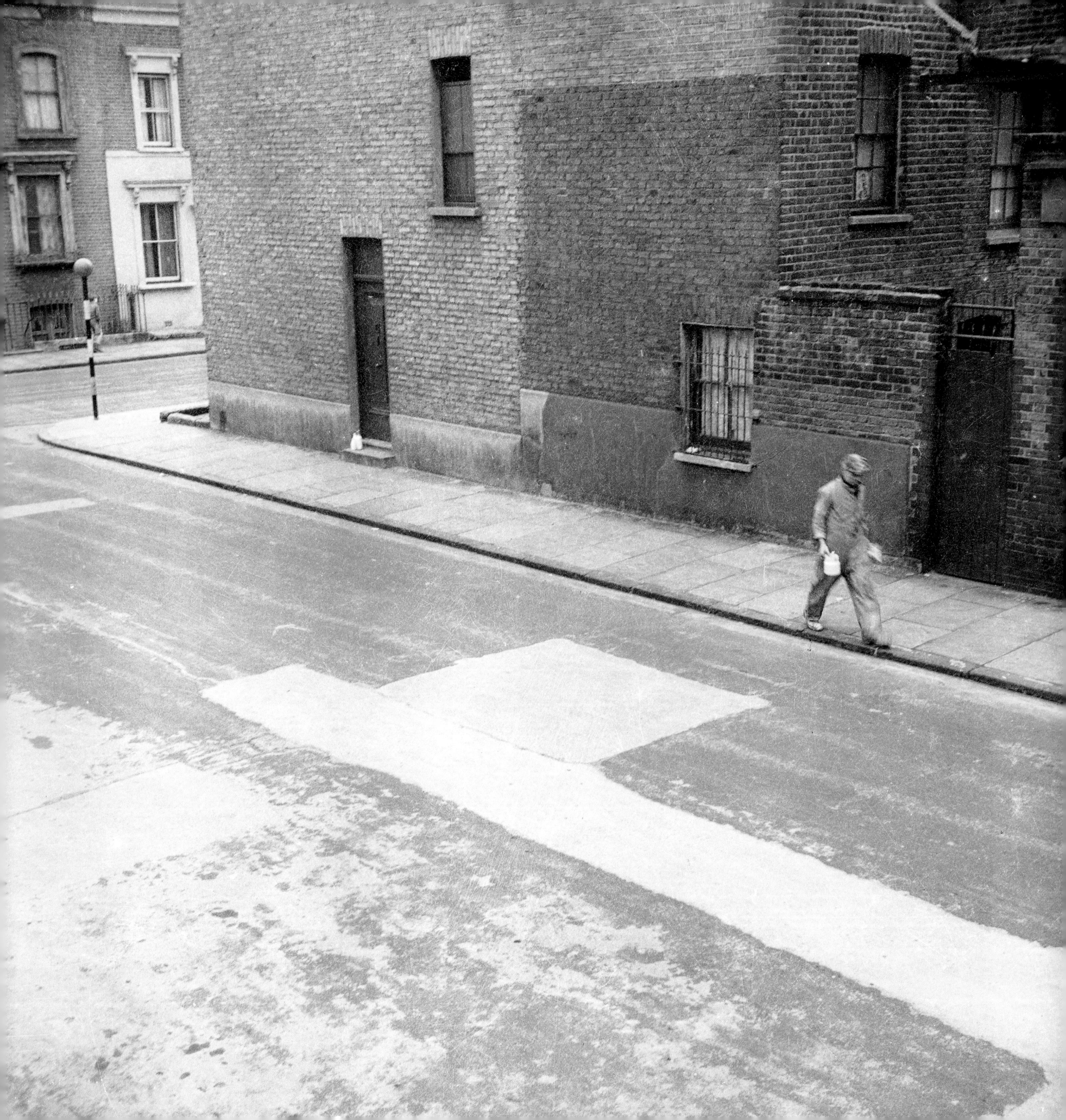

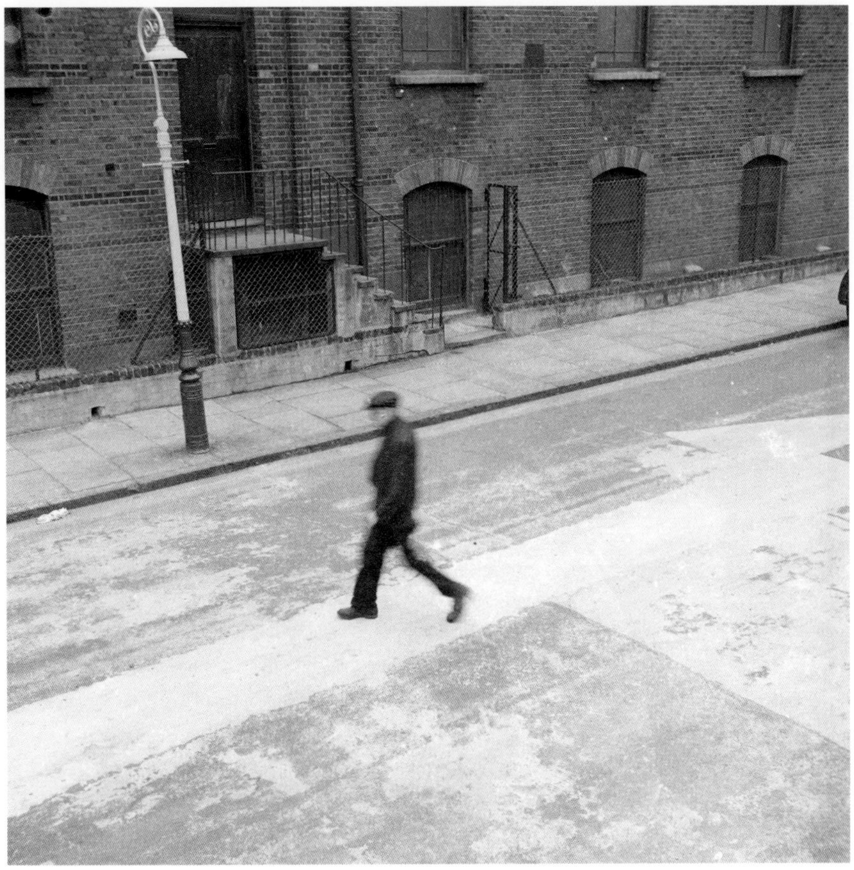

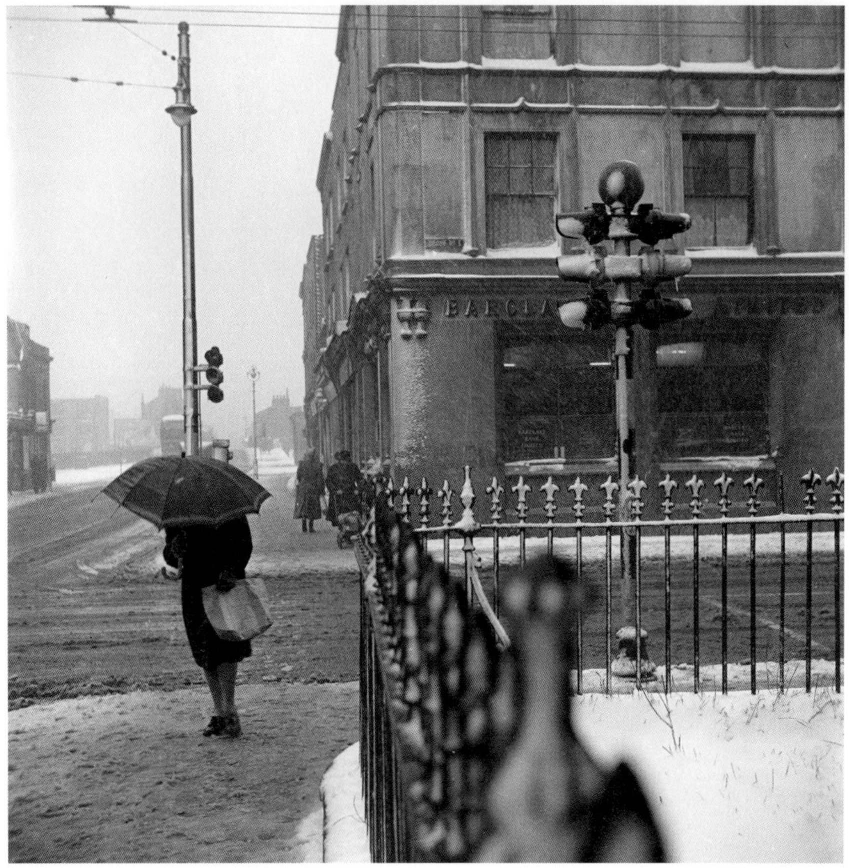

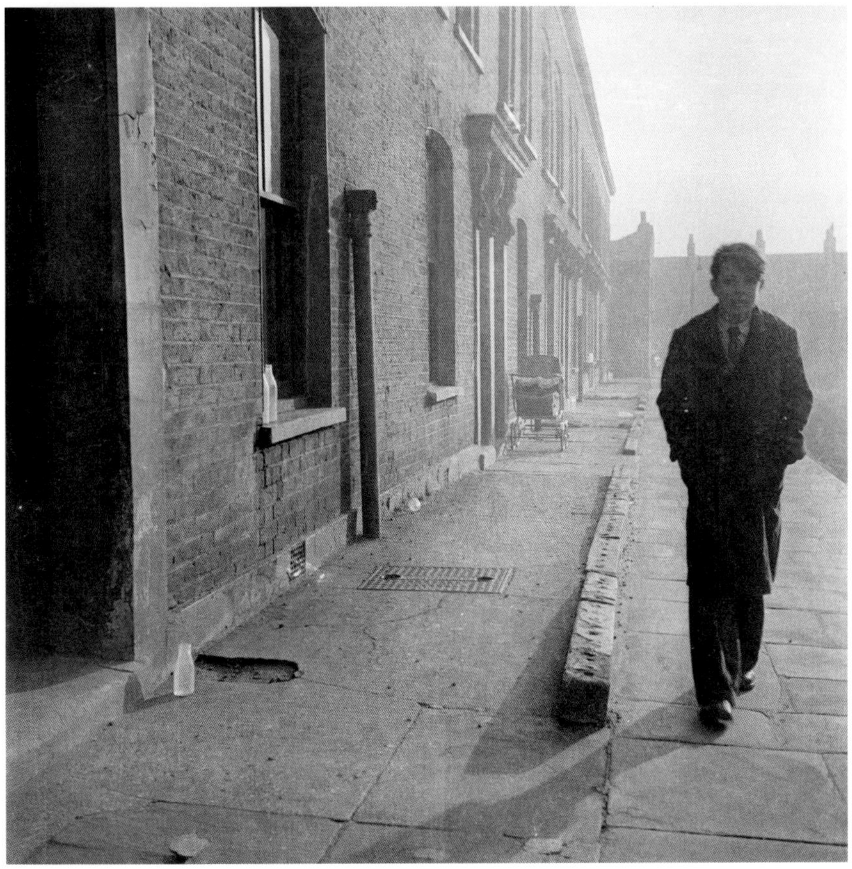

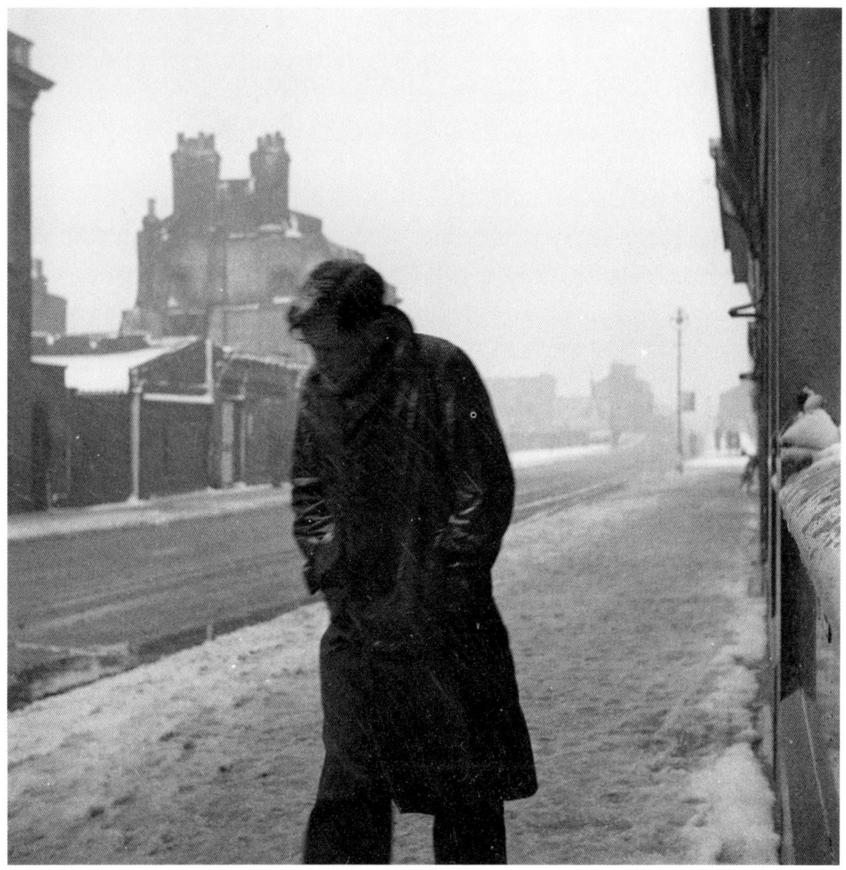

TOP *Man in Bunsen Street, Bethnal Green* 1950

OPPOSITE Man crossing Bunsen Street, Bow E3

TOP Corner of Grove Road and Roman Road, Bow E3

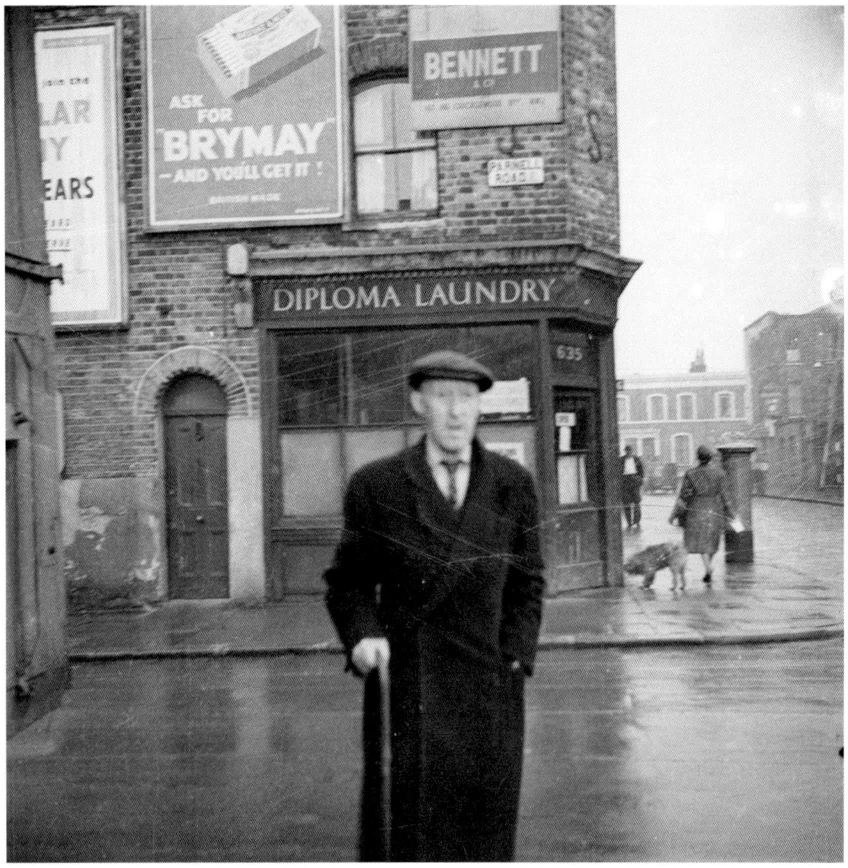

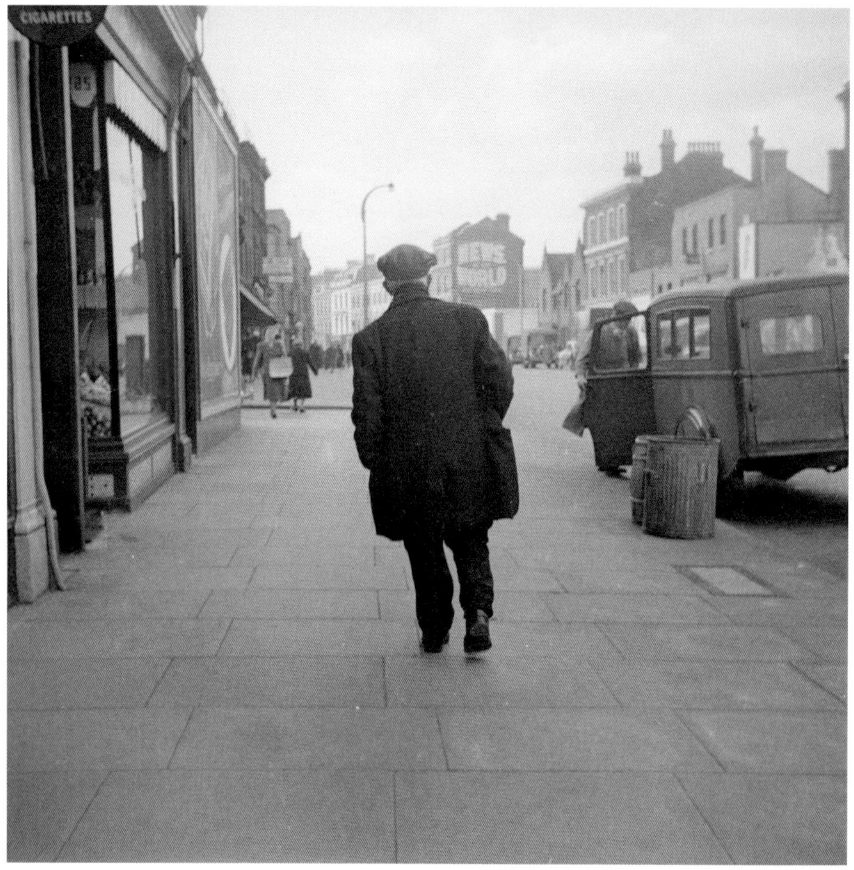

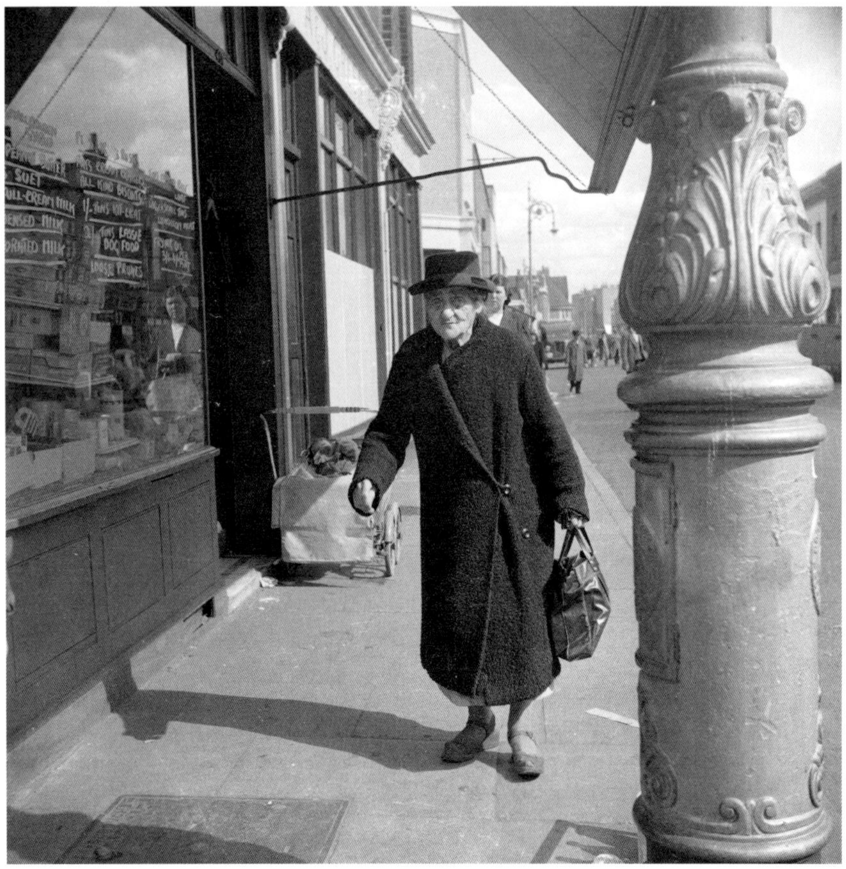

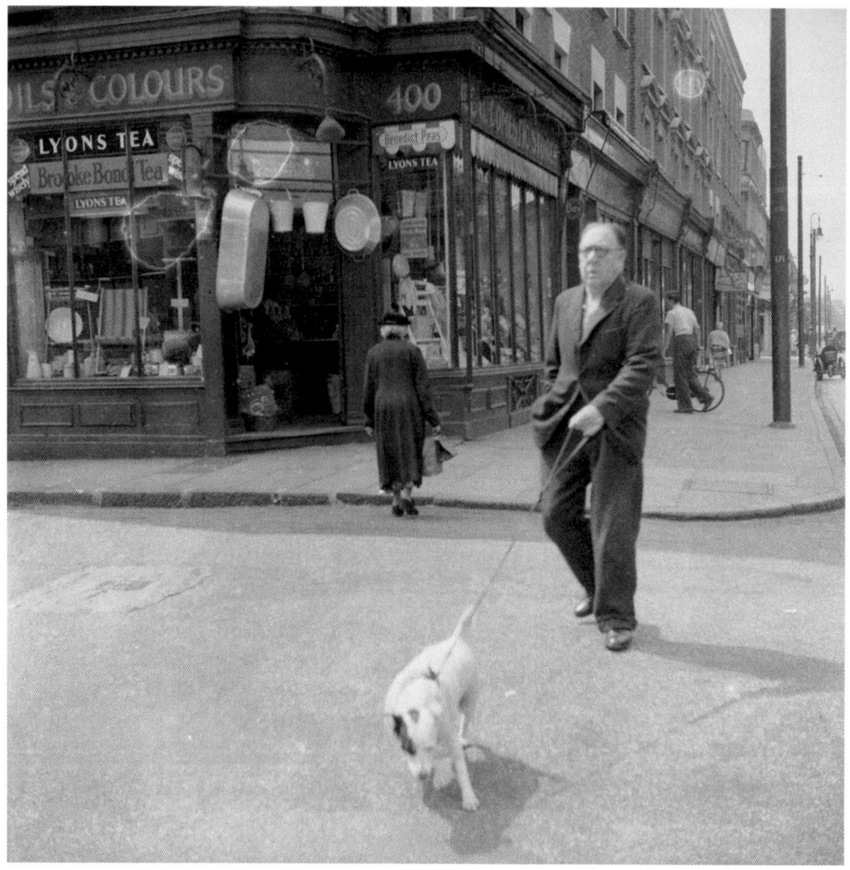

TOP LEFT Roman Road, corner of Parnell Road, Bow E3

BOTTOM LEFT *Old Woman Shopping, Bethnal Green Road.* (Actually Roman Road, Bow E3)

RIGHT 1953

BELOW *Justin Henderson*, outside 46 Chisenhale Road (The Hendersons' home), Bow E3

OVERLEAF

LEFT *Boy before boarded-up Pub, Stepney*

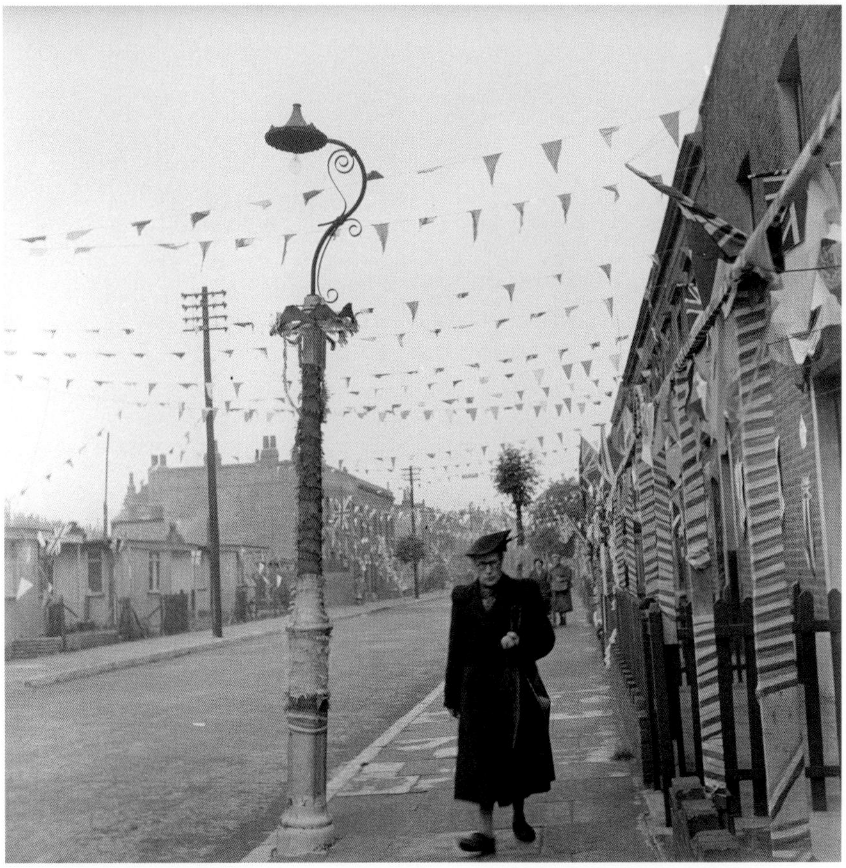

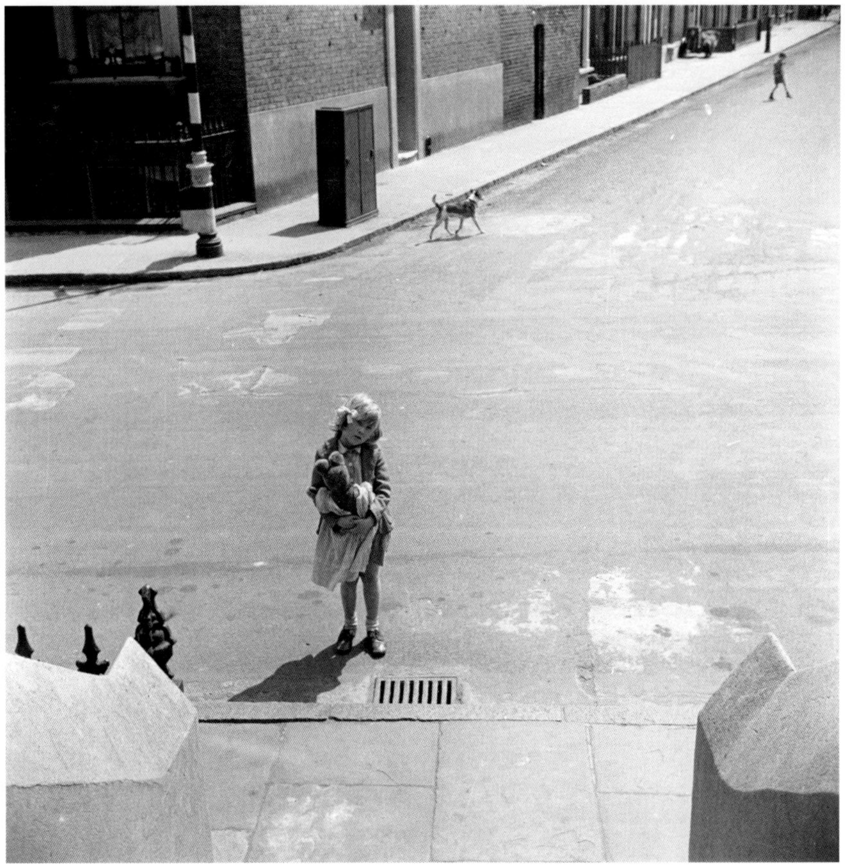

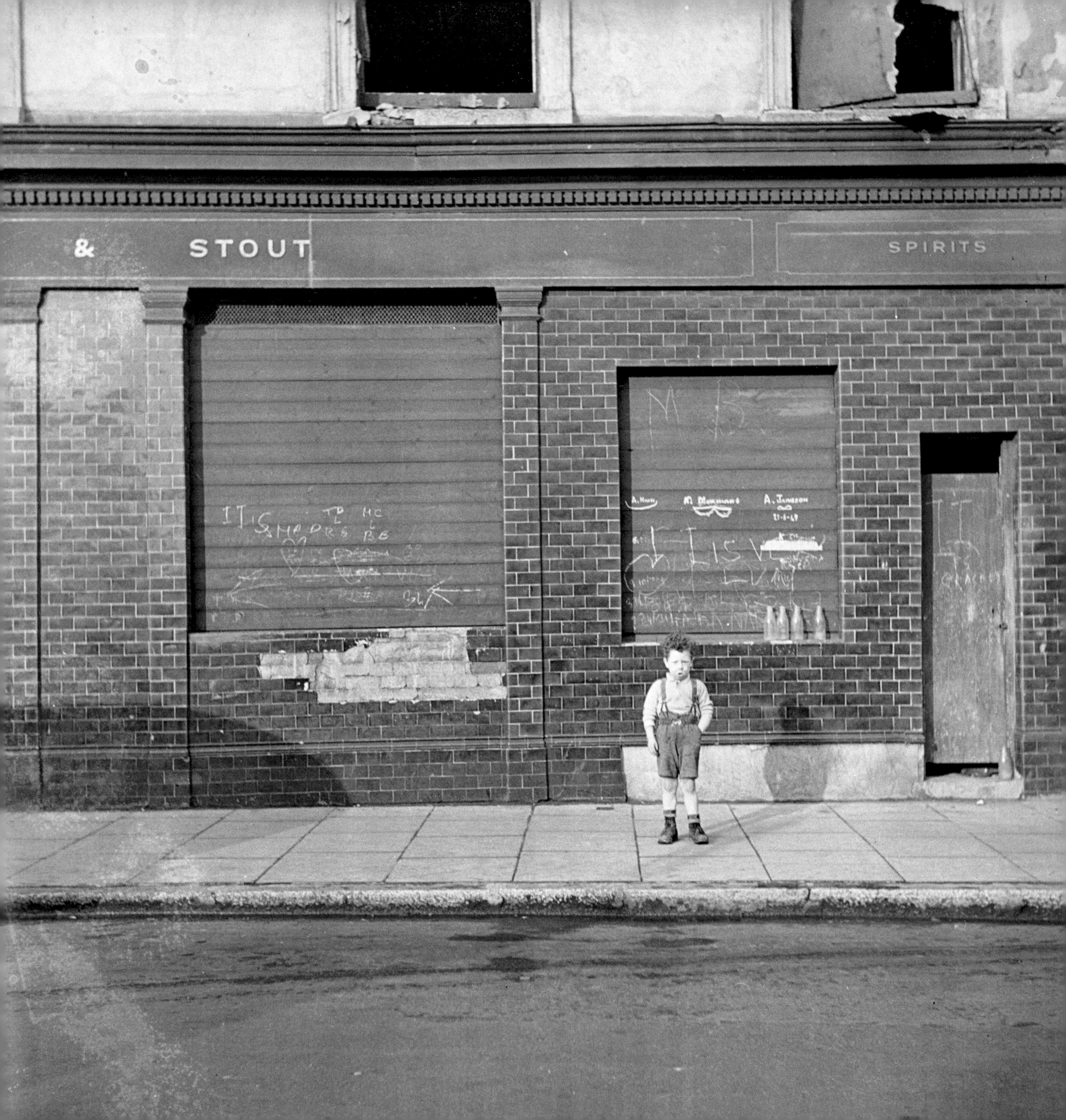
& STOUT
SPIRITS

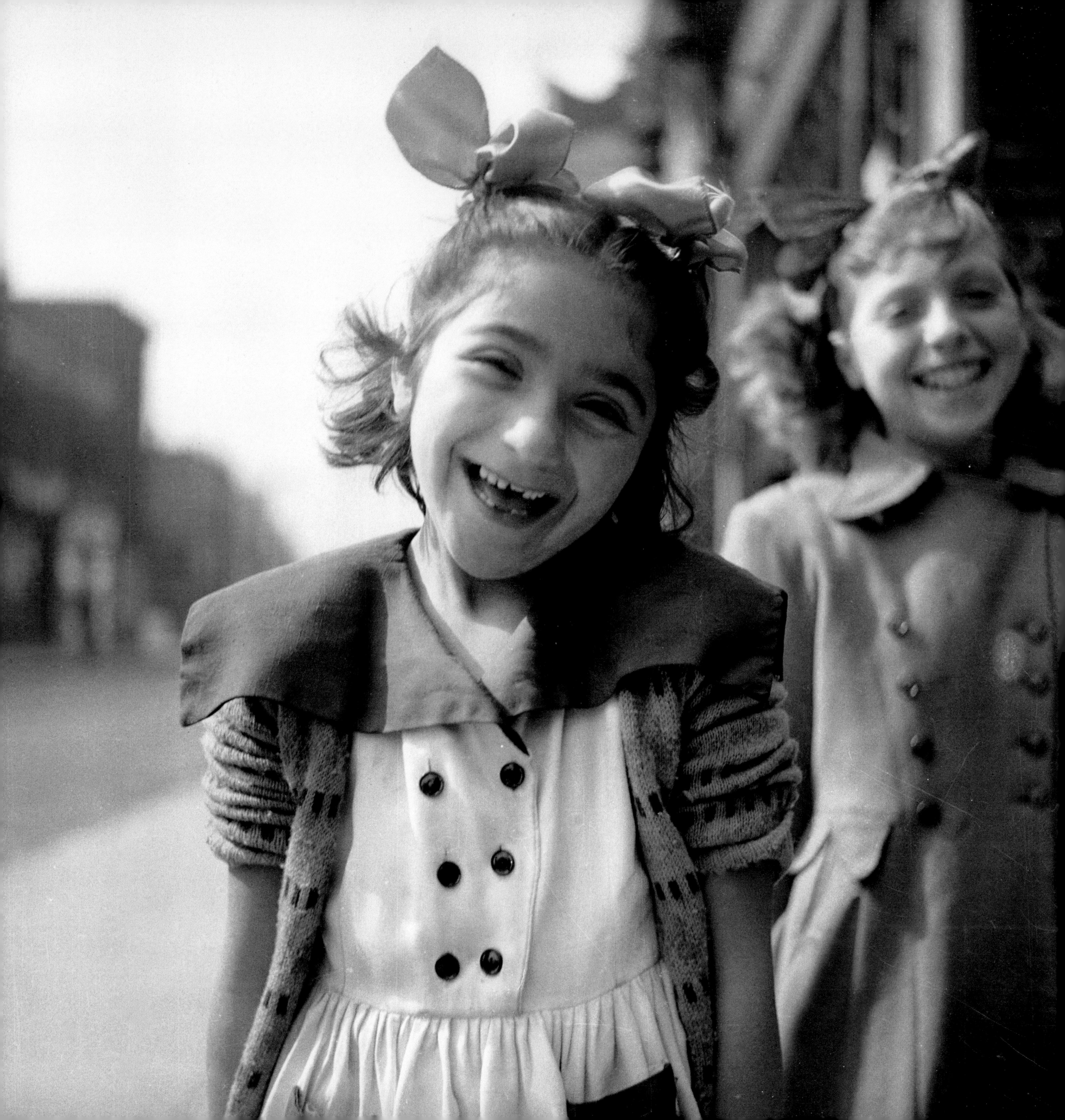

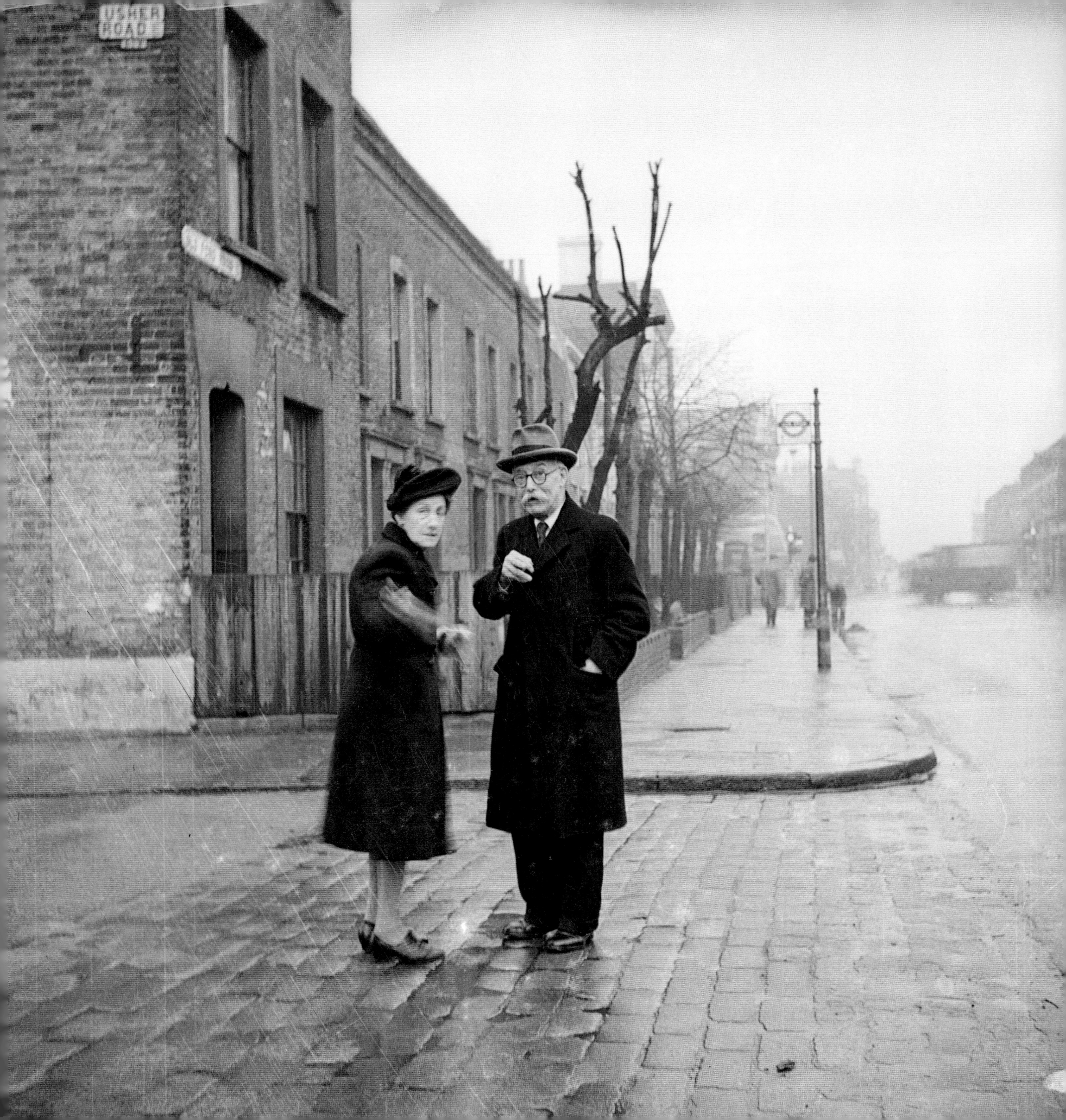
USHER
ROAD

OPPOSITE Couple on the corner of Old Ford Road and Usher Road, Bow E3

BOTTOM RIGHT Peter Samuels (a friend of the Henderson family) and Drussila (Jo) Henderson 1951

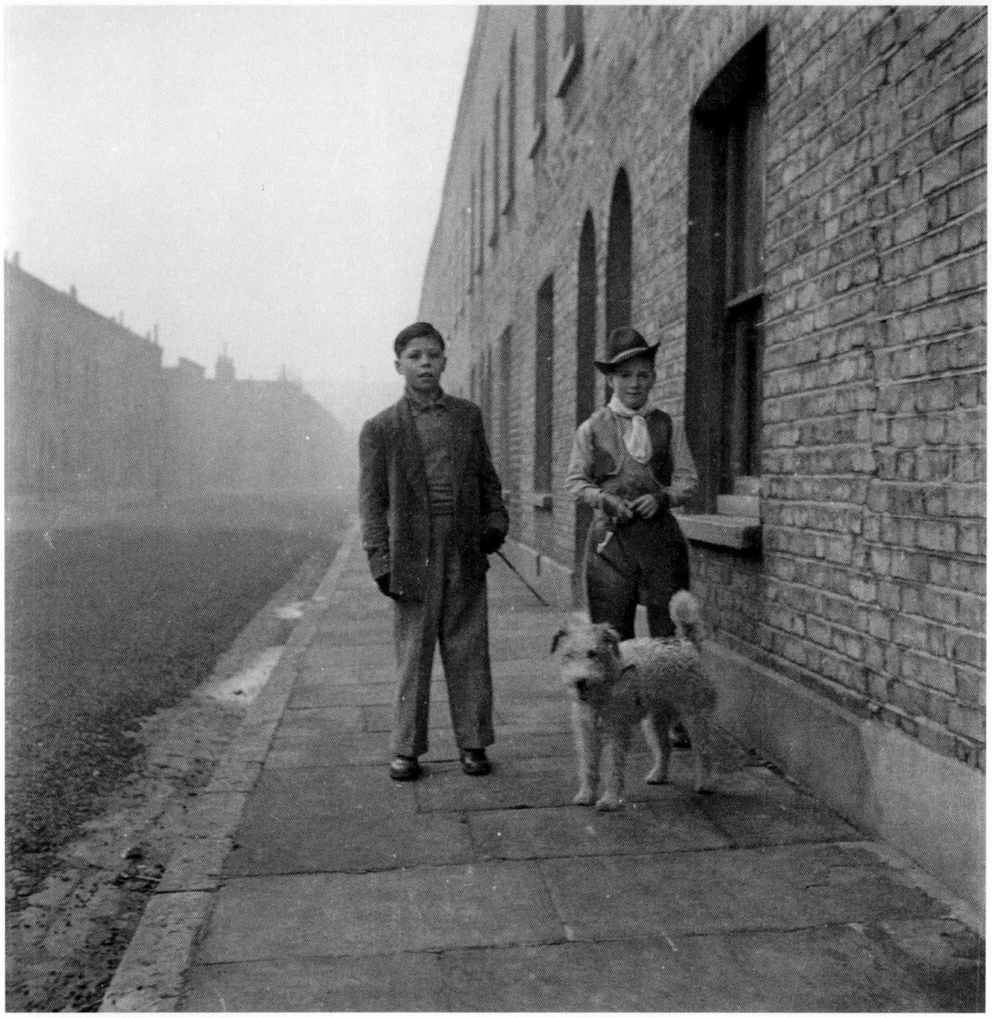

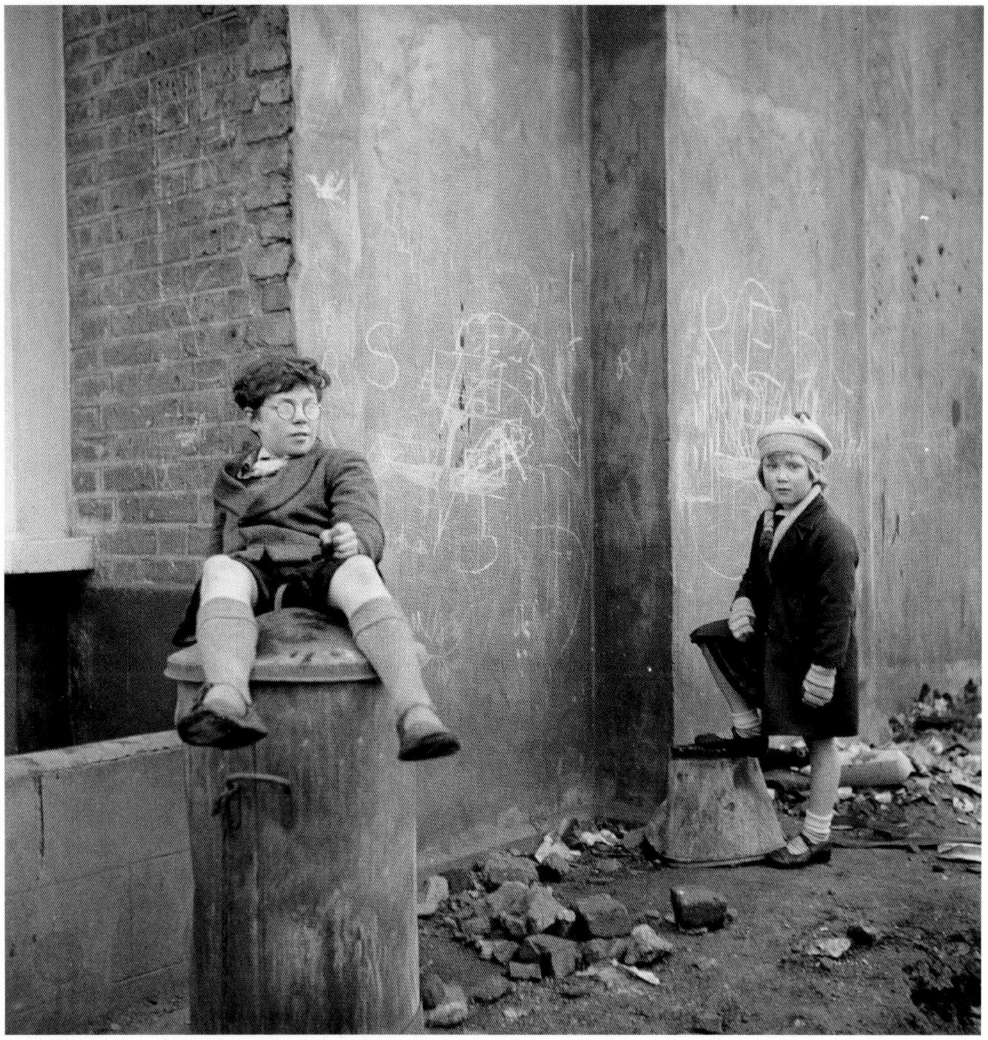

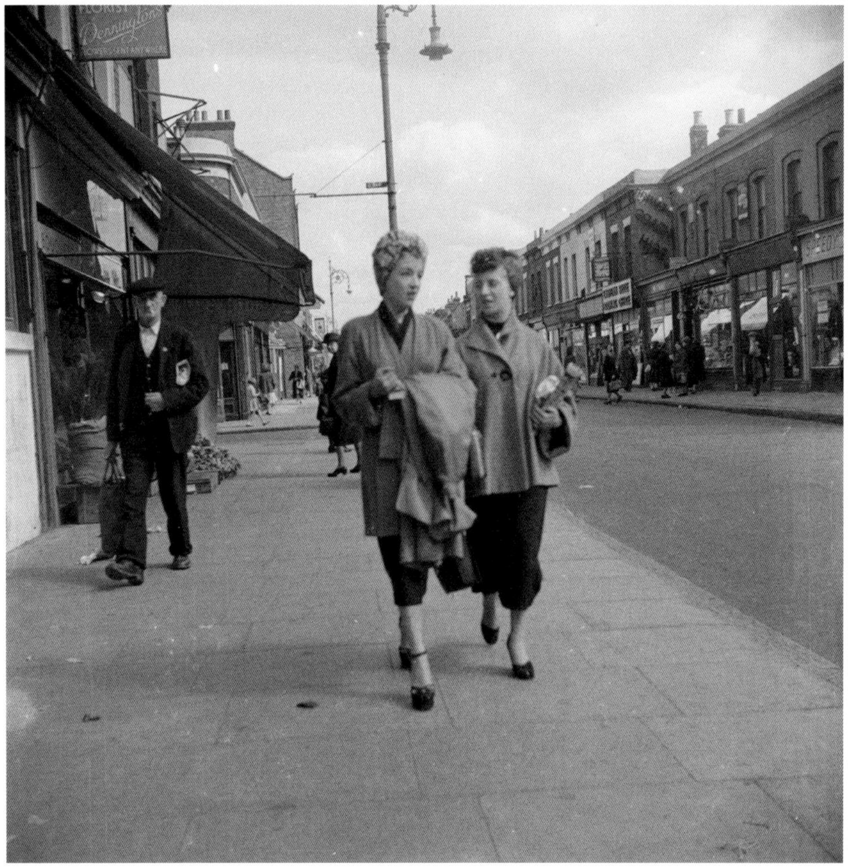

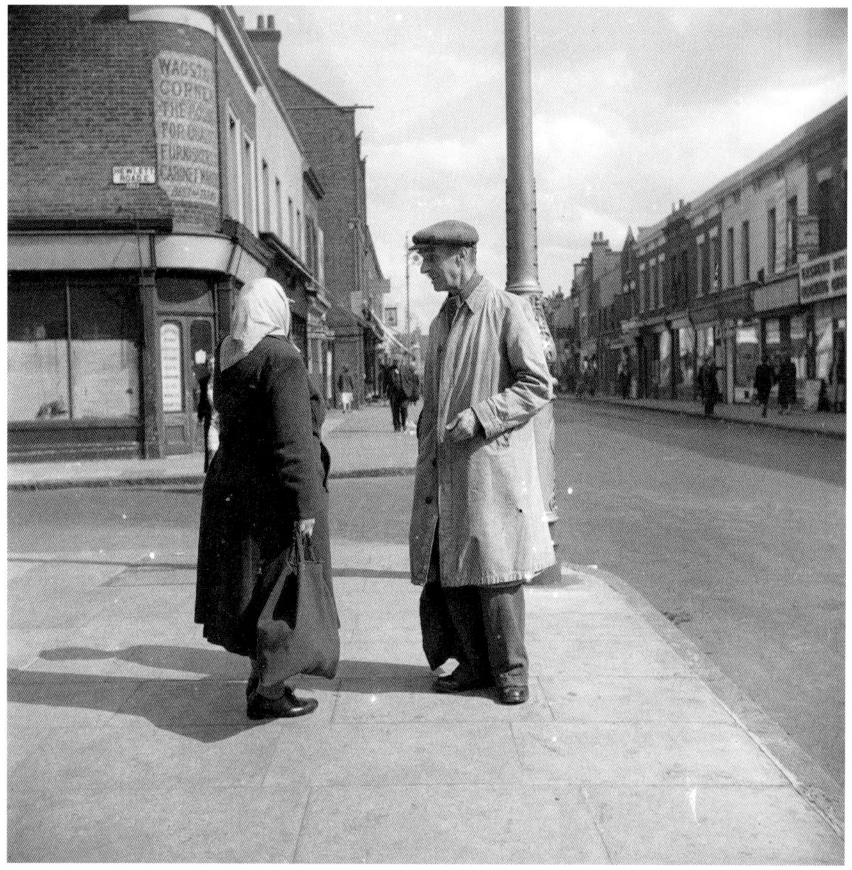

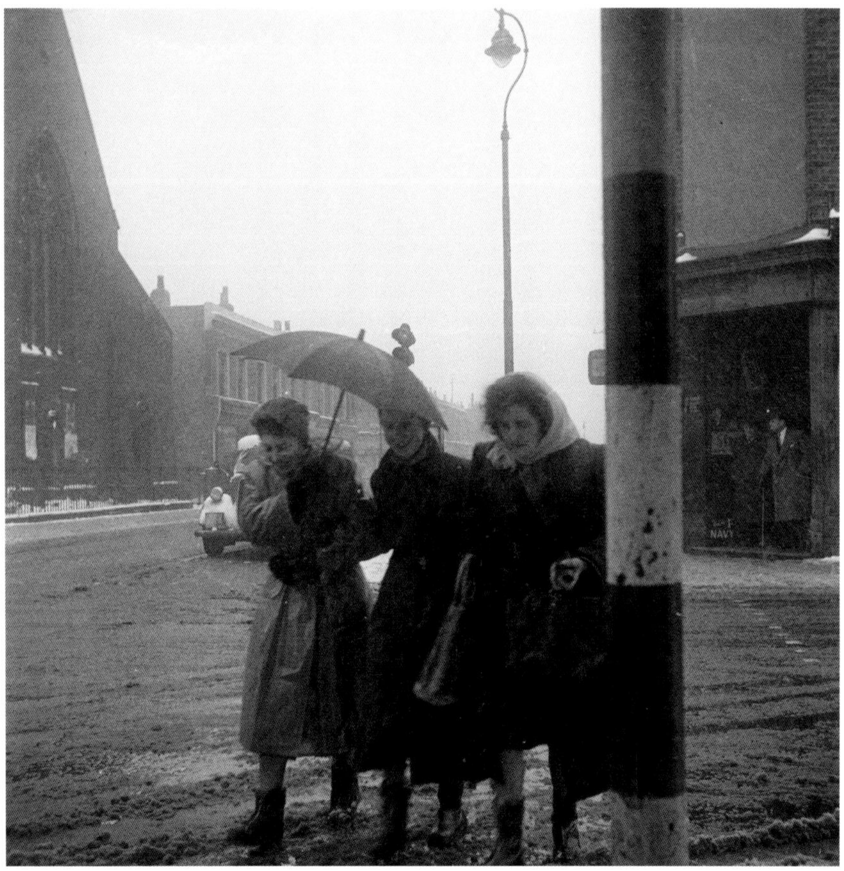

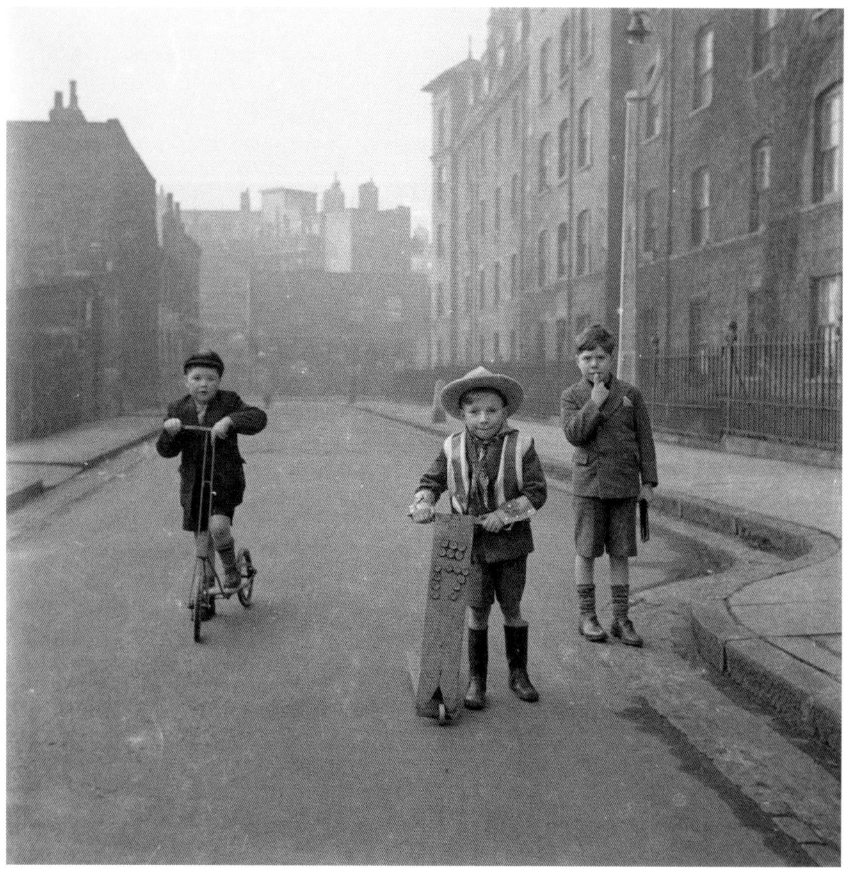

TOP *Bethnal Green Road.* (Actually Roman Road, Bow E3) 1951

TOP Couple on the corner of Roman Road and Hewlett Road, Bow E3

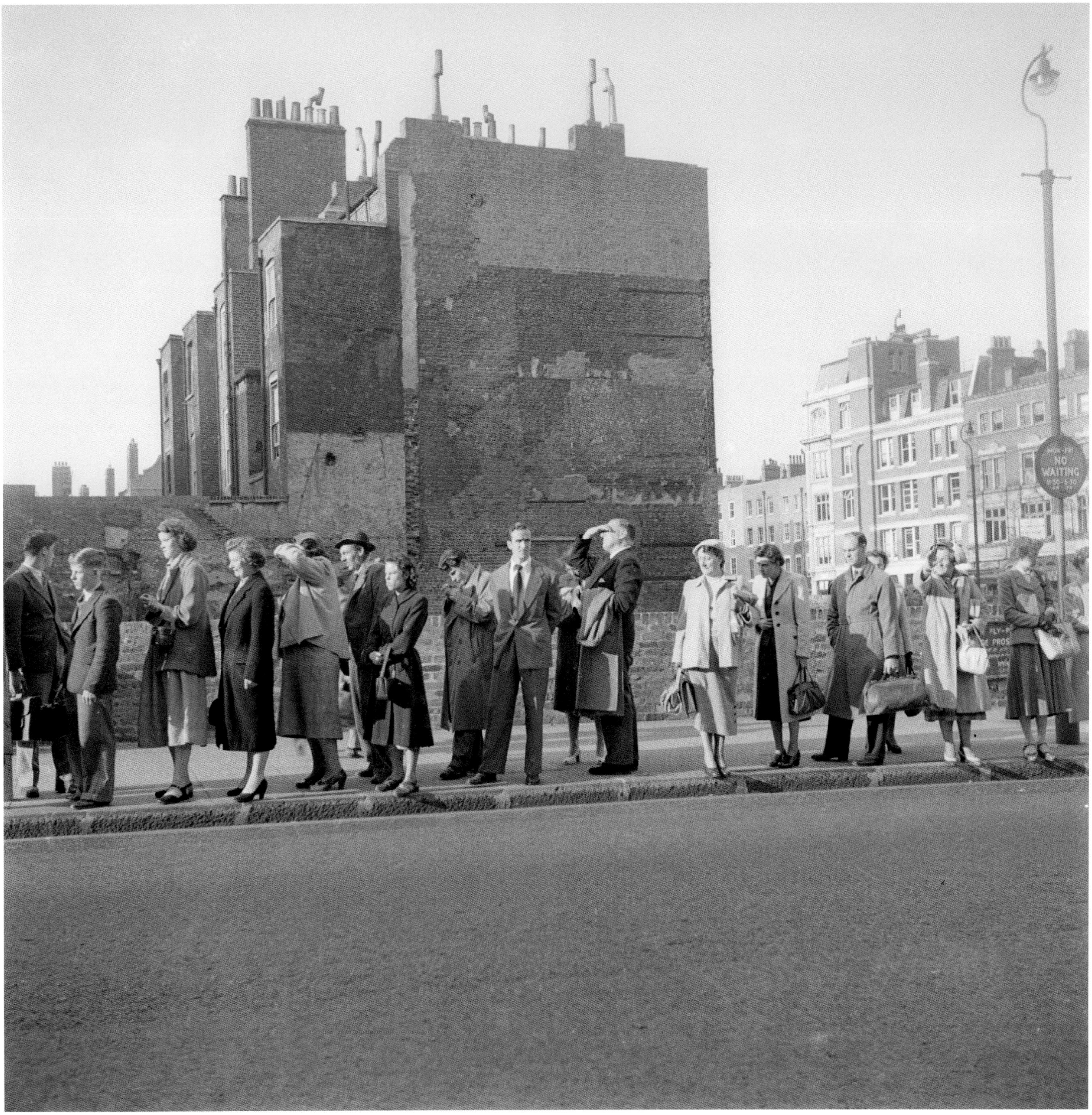

OVERLEAF Workers relaxing in the sun, St Paul's, City of London EC4 (LEFT); A window-cleaner's funeral in Chisenhale Road, Bow E3 (RIGHT)

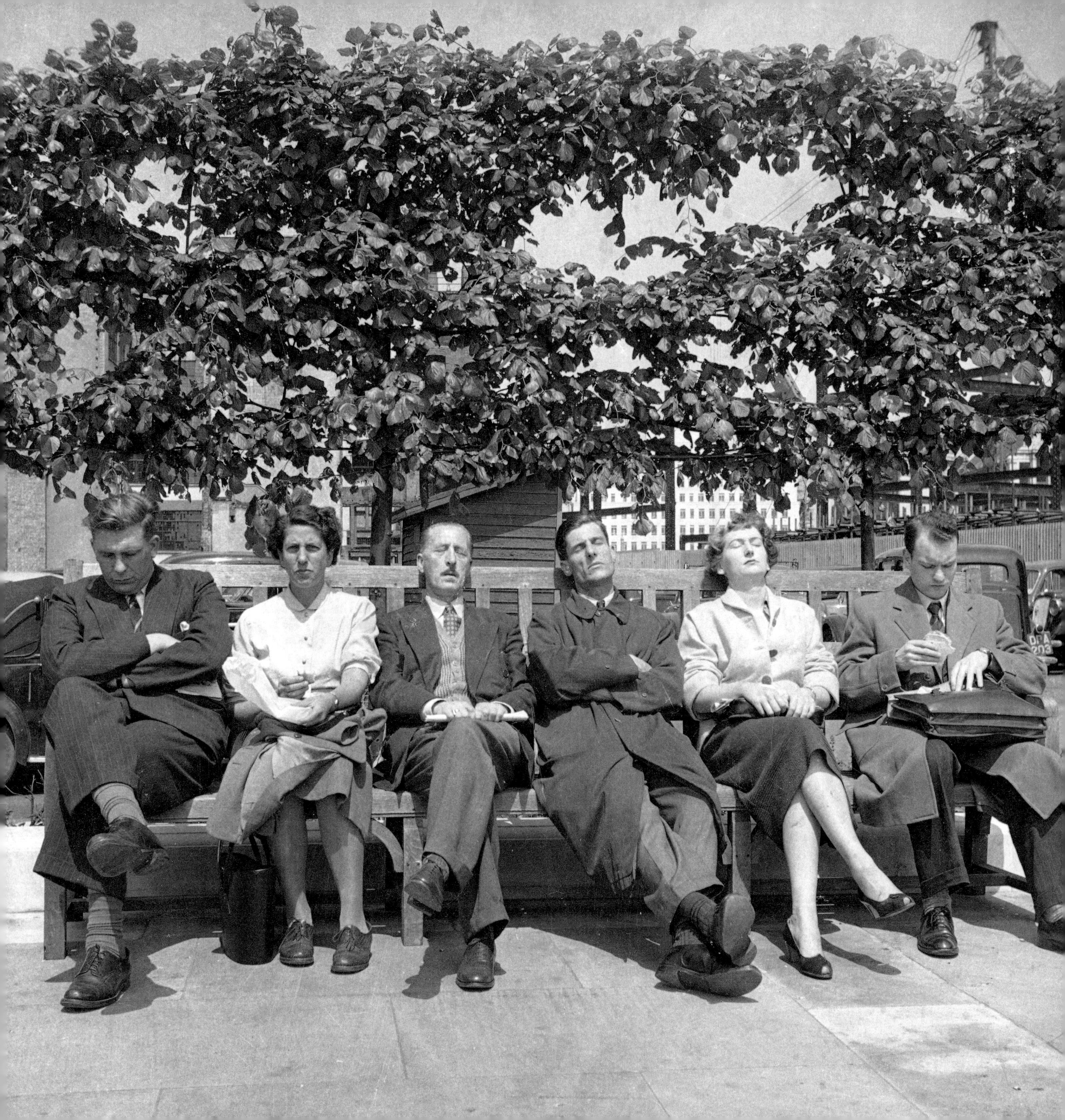

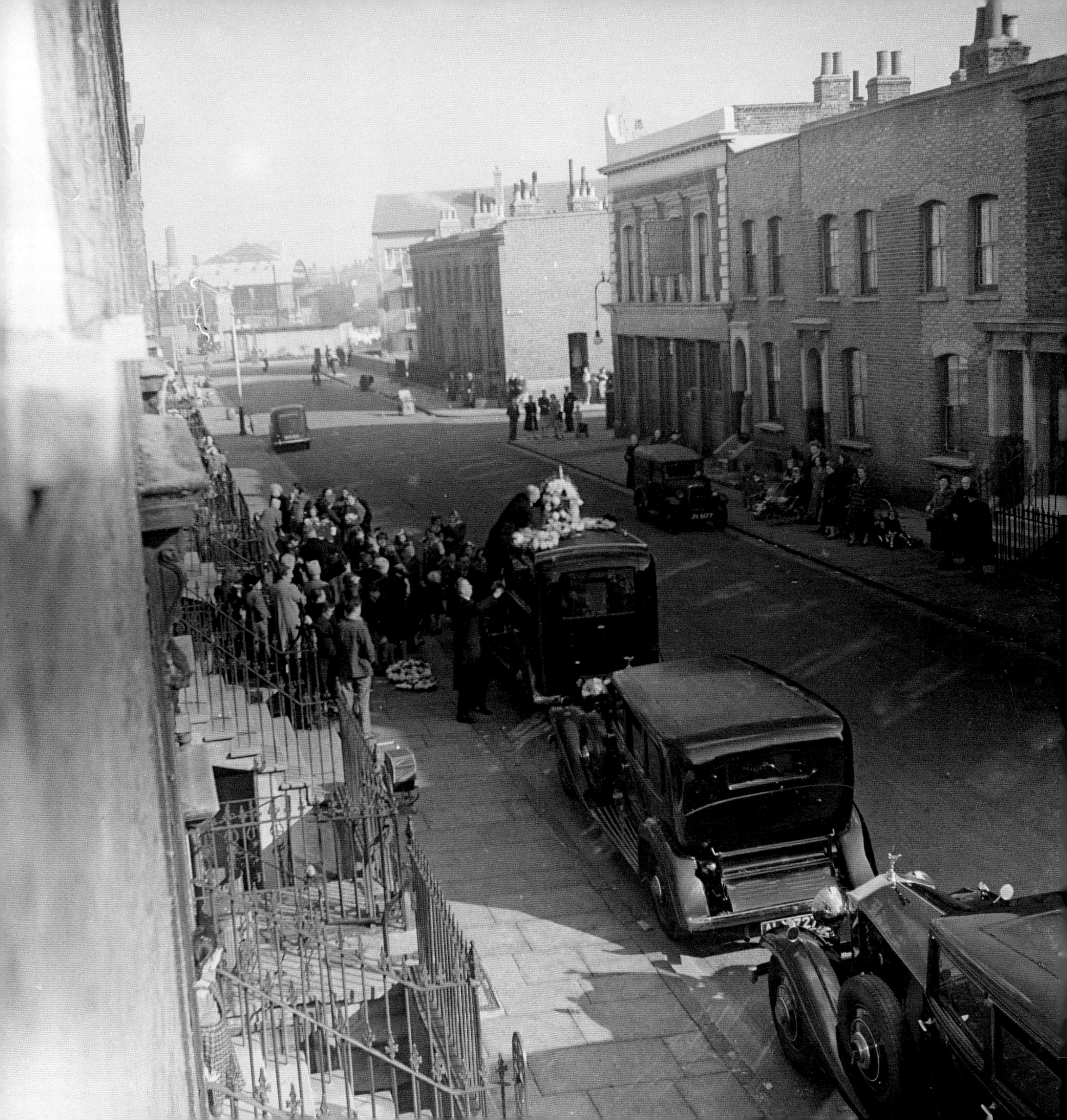

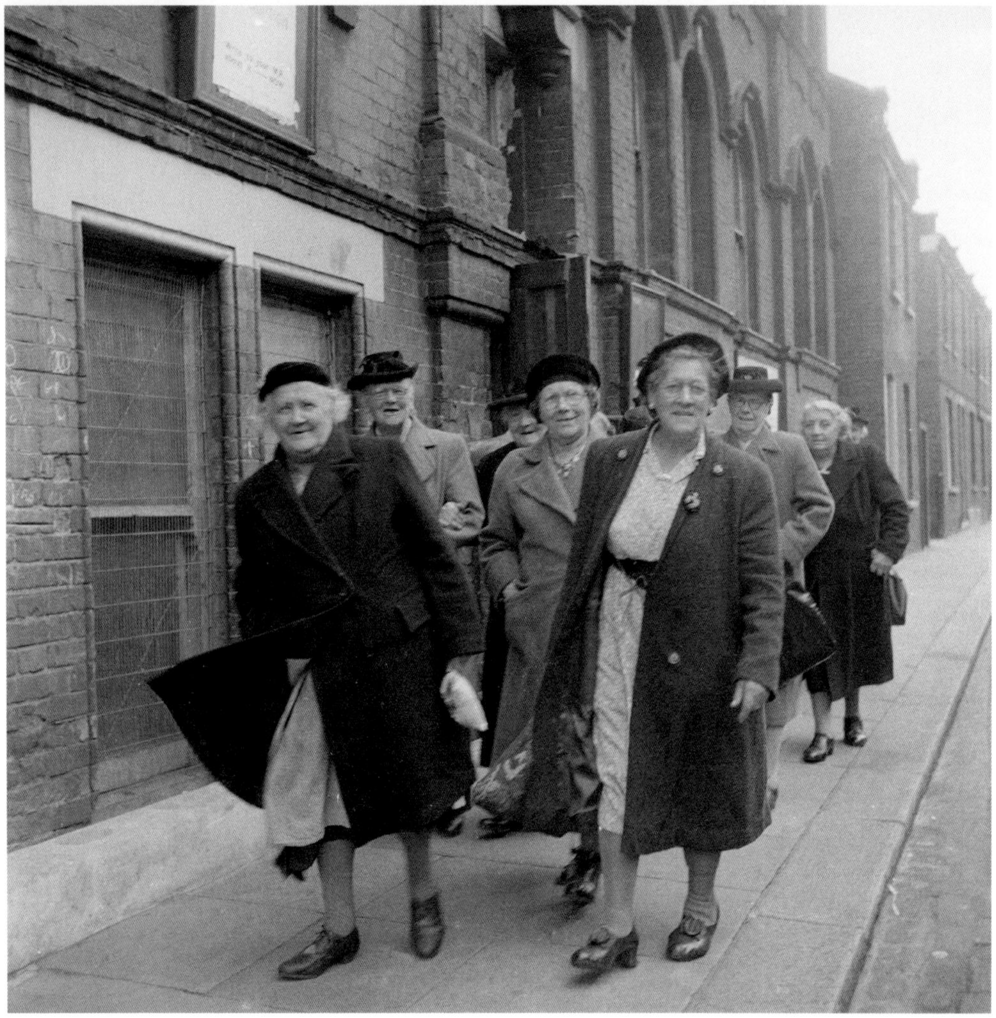

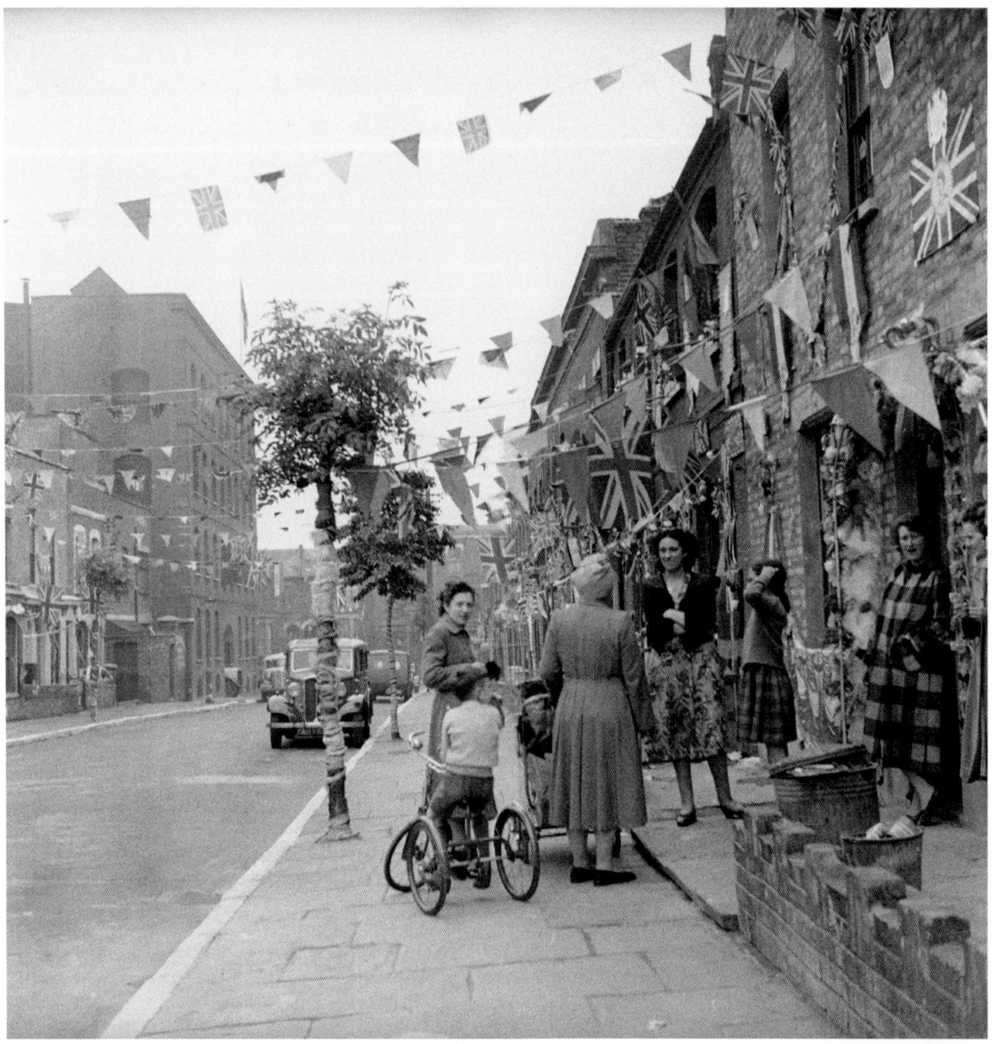

OPPOSITE *The Samuels Family* (from left to right):
Douglas, Peter, Leslie, Brian, Leslie, Doreen and Geoffrey

BOTTOM LEFT 1953

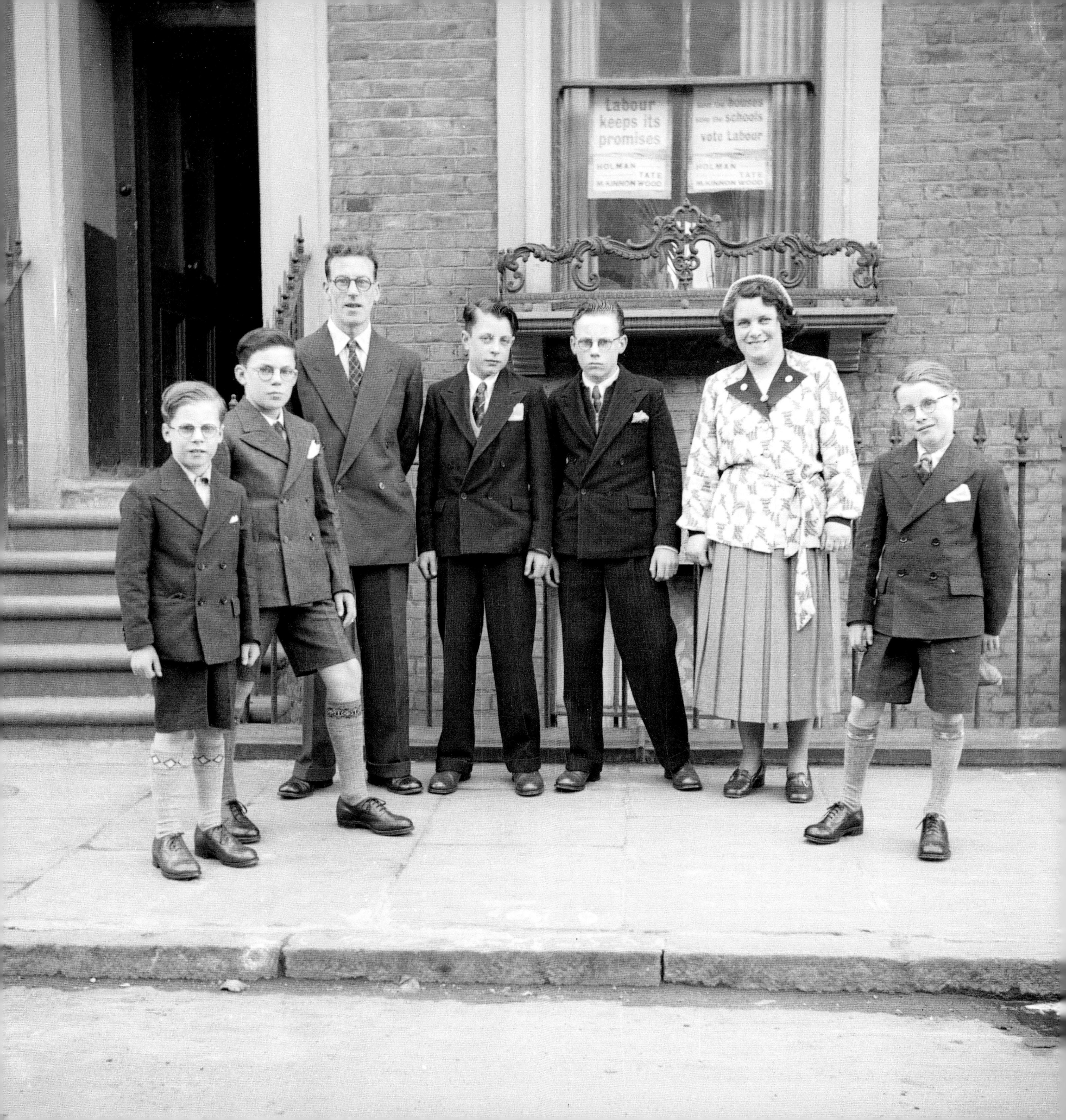
Labour
keeps its
promises
HOLMAN
TATE
McKINNON WOOD
houses
schools
vote Labour
HOLMAN
TATE
McKINNON WOOD

‘One shop front crowds another in that bizarre interplay of trade and sign that contributes to the complex textures of the city. Funeral parlour and ice cream parlour share their universal symbiosis and, from the window niche, the prurient headstone of an angel reassures us that in the midst of death we are in life.’

Shop. S. Lavner, newsagents and tobacconist, 241 Bethnal Green Road, Bethnal Green E2

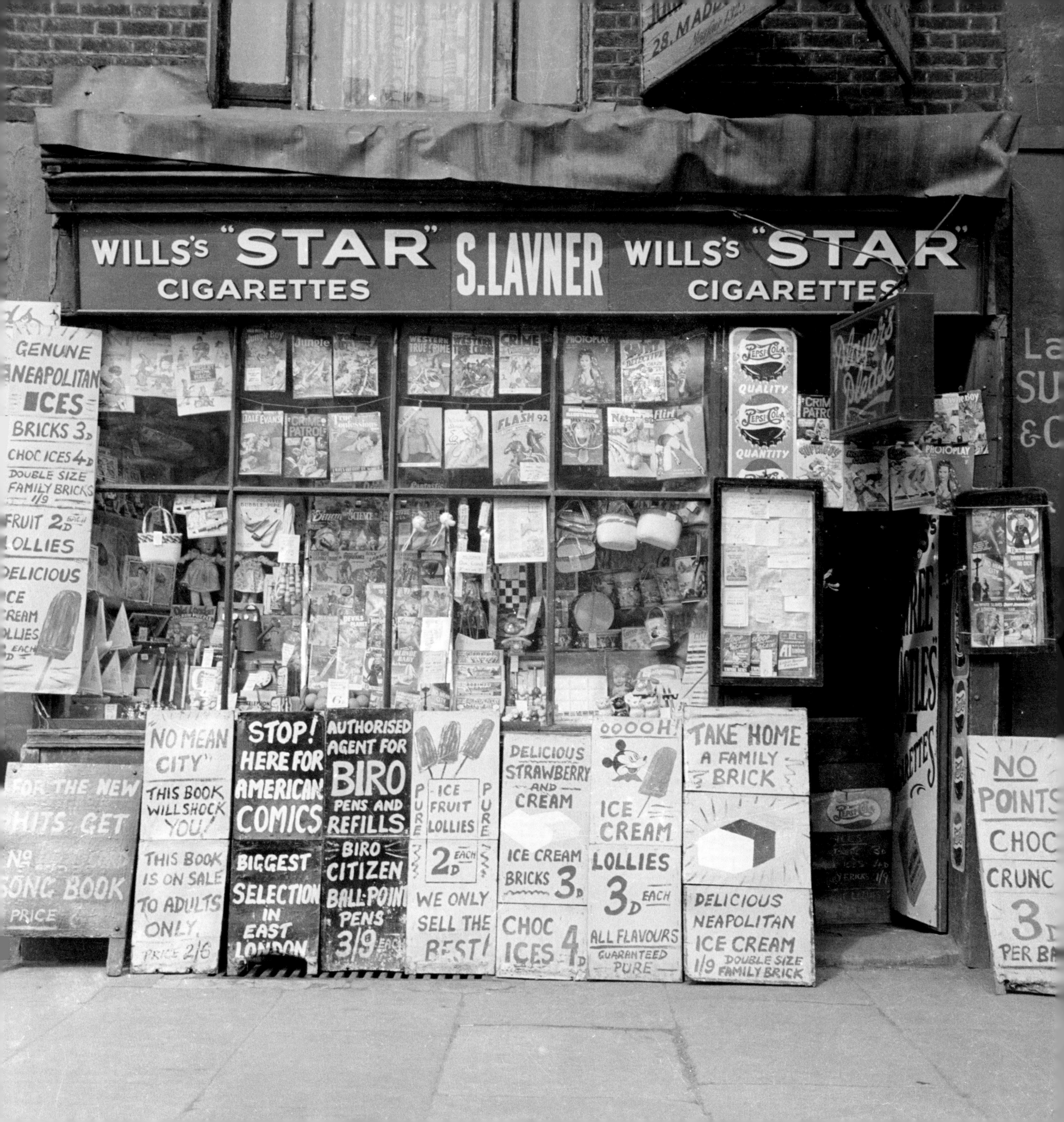
WILLS'S "STAR" CIGARETTES
S. LAVNER
WILLS'S "STAR" CIGARETTES
GENUINE NEAPOLITAN ICES
BRICKS 3D
CHOC ICES 4D
DOUBLE SIZE FAMILY BRICKS 1/9
FRUIT LOLLIES 2D EACH
DELICIOUS ICE CREAM LOLLIES
"NO MEAN CITY"
THIS BOOK WILL SHOCK YOU!
THIS BOOK IS ON SALE TO ADULTS ONLY
PRICE 2/6
STOP! HERE FOR AMERICAN COMICS
BIGGEST SELECTION IN EAST LONDON
AUTHORISED AGENT FOR BIRO PENS AND REFILLS.
BIRO CITIZEN BALL-POINT PENS 3/9
PURE ICE FRUIT LOLLIES PURE
2D EACH
WE ONLY SELL THE BEST!
DELICIOUS STRAWBERRY AND CREAM
ICE CREAM BRICKS 3D
CHOC ICES 4D
OOOOH!
ICE CREAM
LOLLIES 3D EACH
ALL FLAVOURS GUARANTEED PURE
TAKE HOME A FAMILY BRICK
DELICIOUS NEAPOLITAN ICE CREAM
1/9 DOUBLE SIZE FAMILY BRICK
NO POINTS
CHOC
CRUNC
3D
PER BA
PEPSI-COLA
QUALITY
QUANTITY

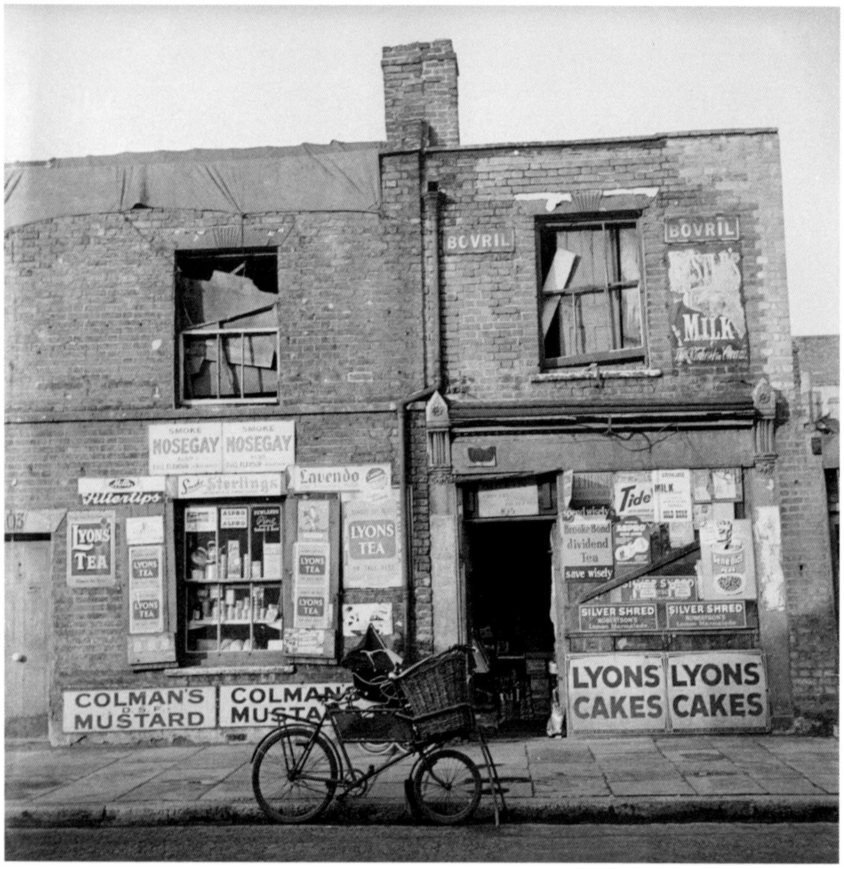

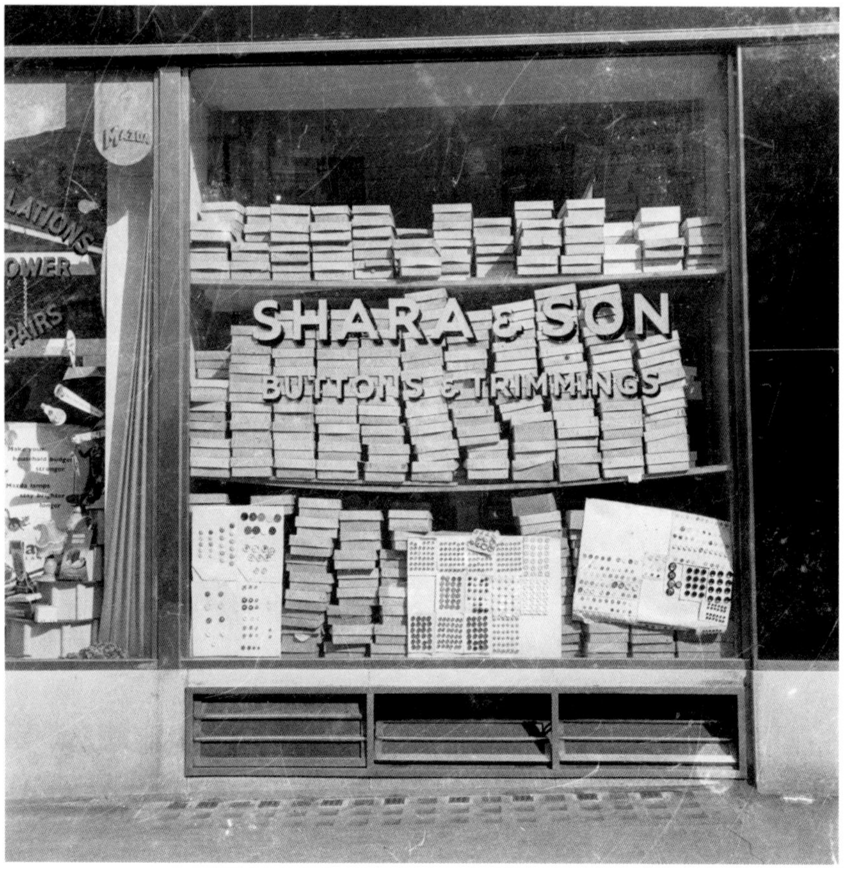

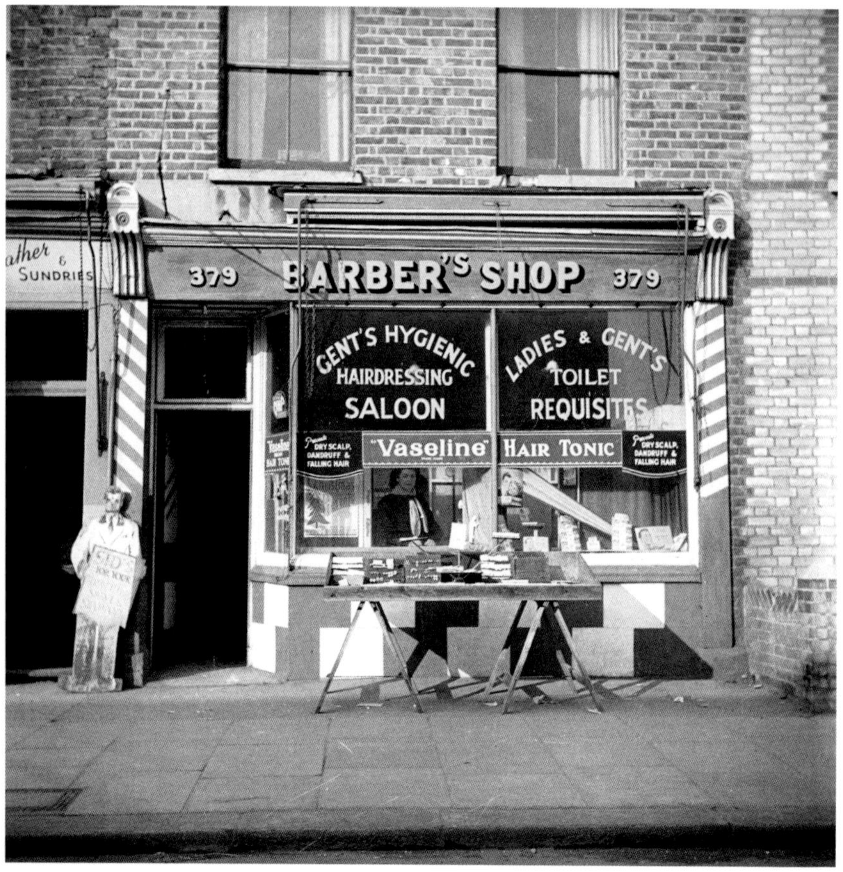

TOP Benjamin Myer Levin, chandlers shop, 105 Cephas Street, Bethnal Green E1
BOTTOM Shara & Son, buttons and trimmings, 3 Leman Street, City of London E1

TOP Mark Klein Library, 308 Stepney Way, Stepney E1
BOTTOM Sydney Myers barber's shop, 379 Roman Road, Bow E3

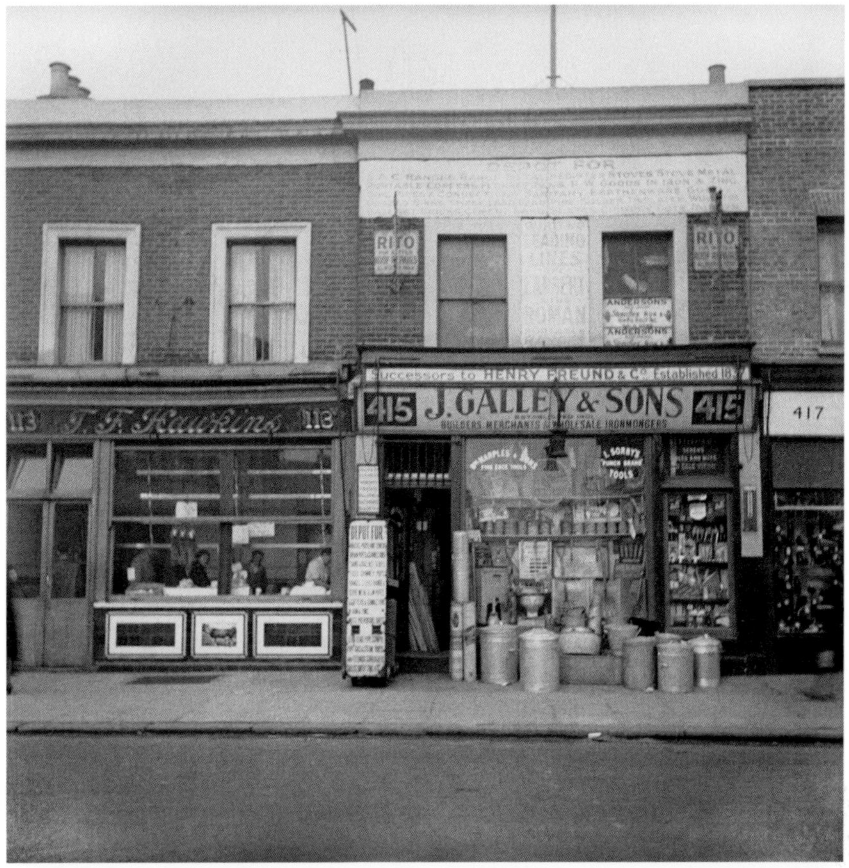

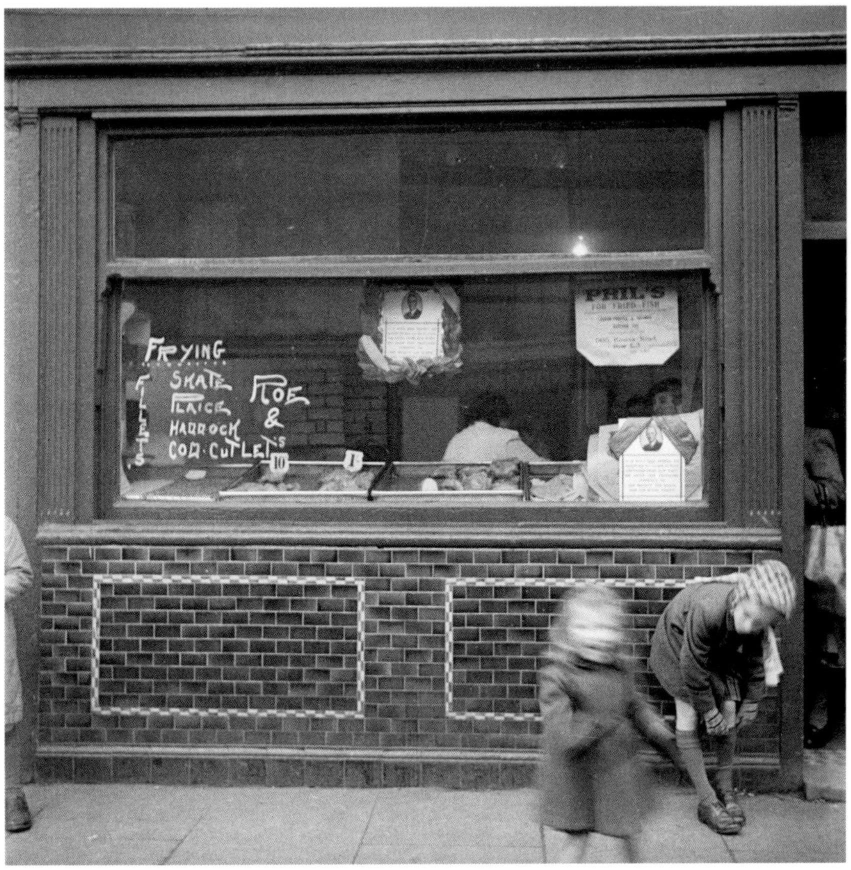

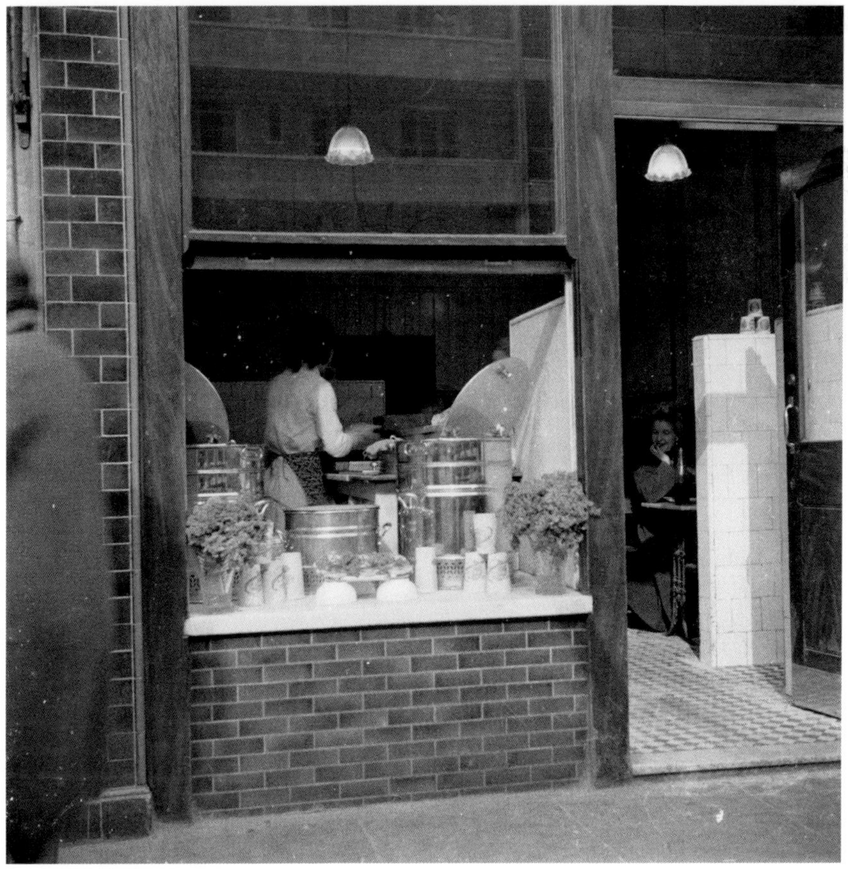

ABOVE *Phil's.* Fish and chip shop, 505 Roman Road, Bow E3 1952

TOP RIGHT T.F Hawkins, butchers and J. Galley & Sons, builders' merchant and wholesale ironmongers, 113 and 415 Roman Road, Bow E3

BOTTOM RIGHT G. Kelly's Pie and Mash, 600 Roman Road, Bow E3

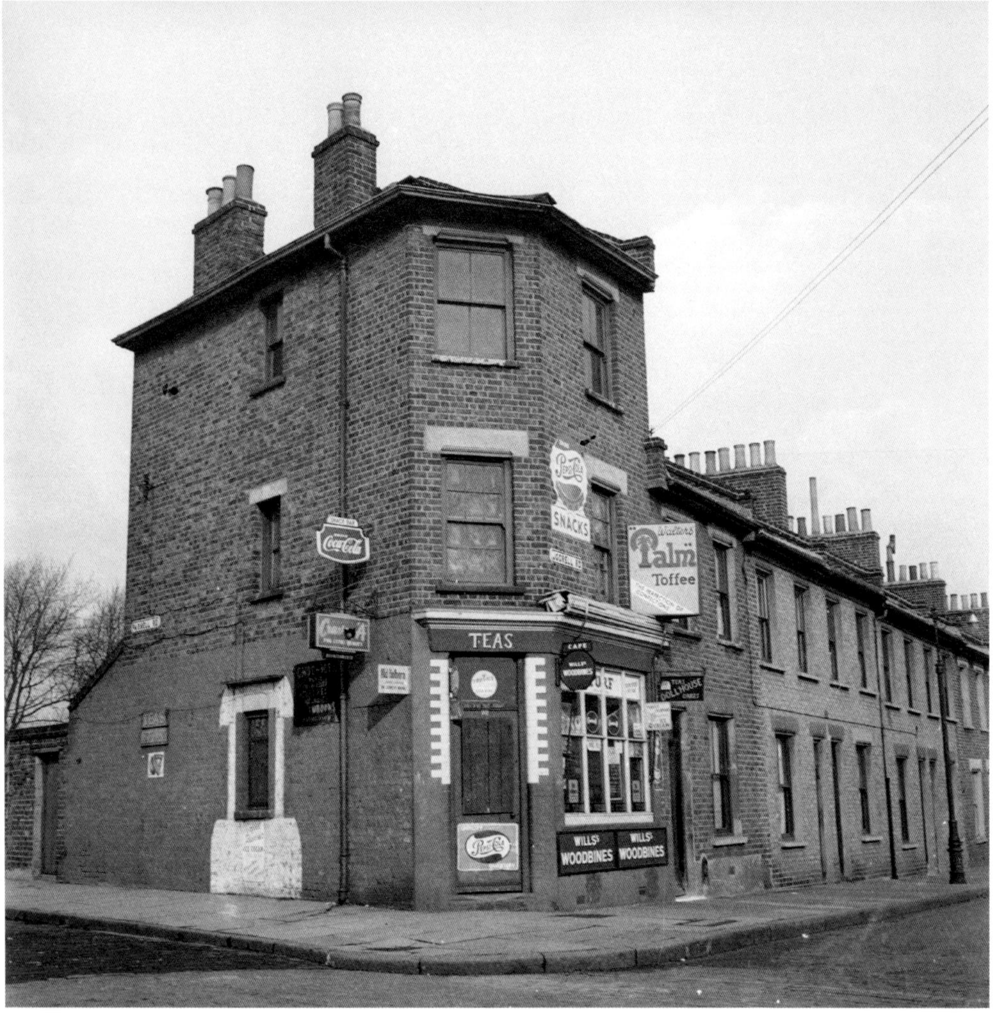

LEFT Joseph T. Griffith, confectioners, 92 Jodrell Road, Bow E3

BELOW J. Day & Co. Derby Works, 237 Roman Road, Bow E3

OPPOSITE Thomas William Clench, newsagent, 51 Emmett Street, Poplar E14

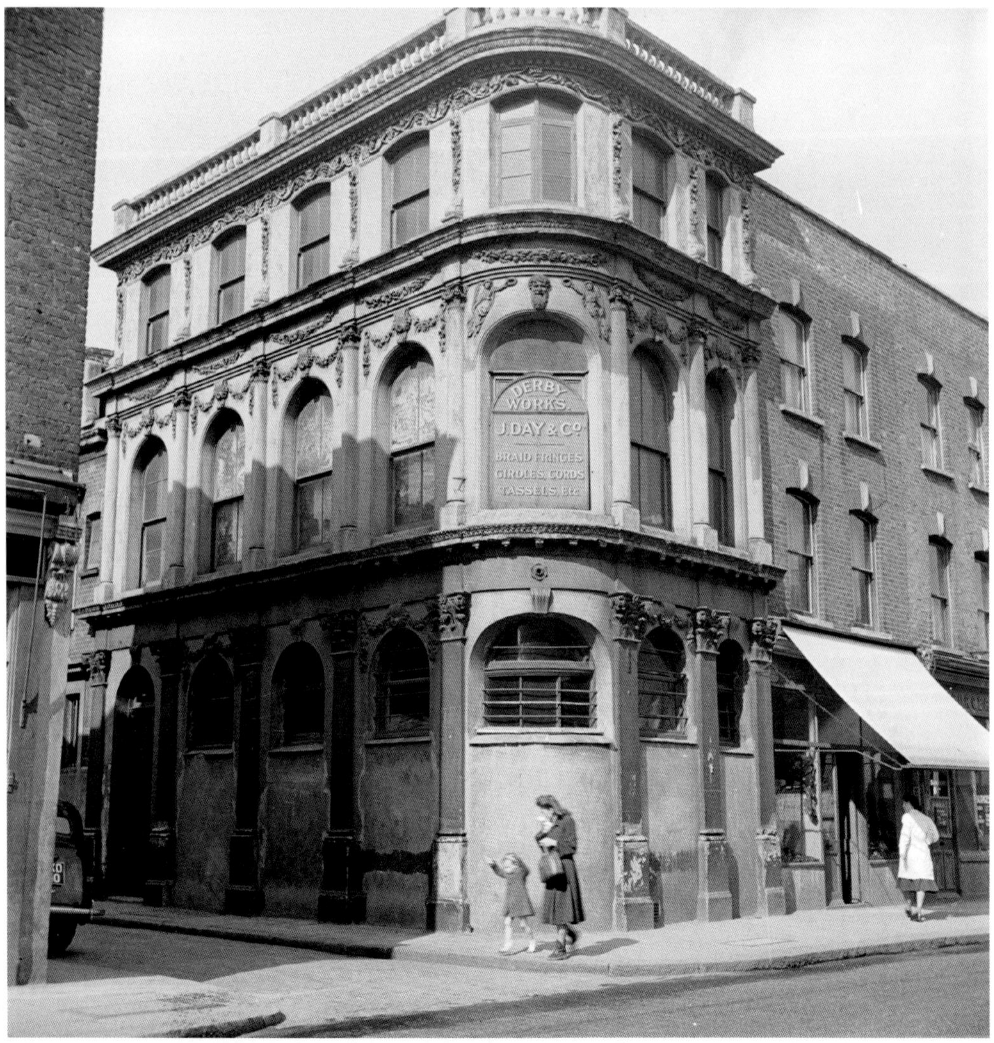

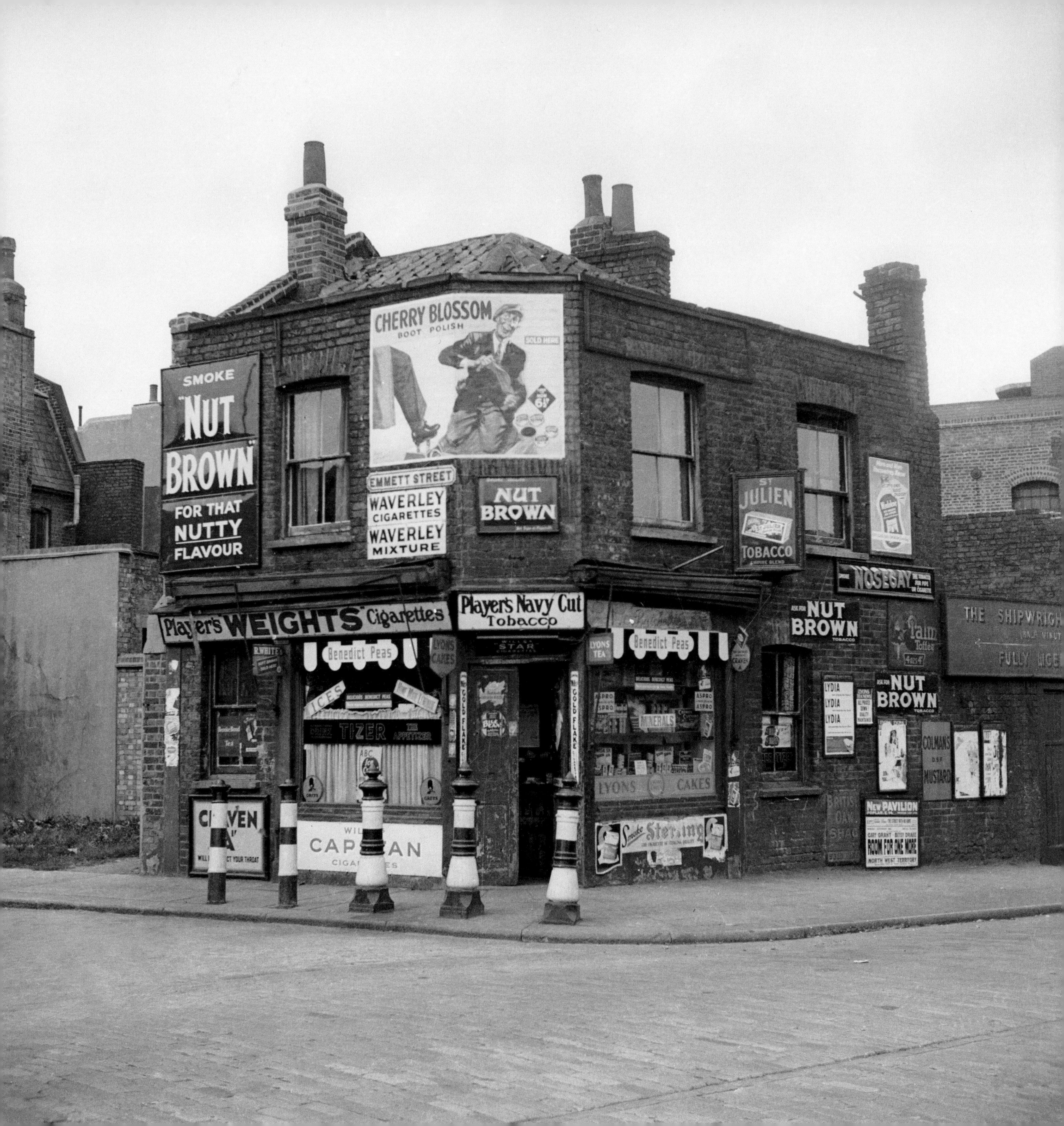

CHERRY BLOSSOM
BOOT POLISH
SOLD HERE
SMOKE
"NUT BROWN"
FOR THAT NUTTY FLAVOUR
EMMETT STREET
WAVERLEY CIGARETTES
WAVERLEY MIXTURE
NUT BROWN
ST JULIEN
TOBACCO
NOSEGAY
Player's WEIGHTS Cigarettes
Player's Navy Cut Tobacco
Benedict Peas
LYONS CAKES
ICES
TIZER
THE APPETIZER
LYONS TEA
Benedict Peas
MINERALS
LYONS CAKES
ASK FOR NUT BROWN TOBACCO
THE SHIPWRIGH
FULLY
NUT BROWN
TOBACCO
LYDIA
LYDIA
LYDIA
COLMANS
MUSTARD
NEW PAVILION
ROOM FOR ONE MORE
CRAVEN "A"
CAPSTAN
CIGARETTES
Smoke Sterling

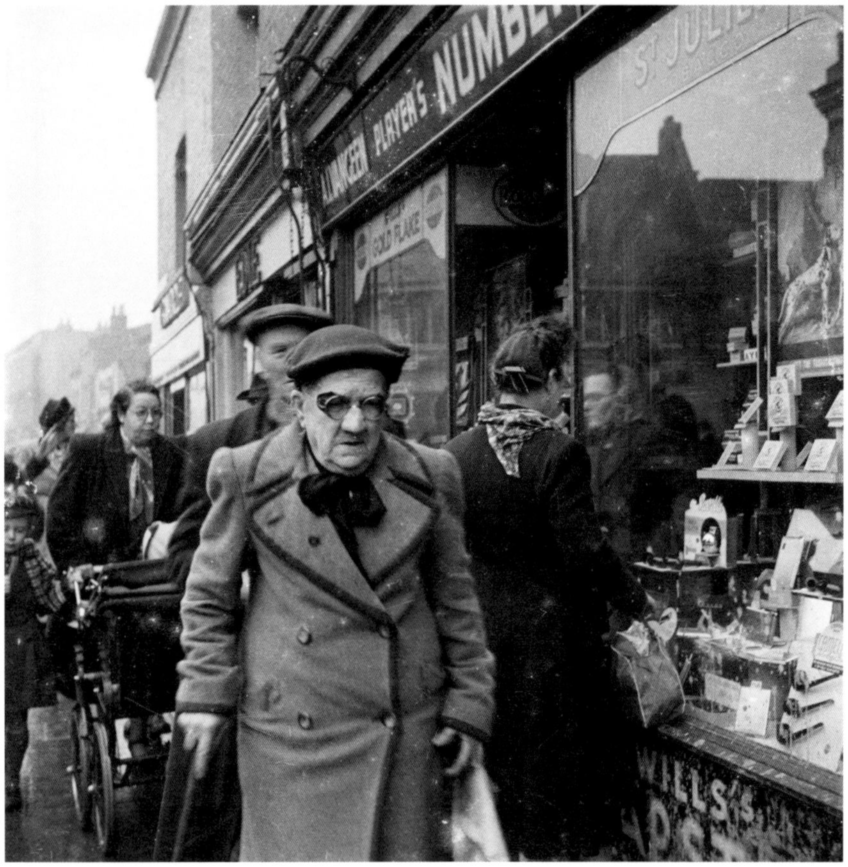

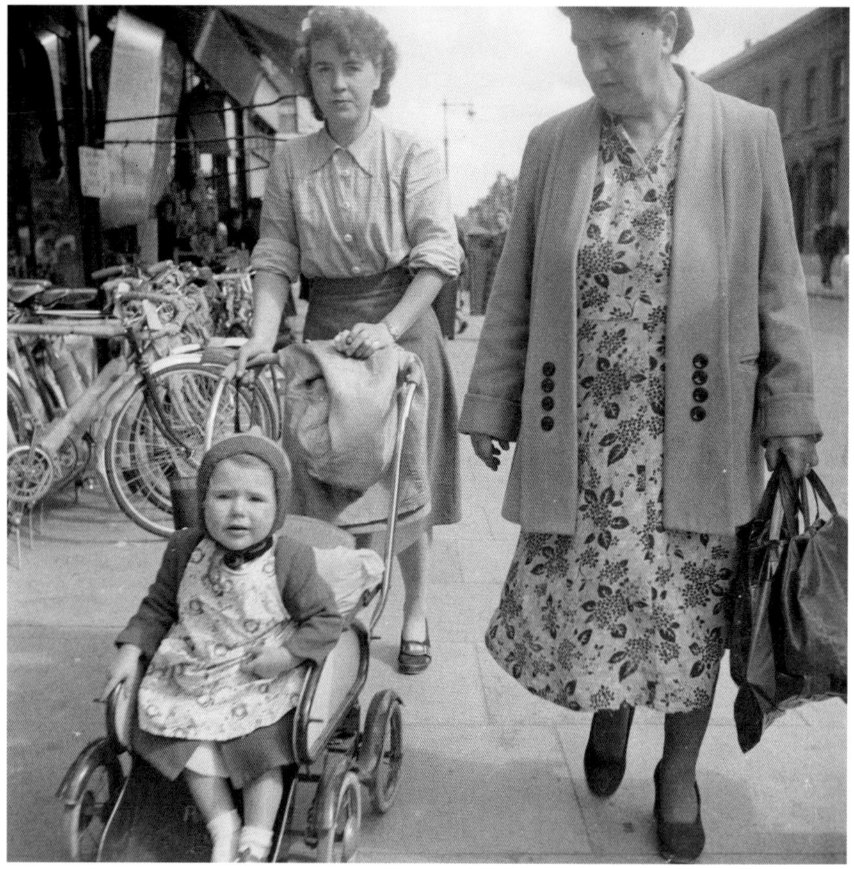

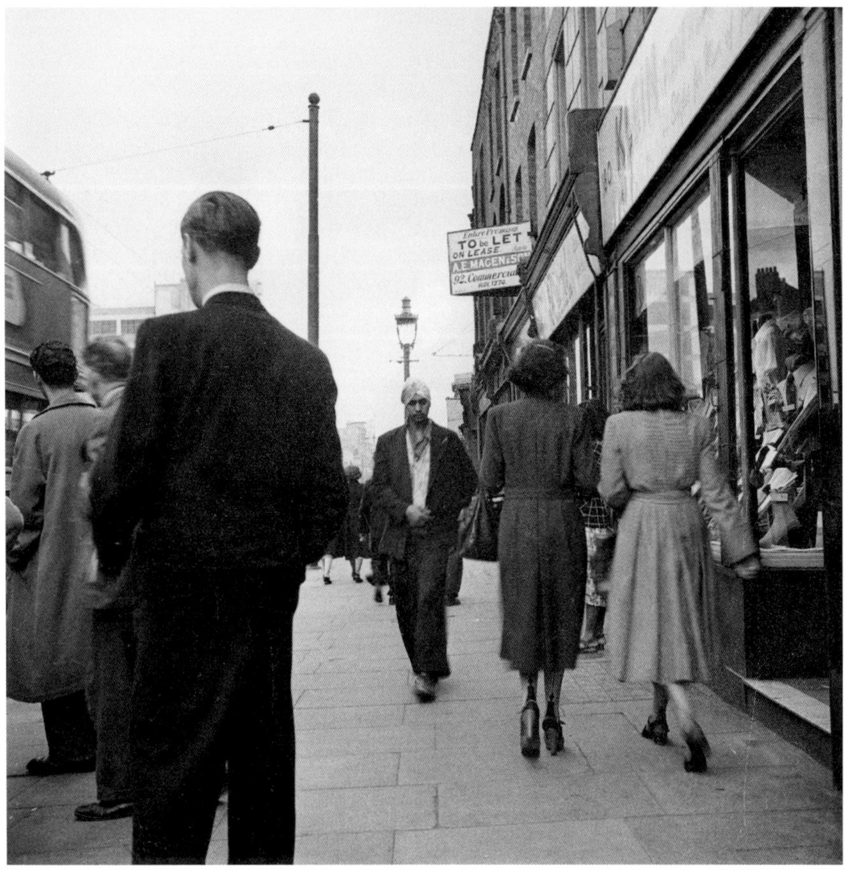

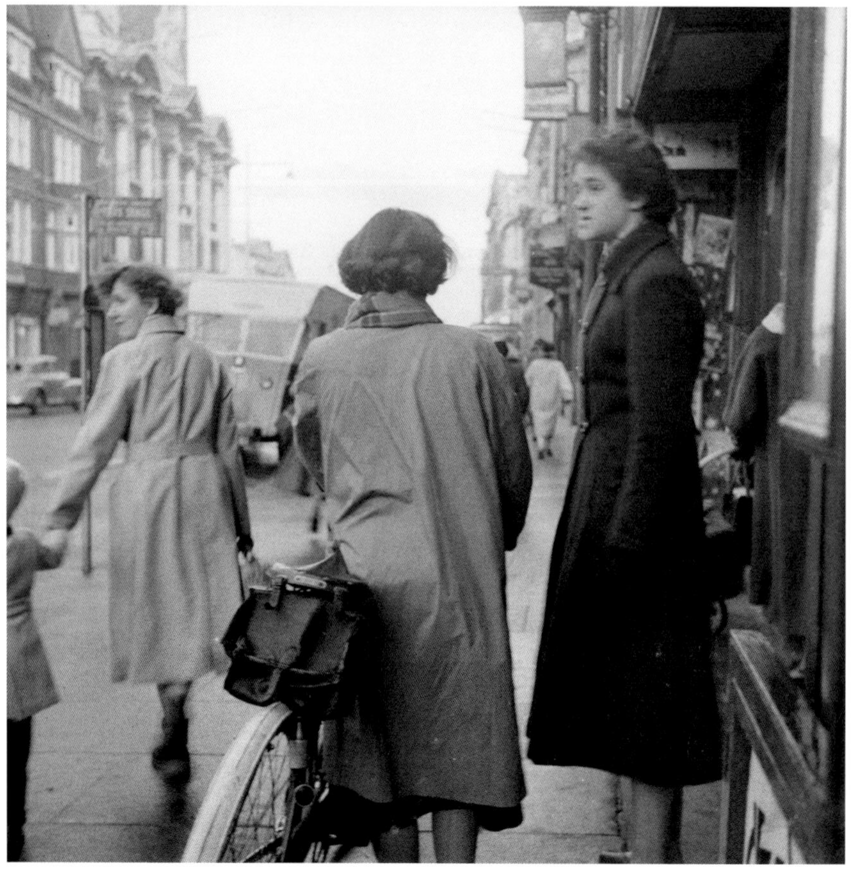

BOTTOM LEFT Commercial Road, Whitechapel E1

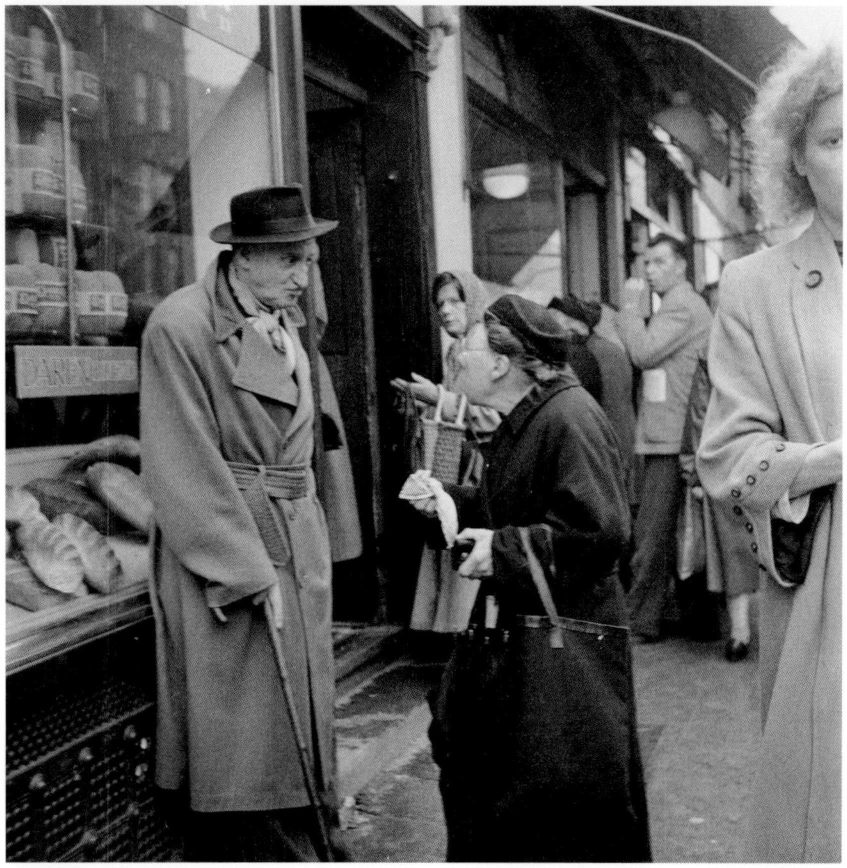

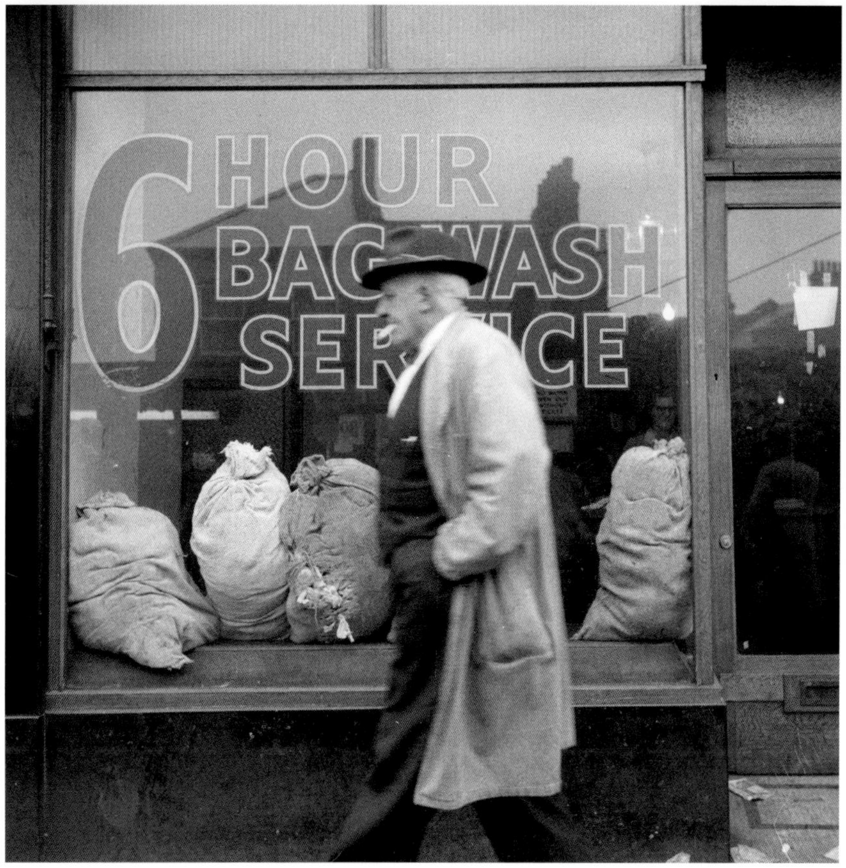

BOTTOM *The Bagwash*

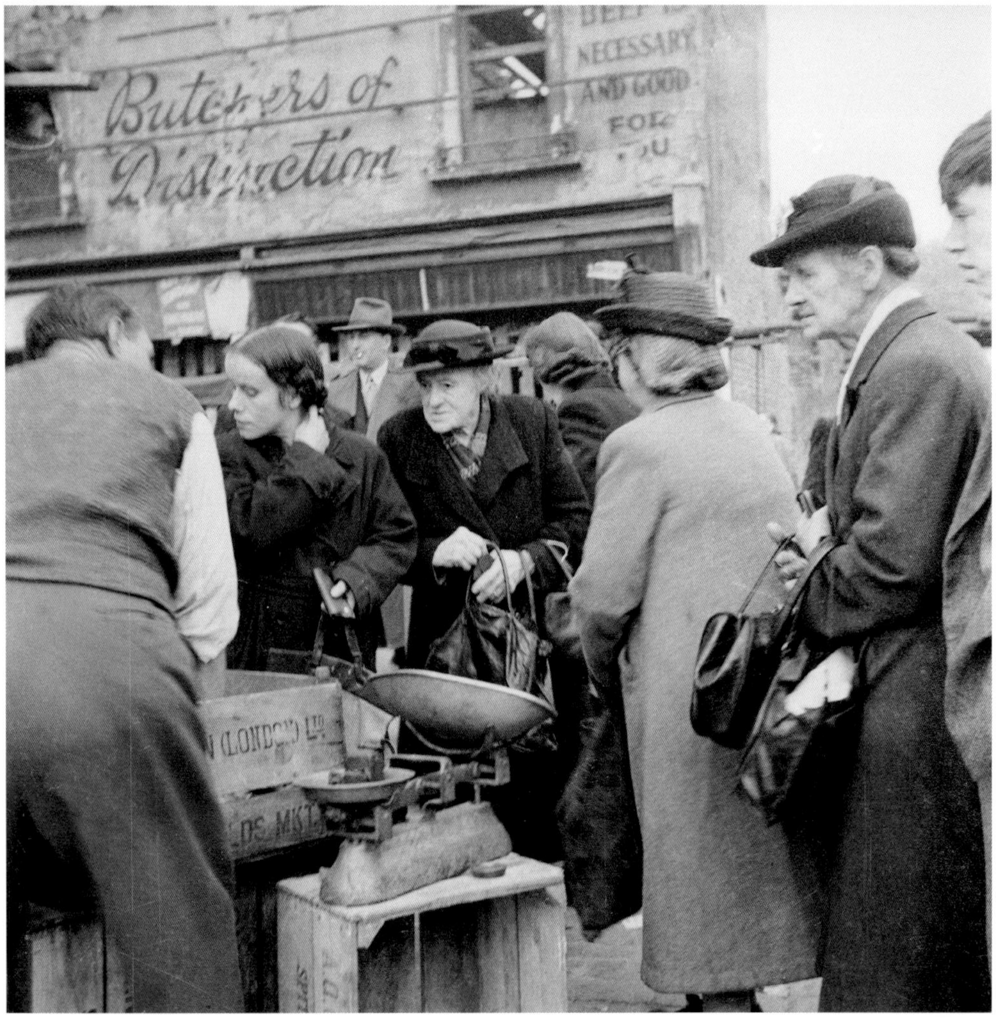
NECESSARY
AND GOOD

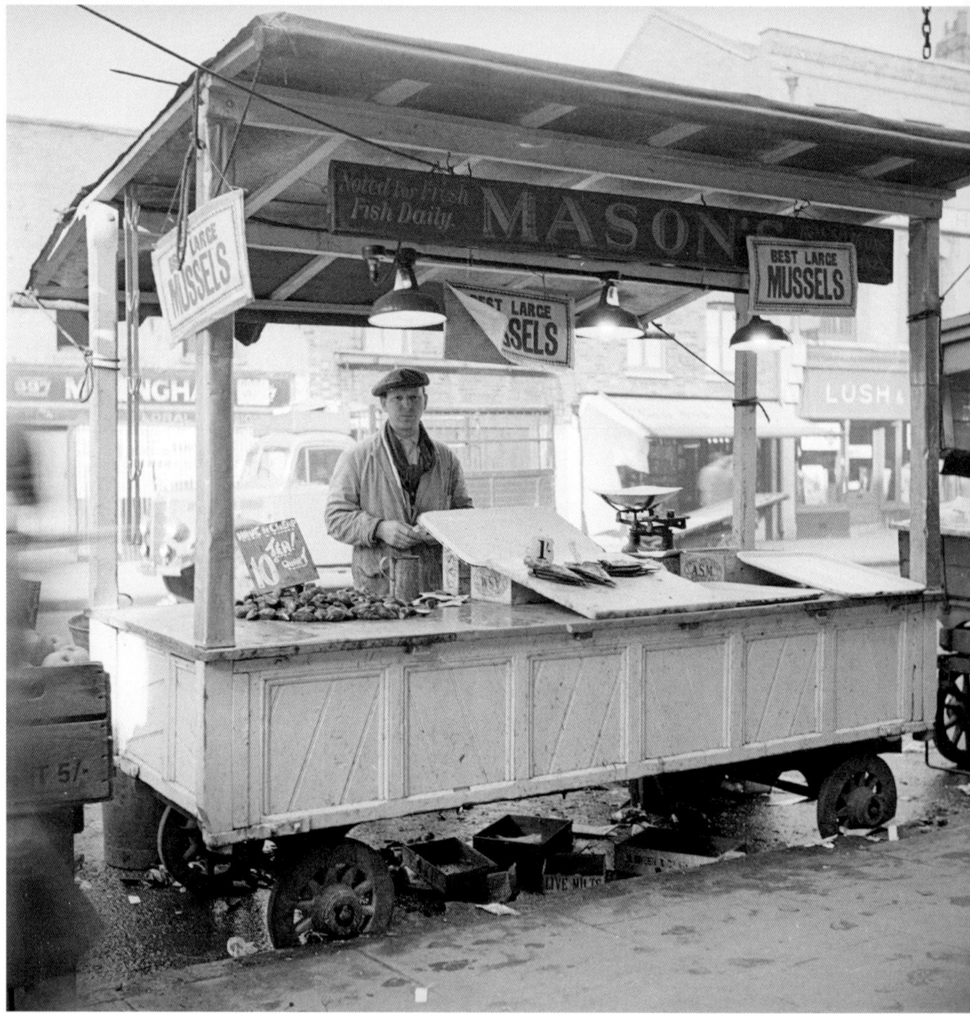
Noted For Fresh Fish Daily
MASON'S
BEST LARGE MUSSELS
LUSH

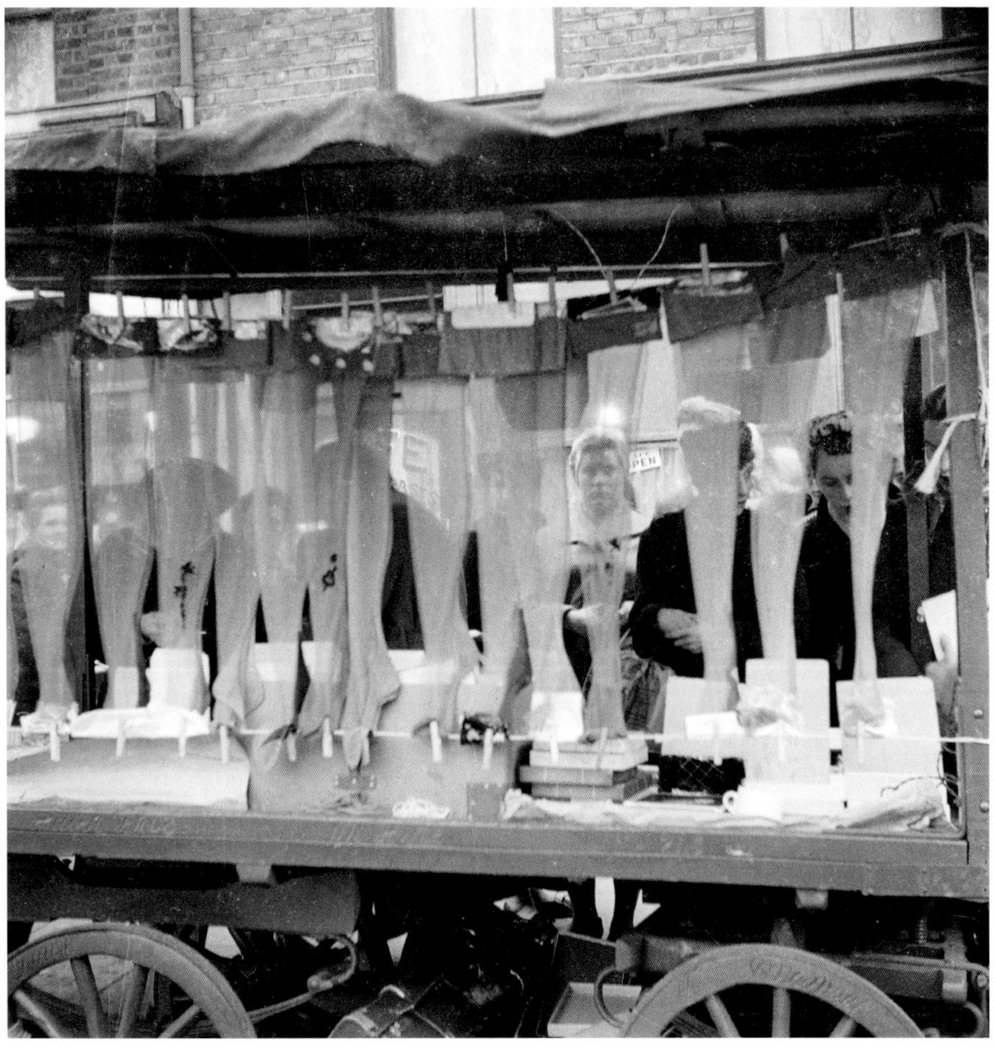

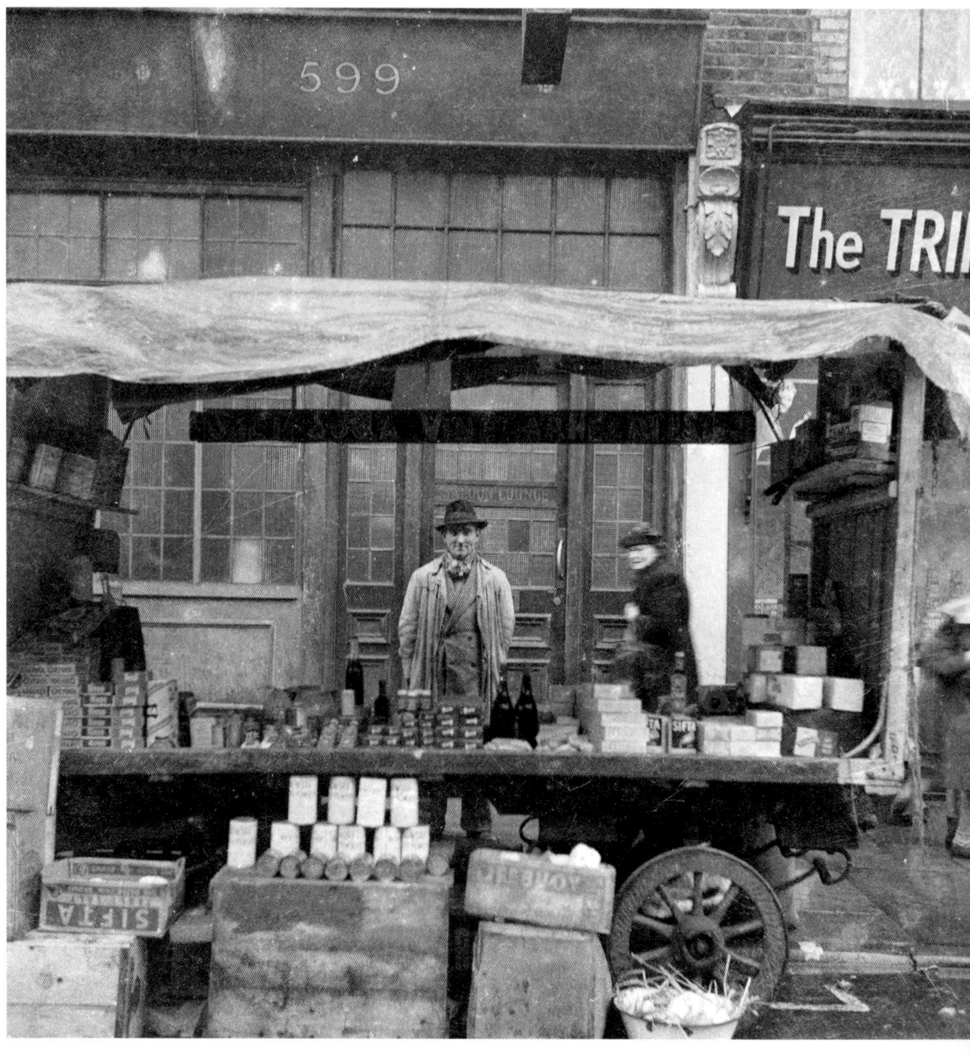
599
The TRIN
SIFTA

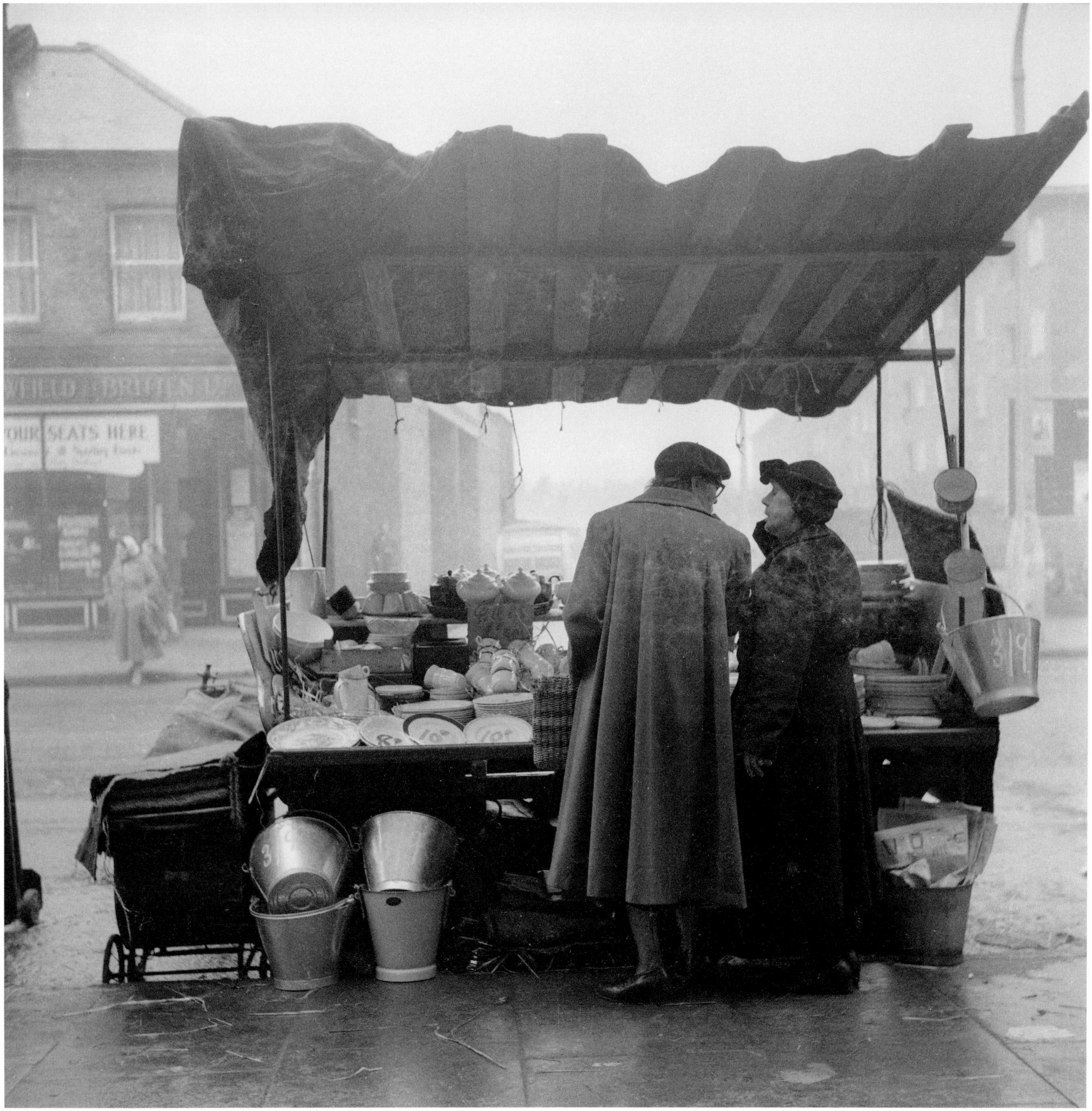

OPPOSITE

TOP LEFT *Housewives Shopping, Roman Road Street Market*

BOTTOM LEFT *Petticoat Lane Market* 1952

TOP RIGHT Mason's fresh fish stall, Bethnal Green Road, Bethnal Green E2

BOTTOM RIGHT Market stall outside 599 Roman Road, Bow E3

ABOVE Kitchenware stall, opposite Canrobert Street, Bethnal Green Road, Bethnal Green E2

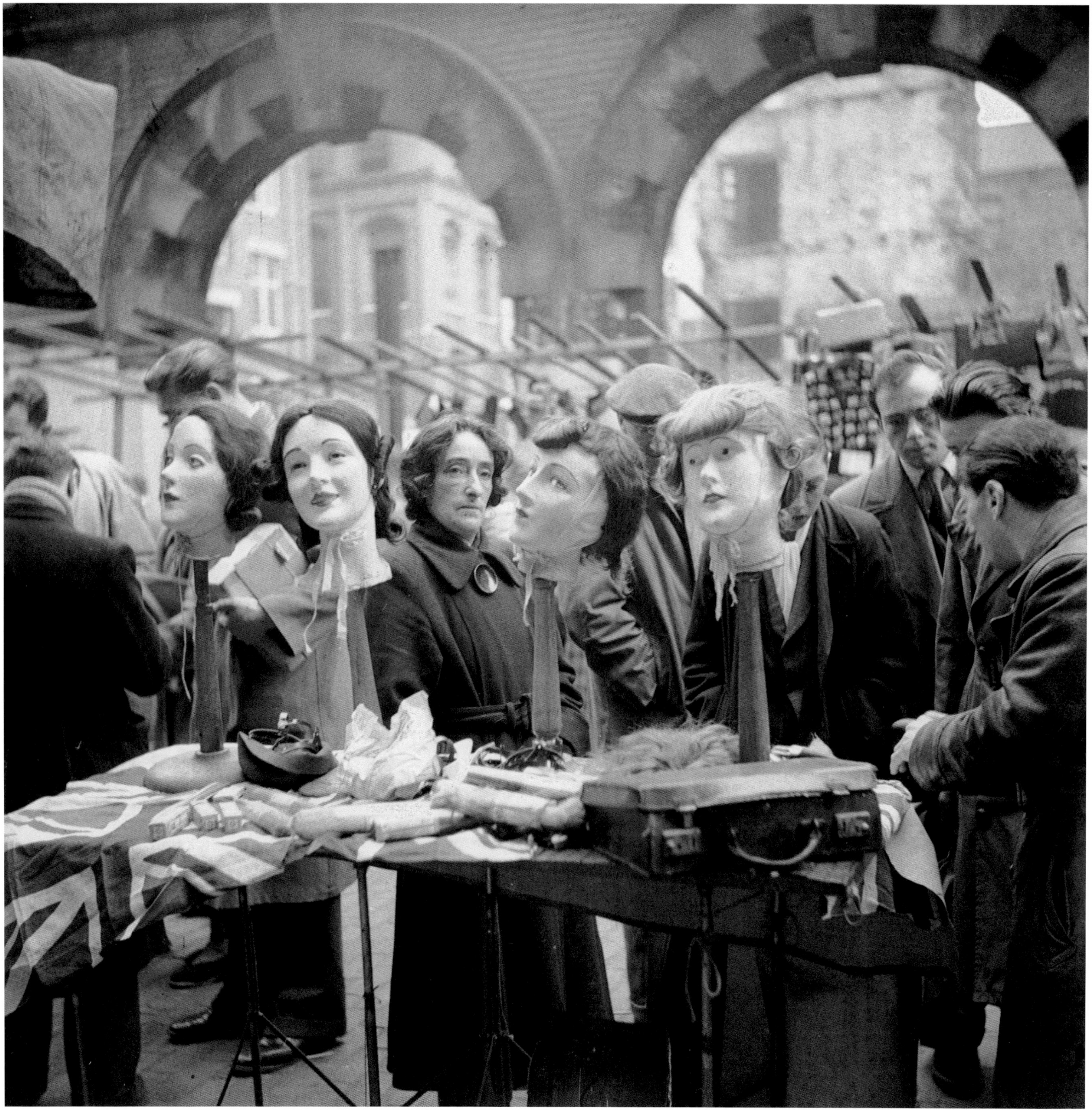

Wig Stall, Petticoat Lane 1952

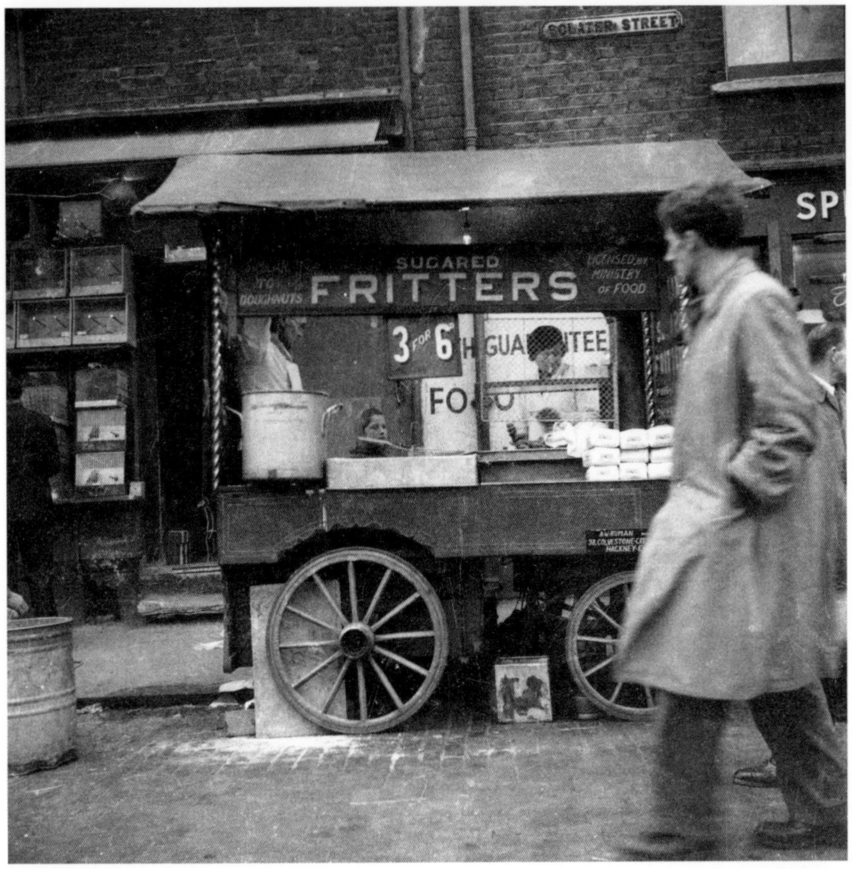

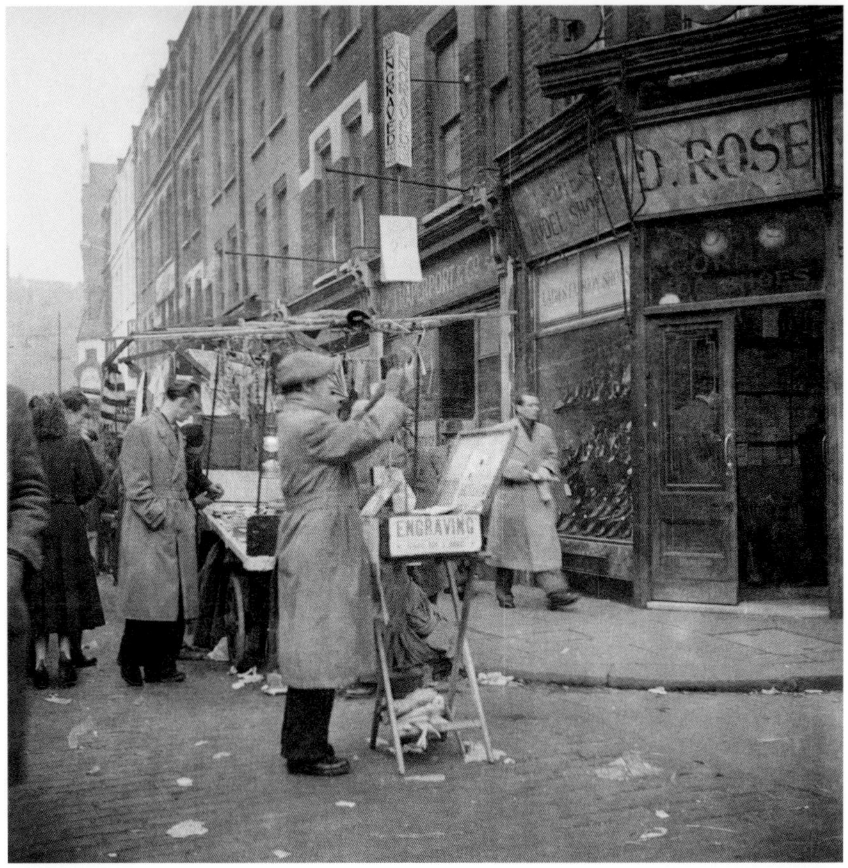

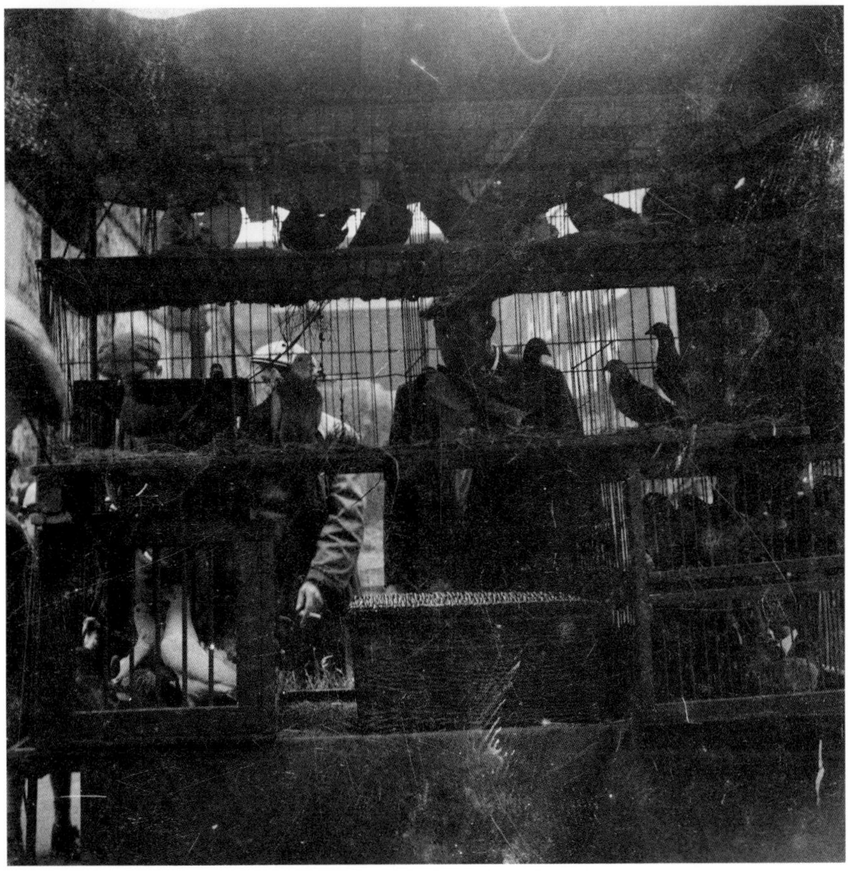

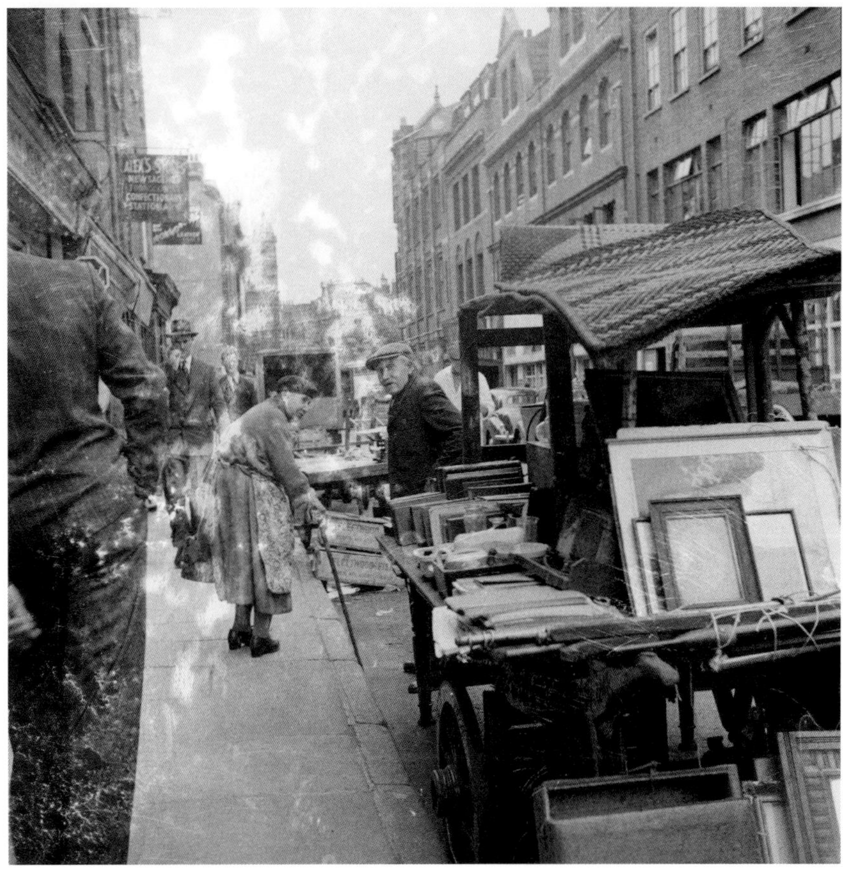

TOP A.W. Roman, sugared fritter seller, Sclater Street, Spitalfields E1

TOP Engraver outside David Rose & Sons Ltd., boot and shoe distributor, 52 Middlesex Street, corner of New Goulston Street, Spitalfields E1

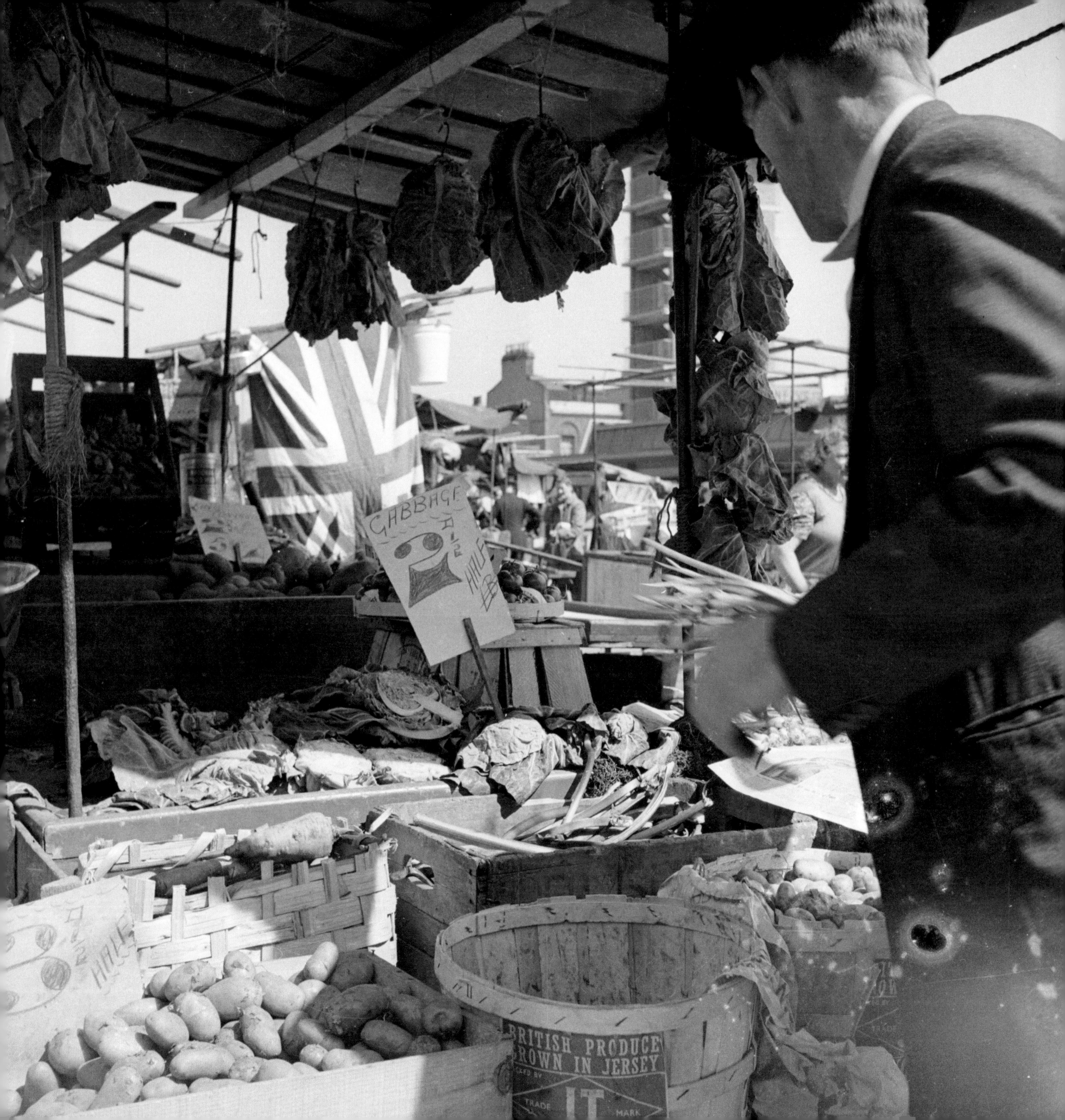
CABBAGE
BRITISH PRODUCE
GROWN IN JERSEY
TRADE
MARK

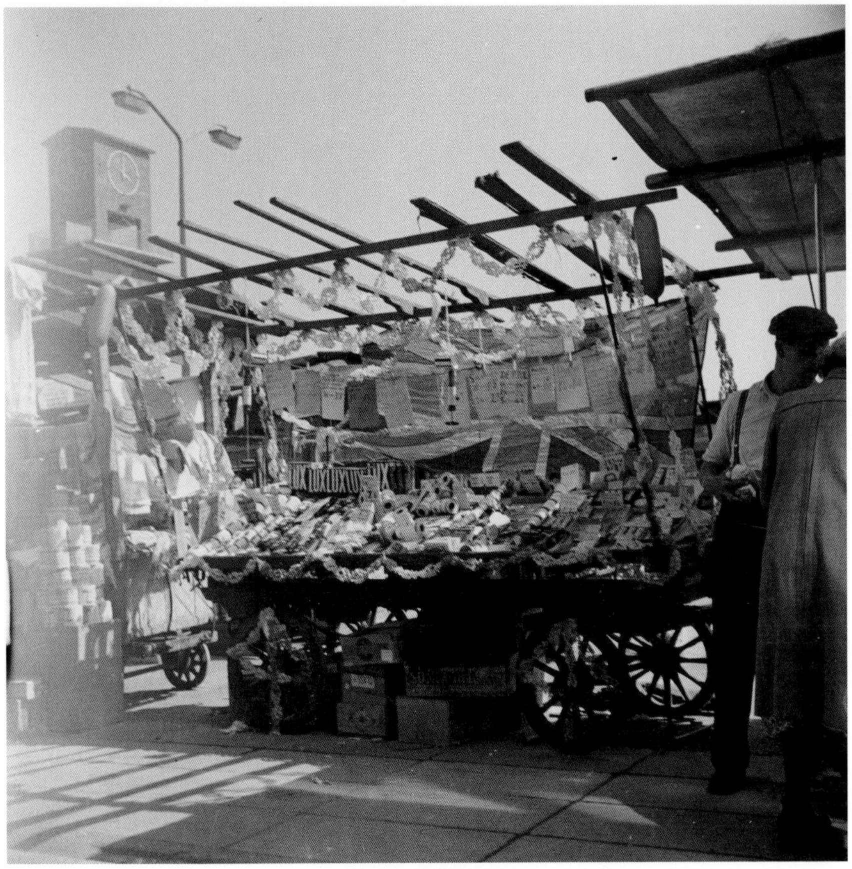

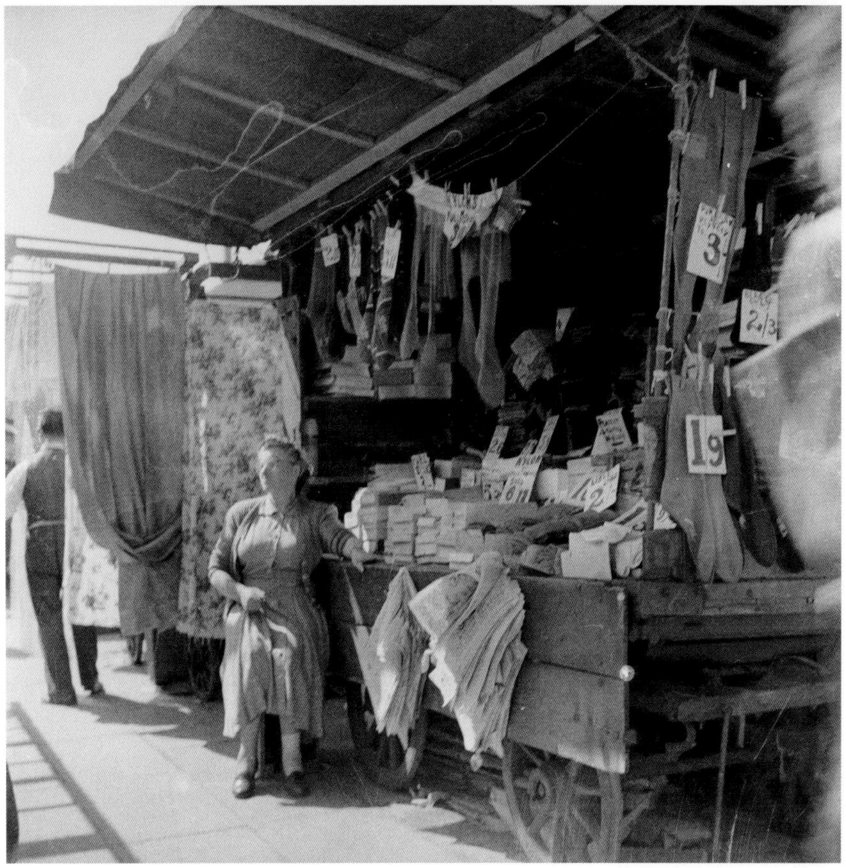

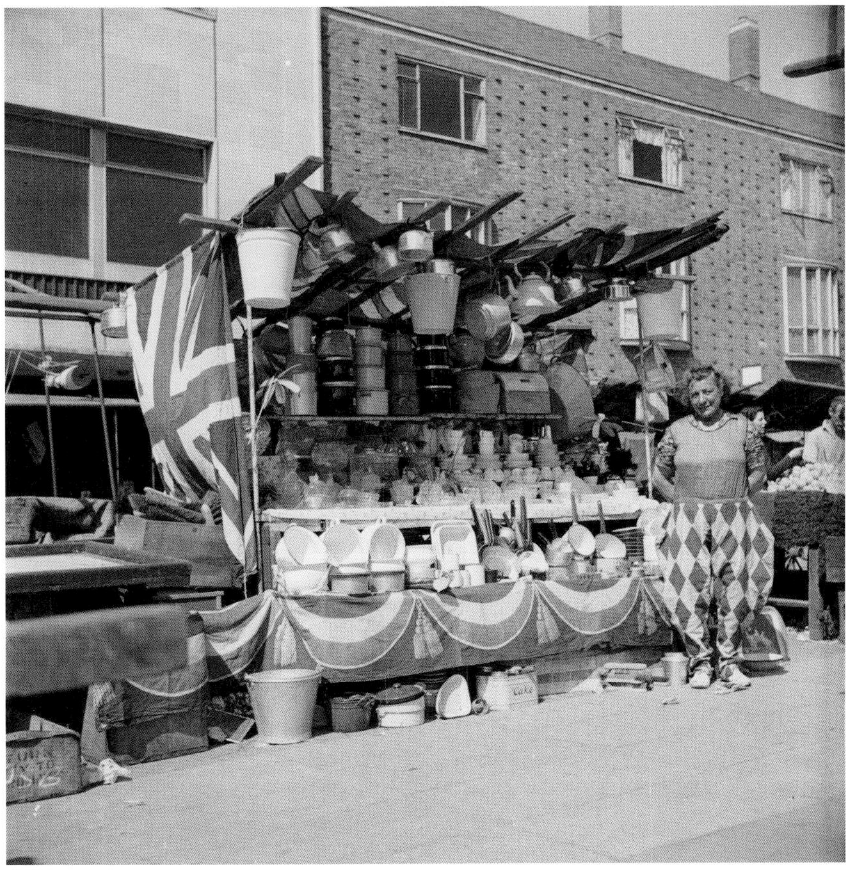

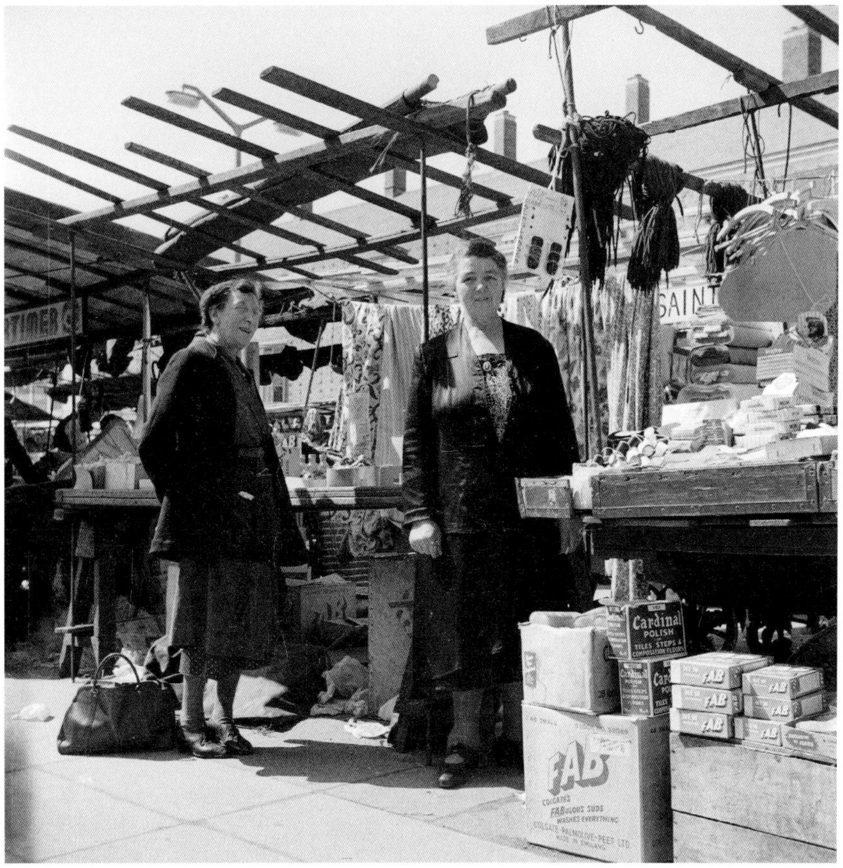

Chrisp Street Market, Poplar E14 1951

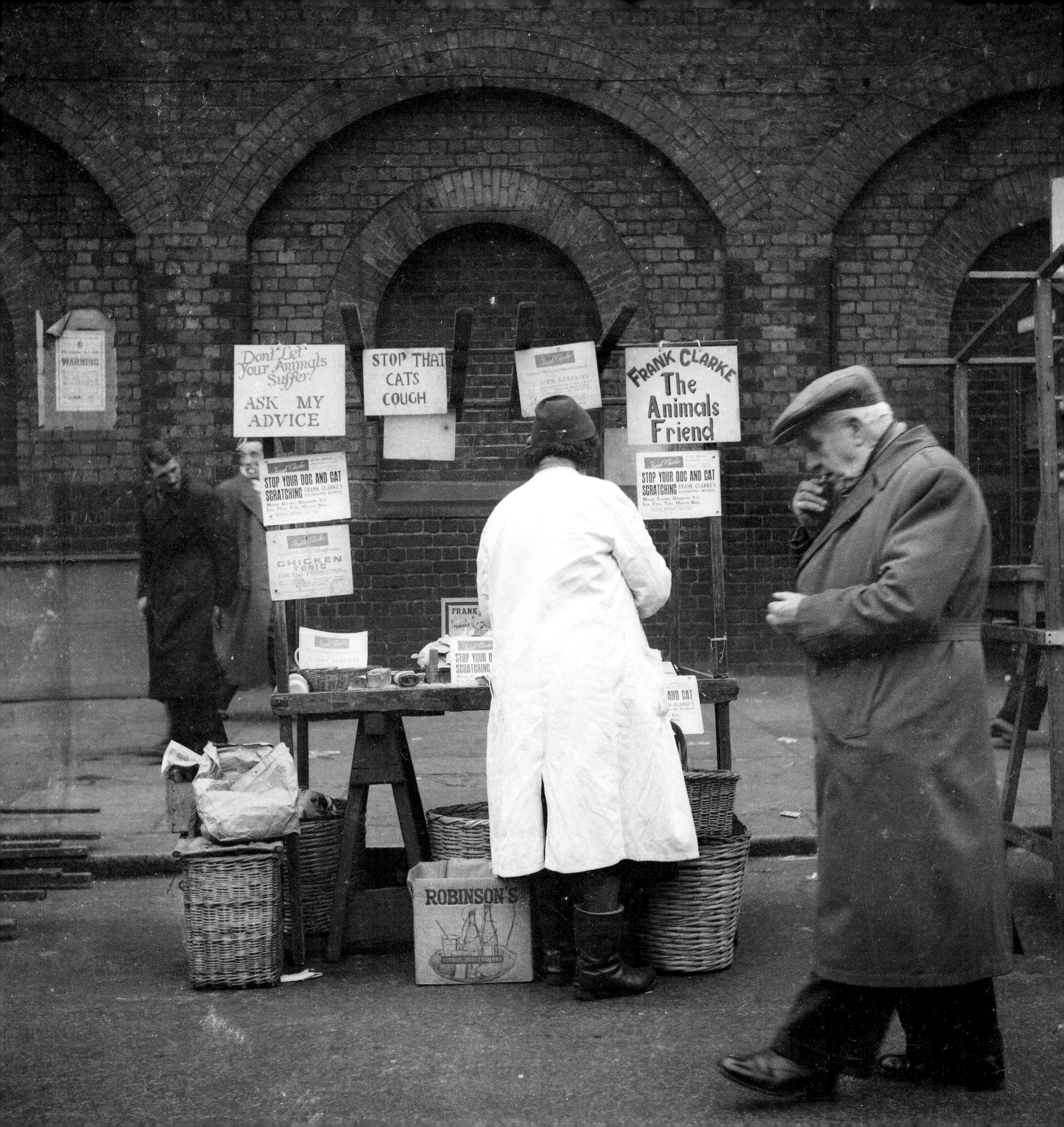
WARNING
Don't Let Your Animals Suffer!
ASK MY ADVICE
STOP THAT CATS COUGH
BIRD REMEDIES
FRANK CLARKE
The Animals Friend
STOP YOUR DOG AND CAT SCRATCHING
FRANK CLARKE'S
STOP YOUR DOG AND CAT SCRATCHING
FRANK CLARKE'S
CHICKEN TONIC
FOR EGG PRODUCTION
ROBINSON'S

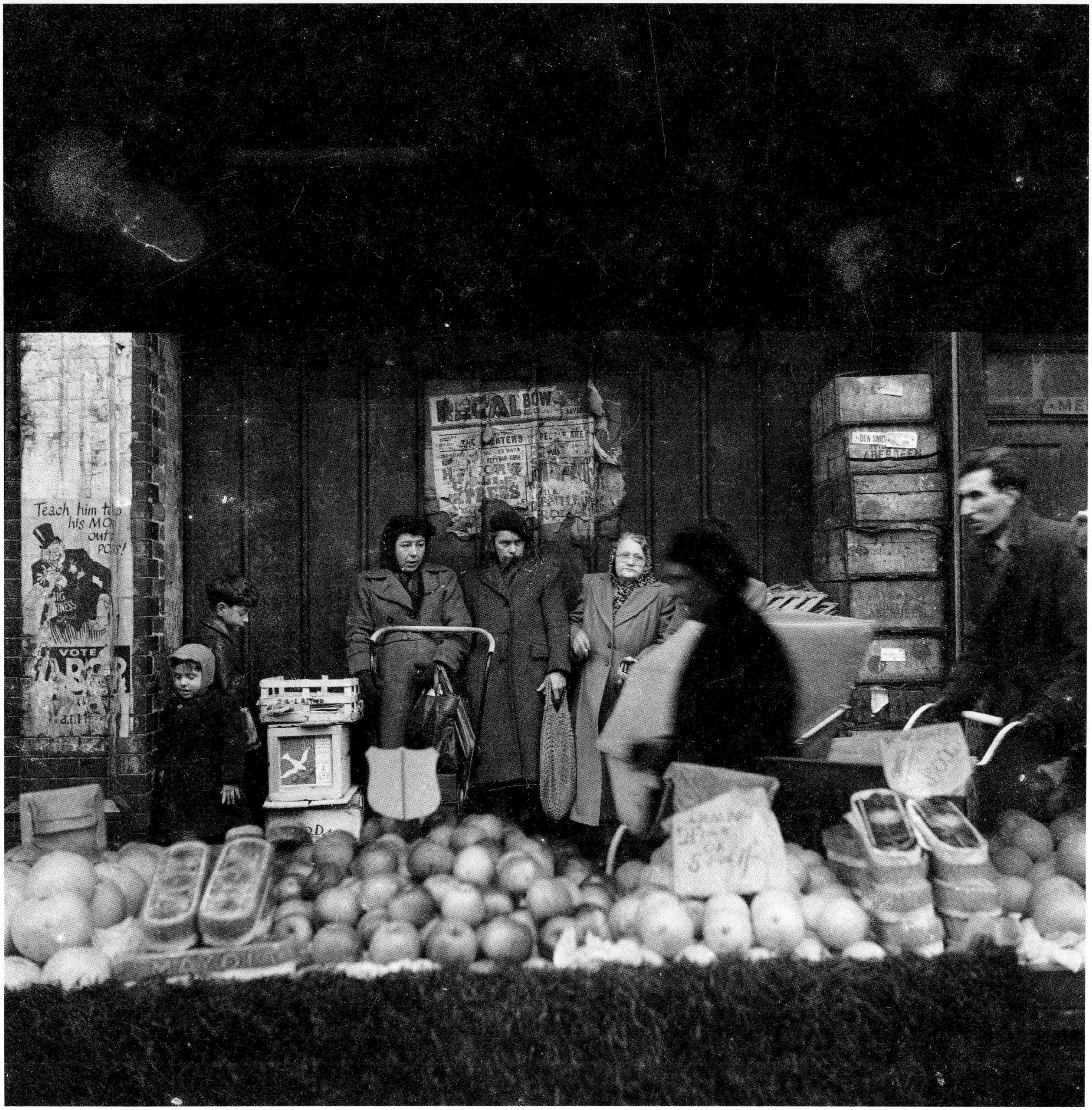

OPPOSITE Pet stall, Bethnal Green Road, Spitalfields E1

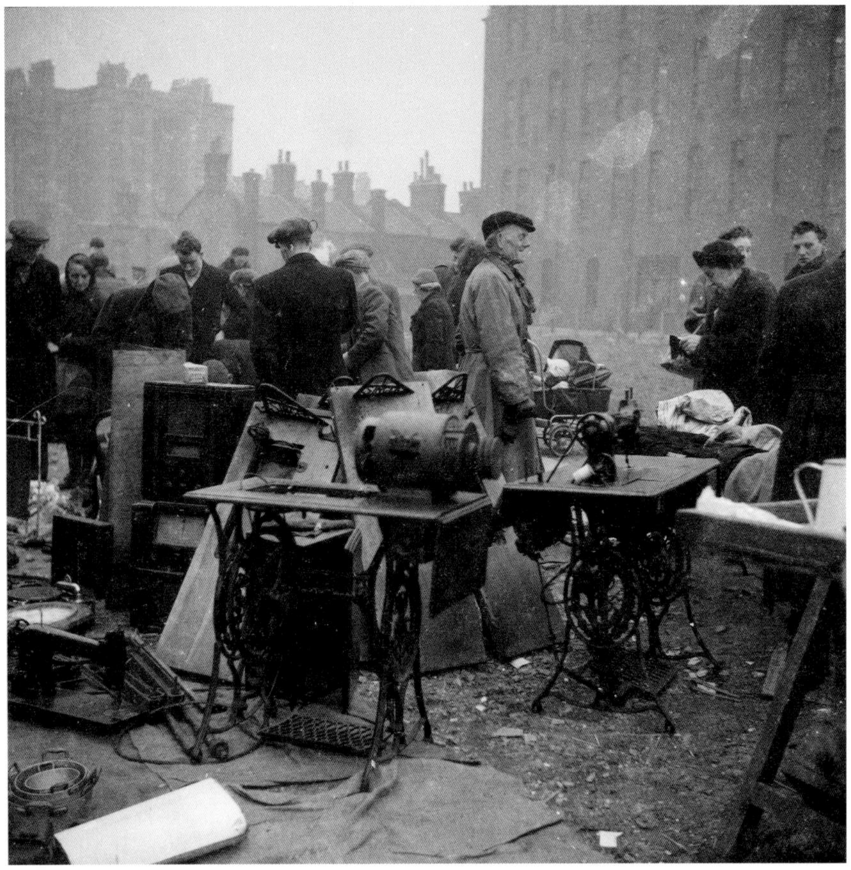

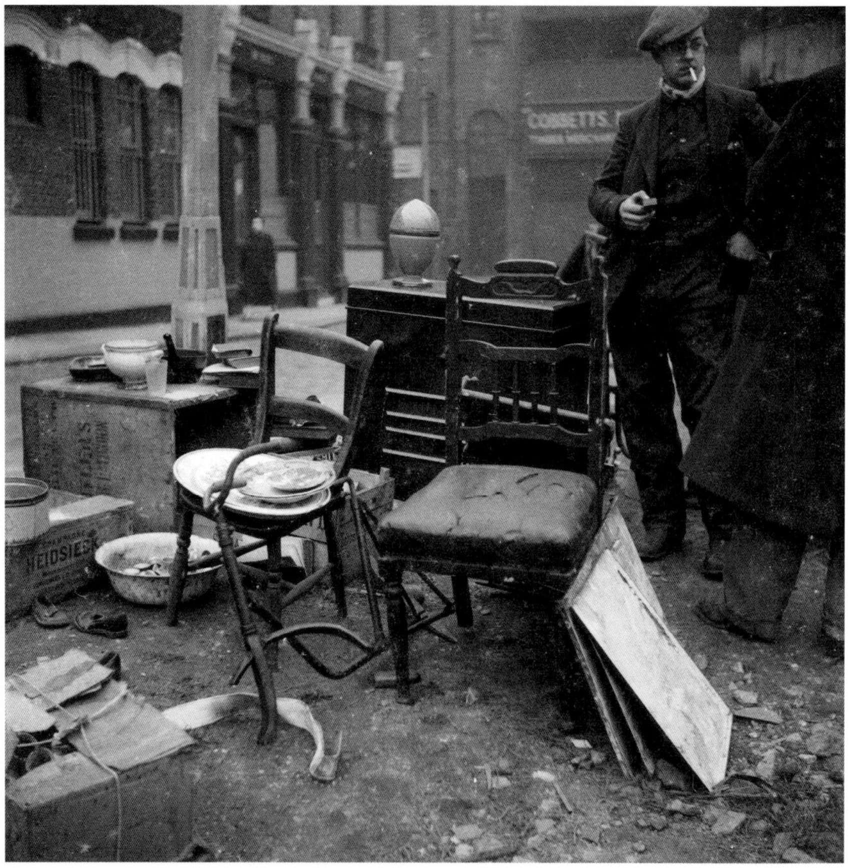

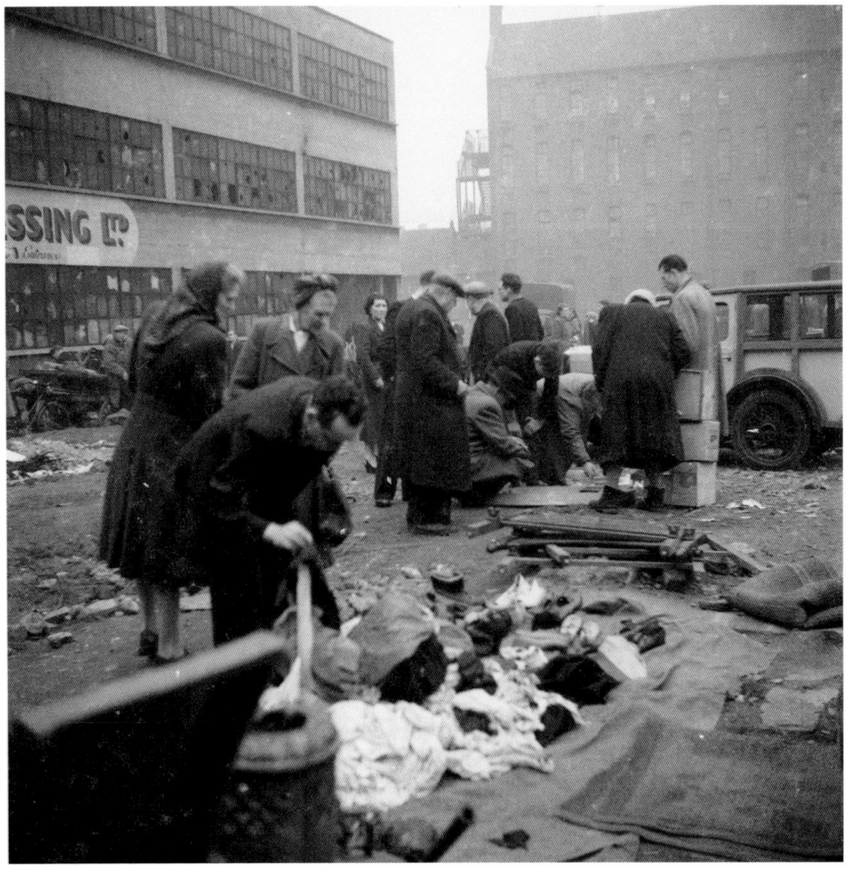

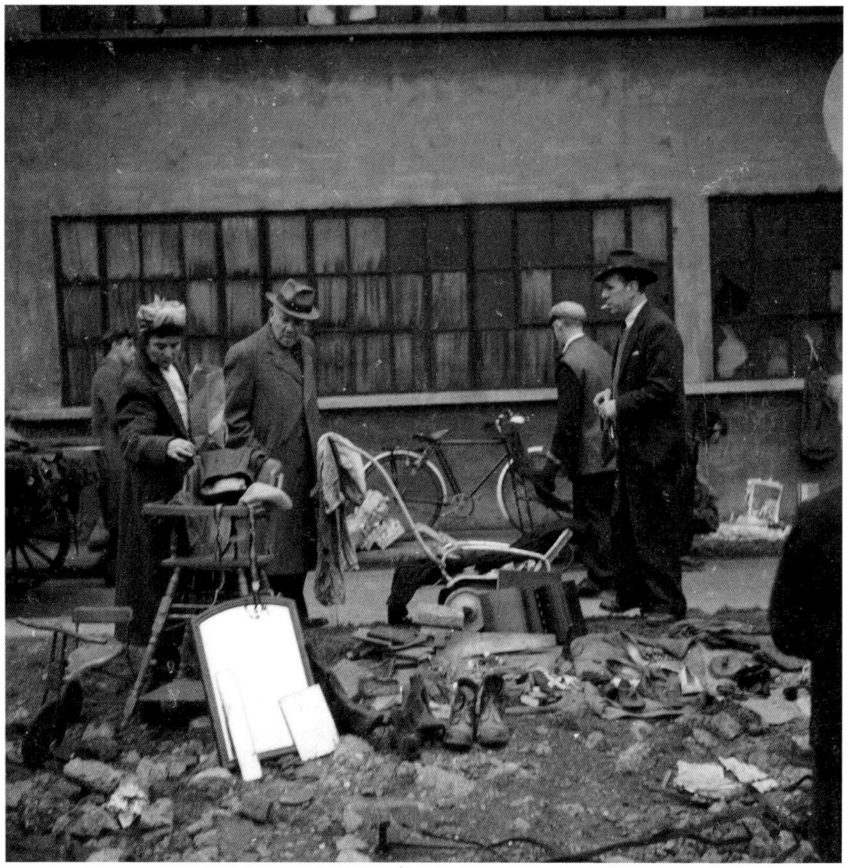

Flea market off Virginia Road, Bethnal Green E2

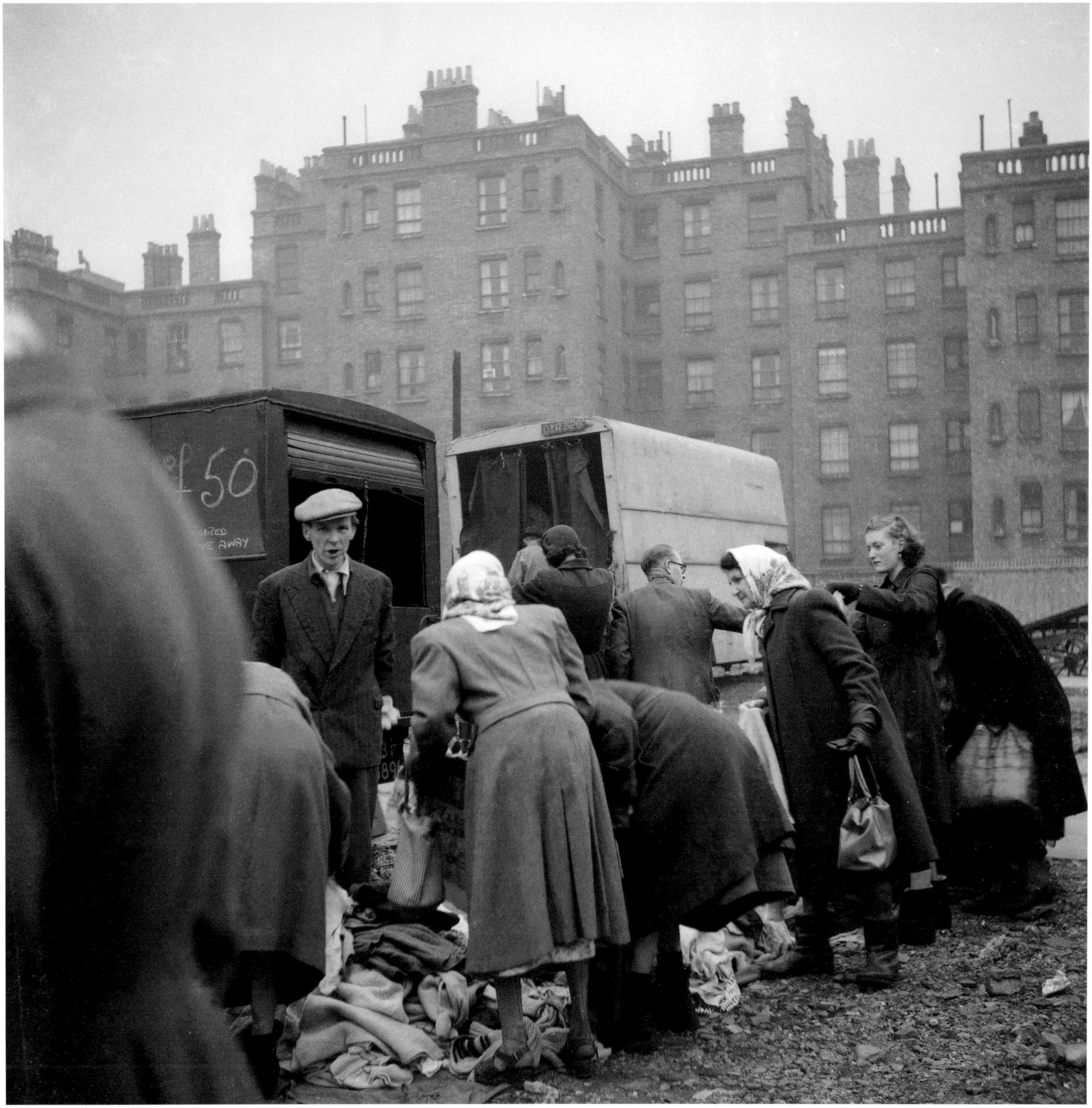

'It didn't occur to me to take photographs when I went to Bethnal Green. I just walked and walked and kept staring at everything. And it occurred to me after a little while...to make a collection of different shots about the very strong and coherent images of Bethnal Green.'

'I realised that my objective was usually to 'cover' the situation interesting me, which was often of a fugitive nature, and to take it back to my darkroom (like a dog with a bone) and scrutinise it.'

Teenagers outside W&F. Riley, newsagent, 76 Cleaveland Way, Bethnal Green E1 1951

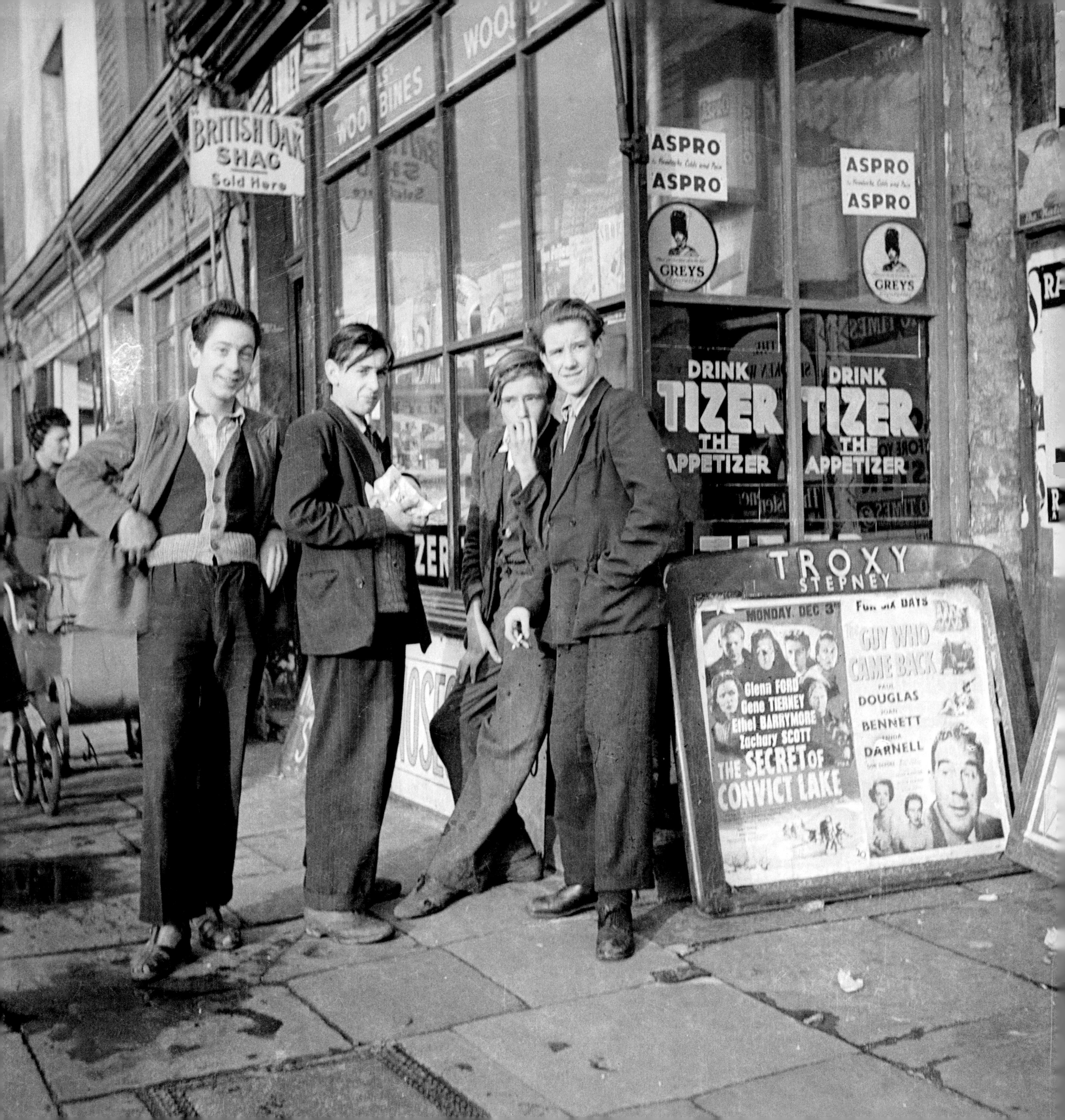
BRITISH OAK
SHAG
Sold Here
WOODBINES
ASPRO
ASPRO
GREYS
ASPRO
ASPRO
GREYS
DRINK
TIZER
THE
APPETIZER
DRINK
TIZER
THE
APPETIZER
TROXY
STEPNEY
MONDAY, DEC 3rd
FOR SIX DAYS
Glenn FORD
Gene TIERNEY
Ethel BARRYMORE
Zachary SCOTT
THE SECRET OF
CONVICT LAKE
GUY WHO
CAME BACK
PAUL
DOUGLAS
JOAN
BENNETT
DARNELL

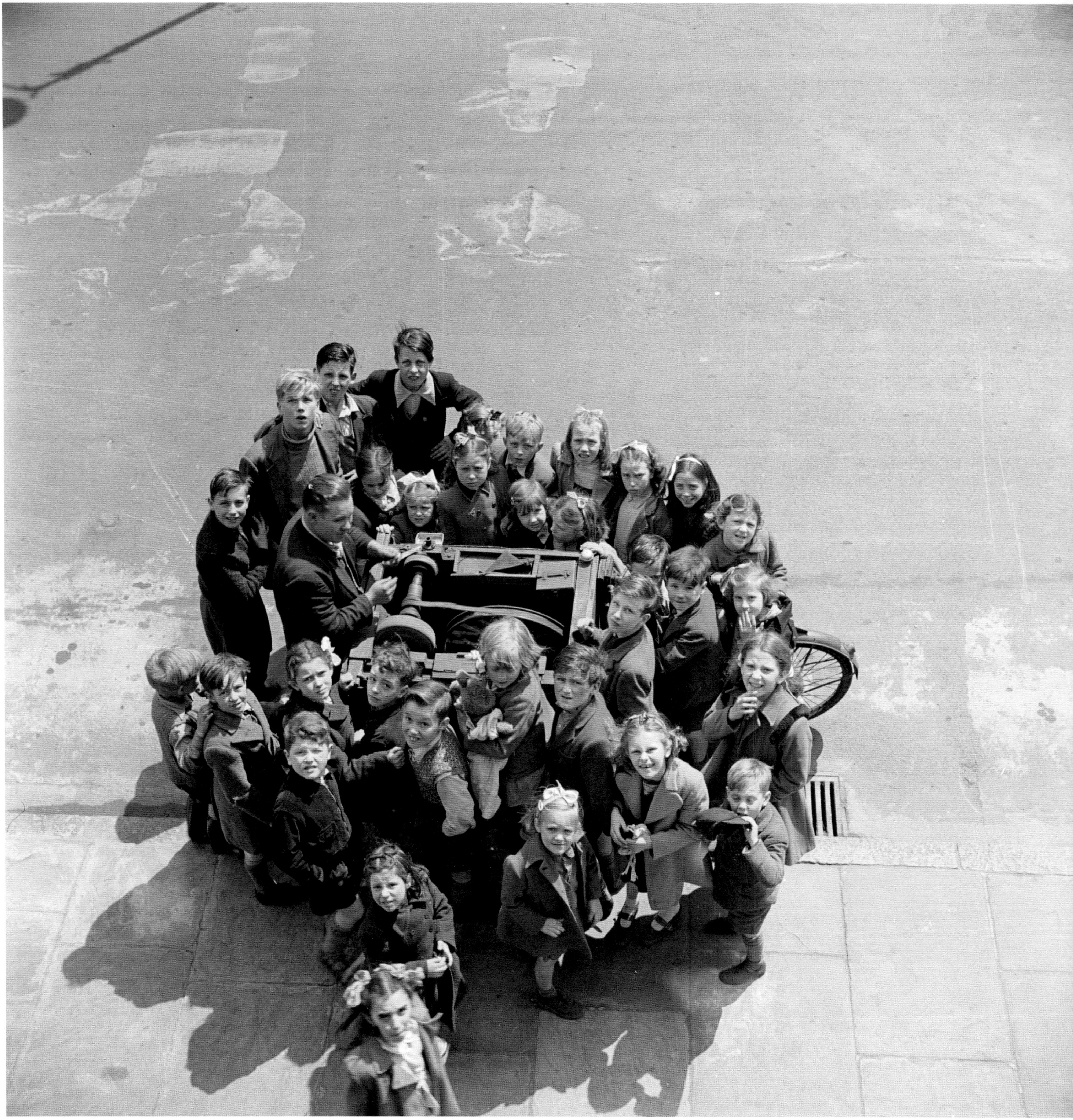

OPPOSITE *Bert Smith*, surrounded by children, outside 46 Chisenhale Road, Bow E3

TOP RIGHT Peter Samuels climbing a lamp post

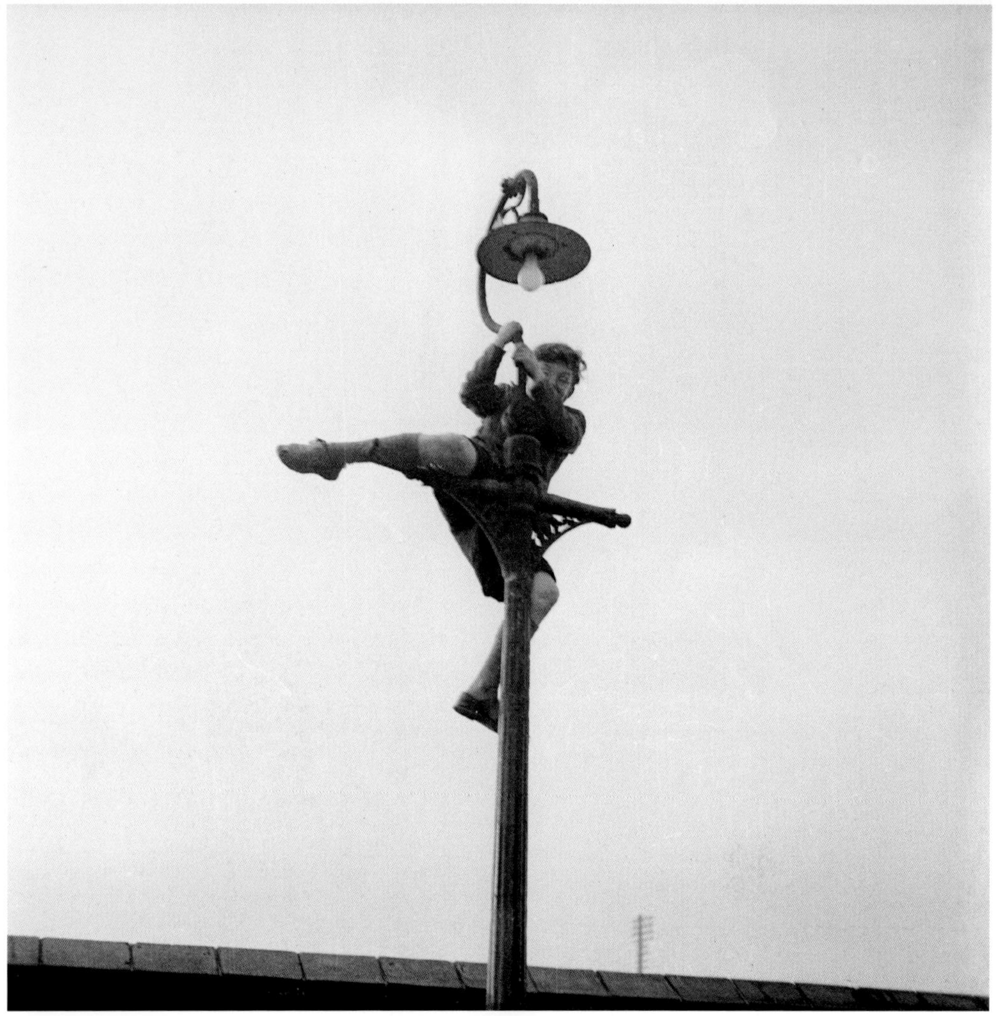

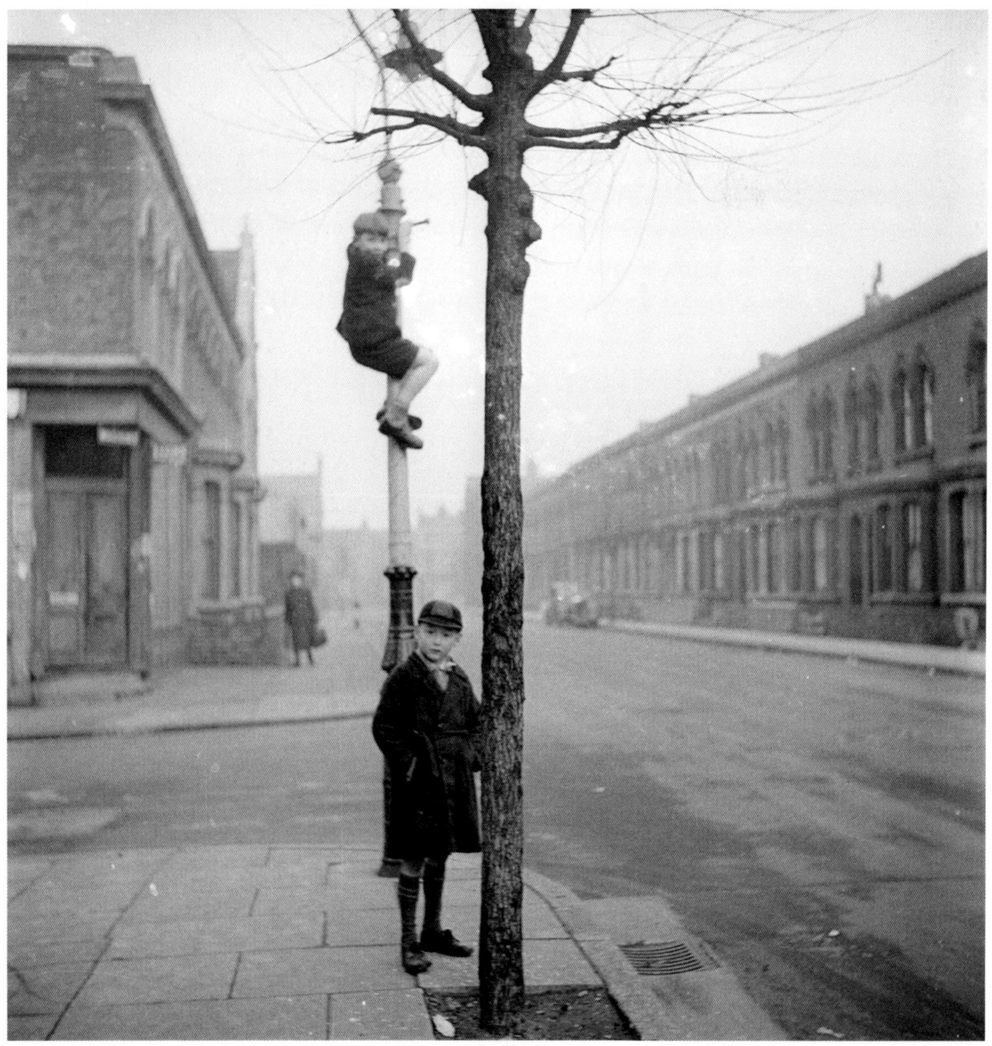

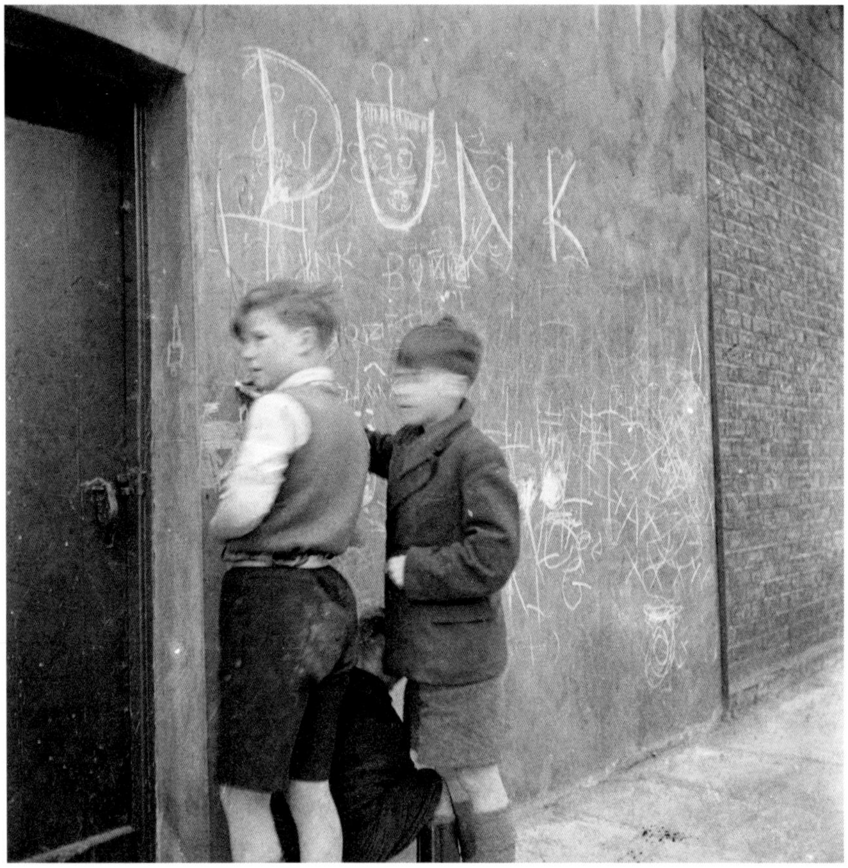

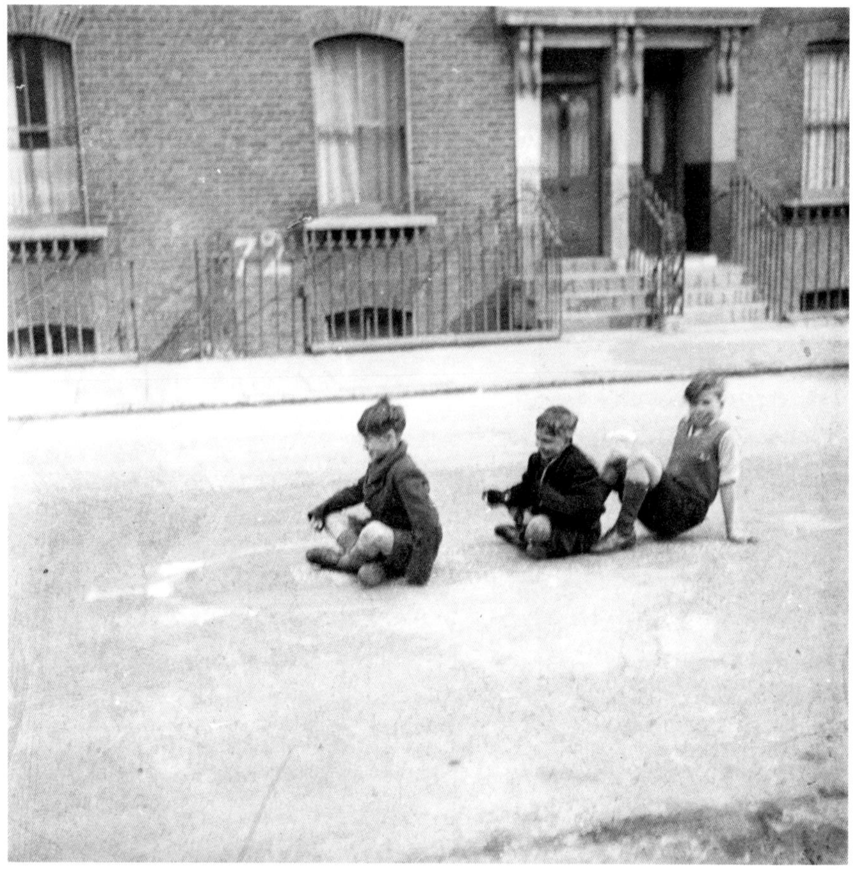

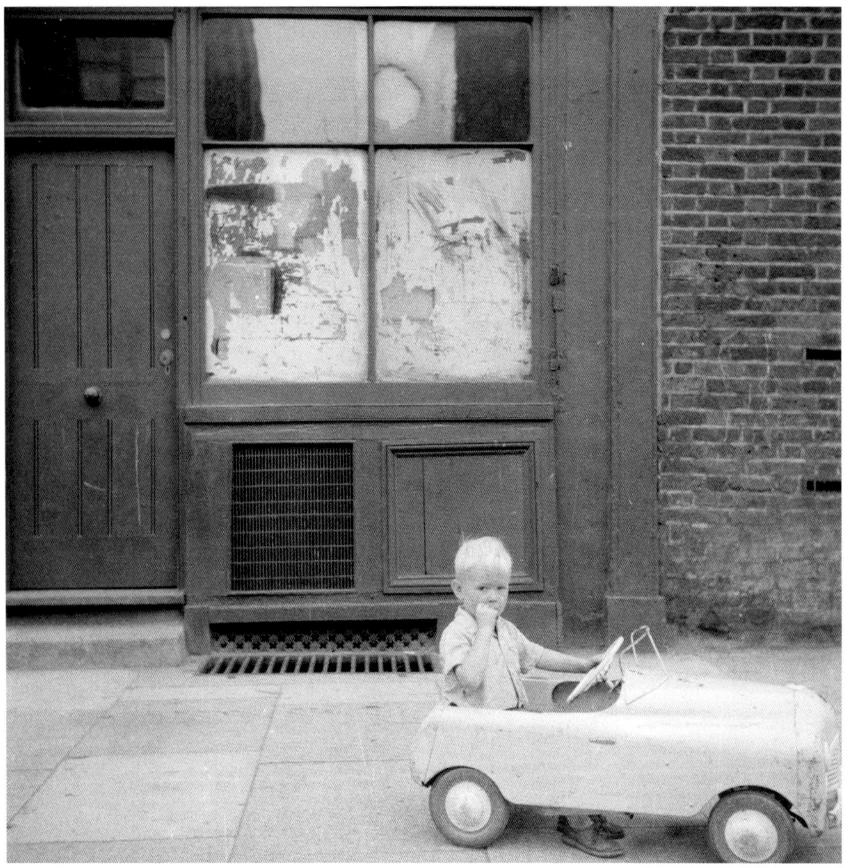

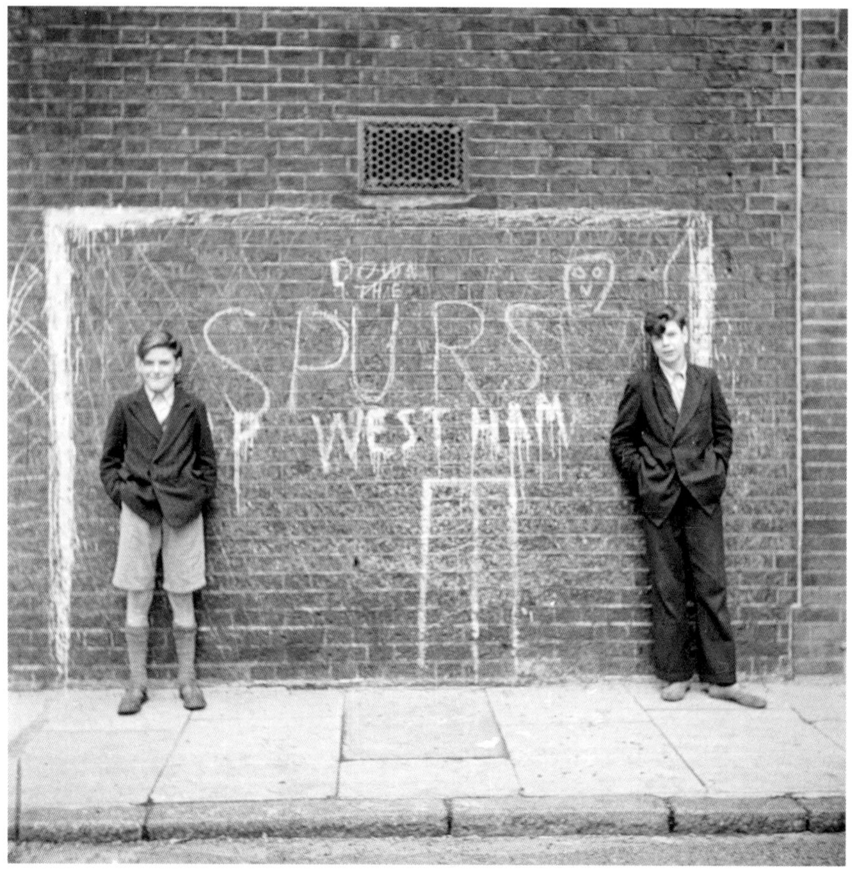

TOP RIGHT Boys playing in Chisenhale Road, Bow E3

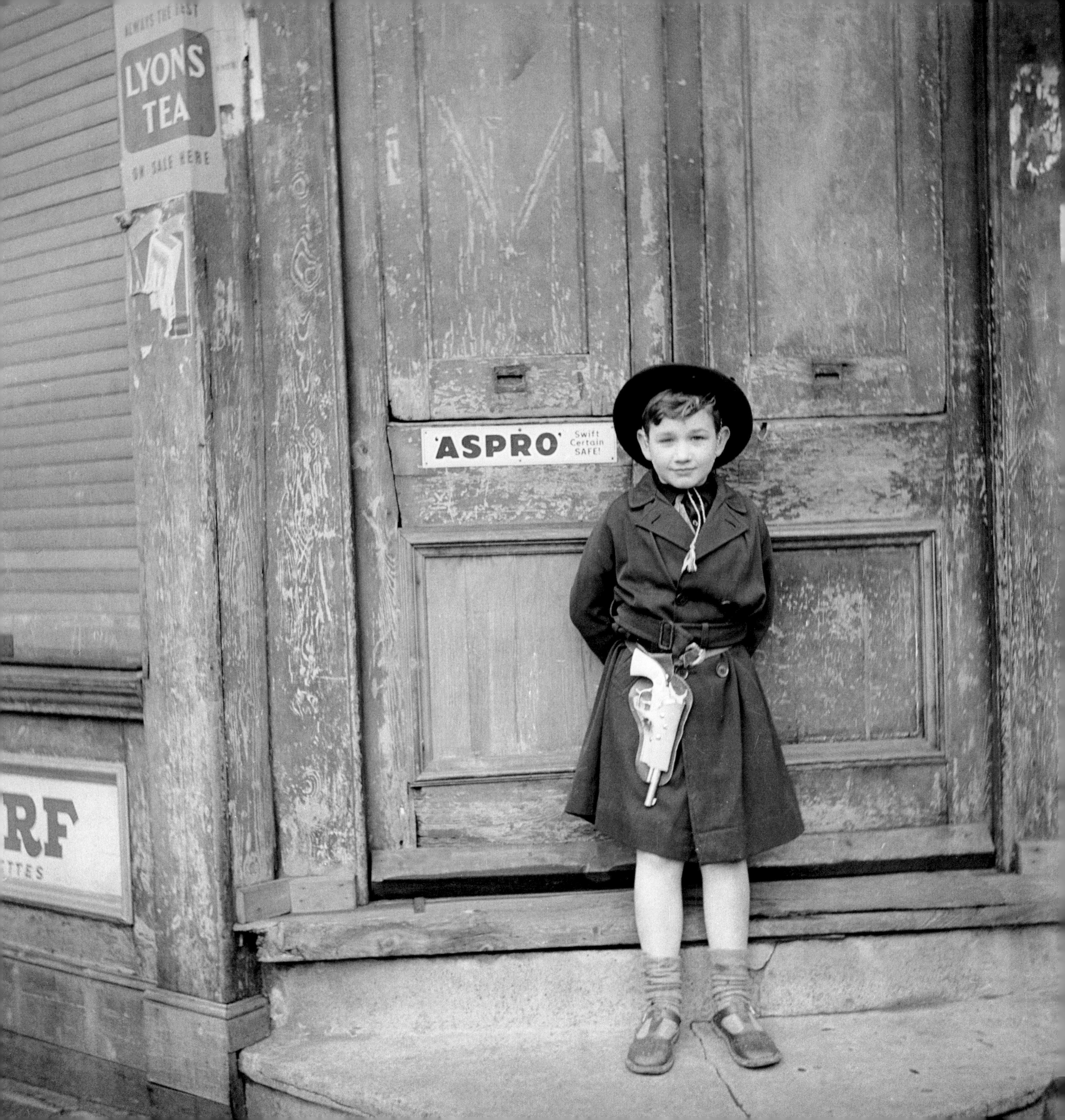
ALWAYS THE BEST
LYONS TEA
ON SALE HERE
'ASPRO' Swift Certain SAFE!
RF
TTES

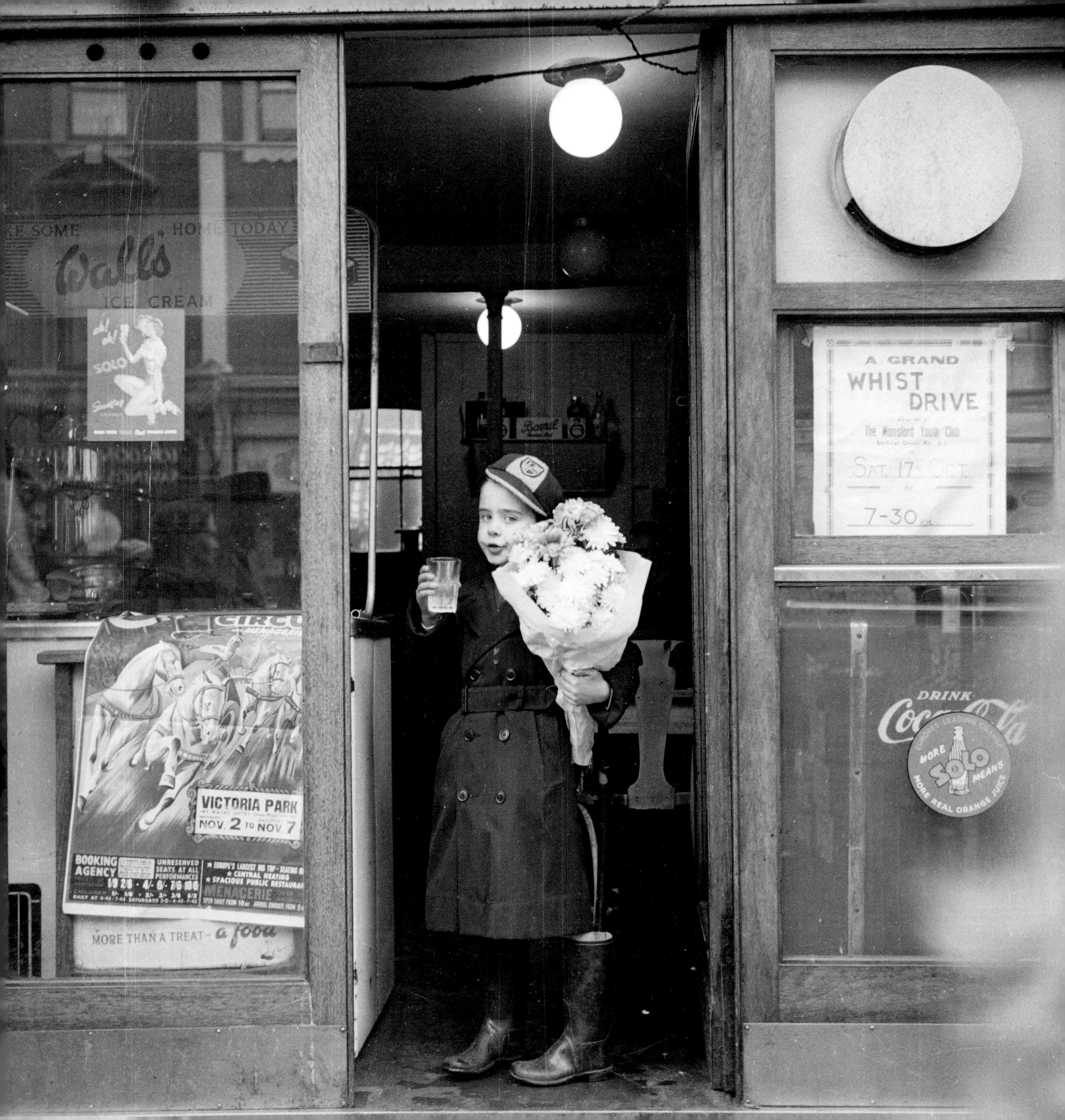
Wall's
ICE CREAM
SOLO
A GRAND
WHIST
DRIVE
The Mansford Youth Club
SAT. 17th OCT.
7-30 PM
VICTORIA PARK
NOV. 2 TO NOV. 7
BOOKING AGENCY
UNRESERVED SEATS AT ALL PERFORMANCES
EUROPE'S LARGEST BIG TOP
CENTRAL HEATING
SPACIOUS PUBLIC RESTAURANT
MENAGERIE
MORE THAN A TREAT – a food
DRINK
MORE SOLO MEANS MORE REAL ORANGE JUICE

RIGHT Camera crew filming on Derbyshire Street, Bethnal Green E2

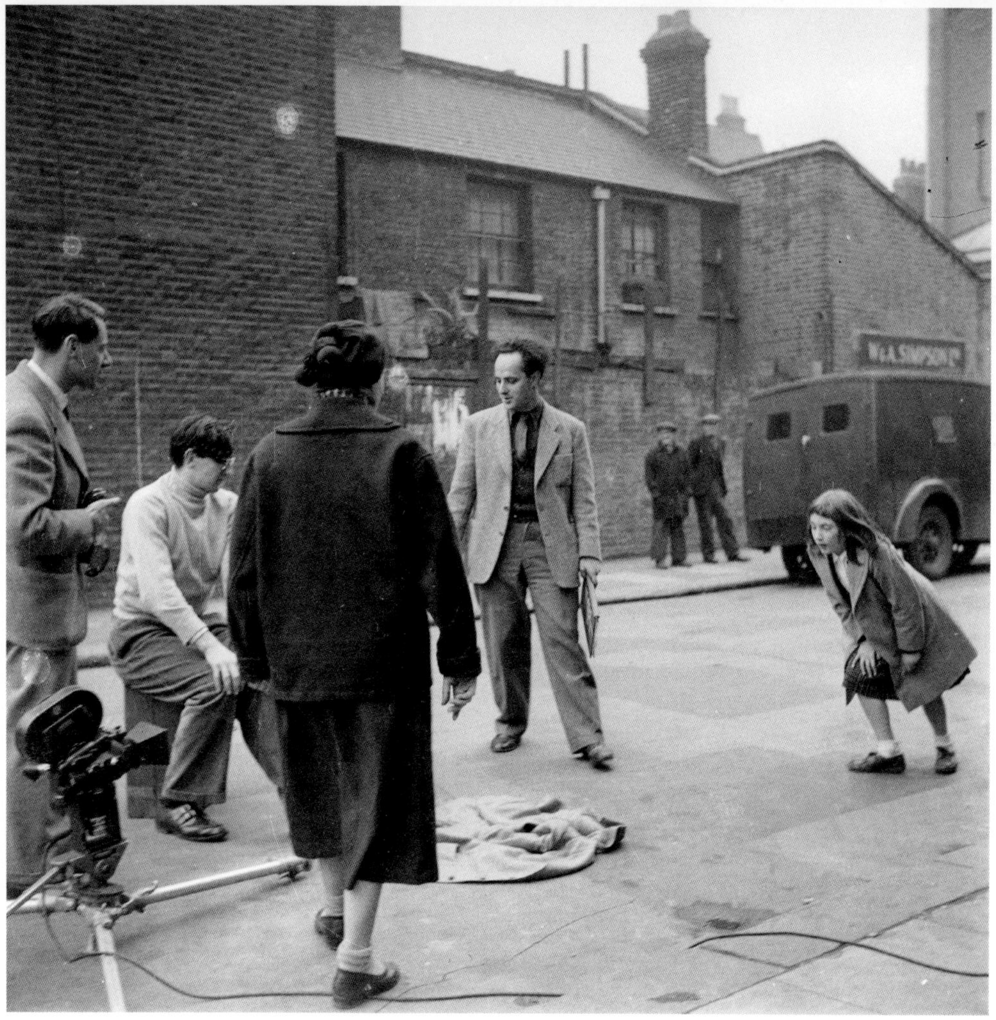

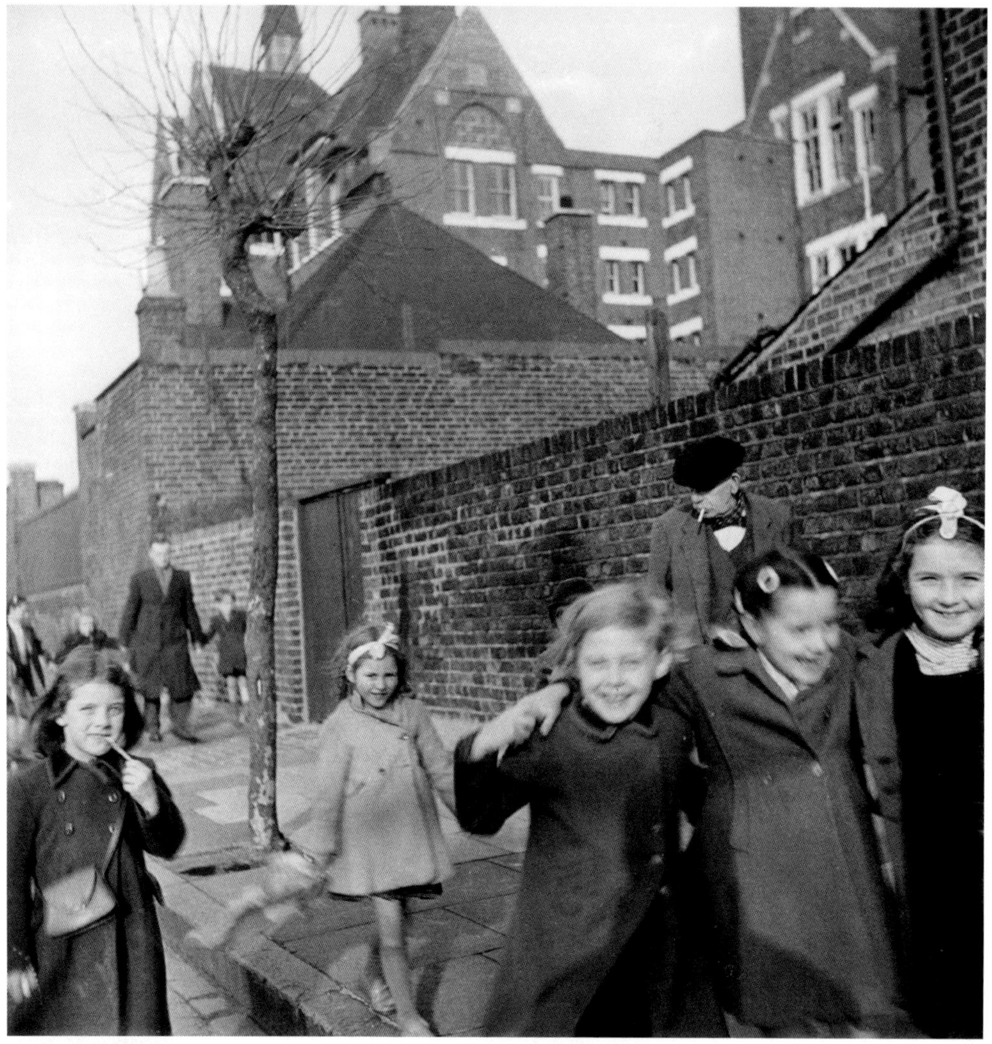

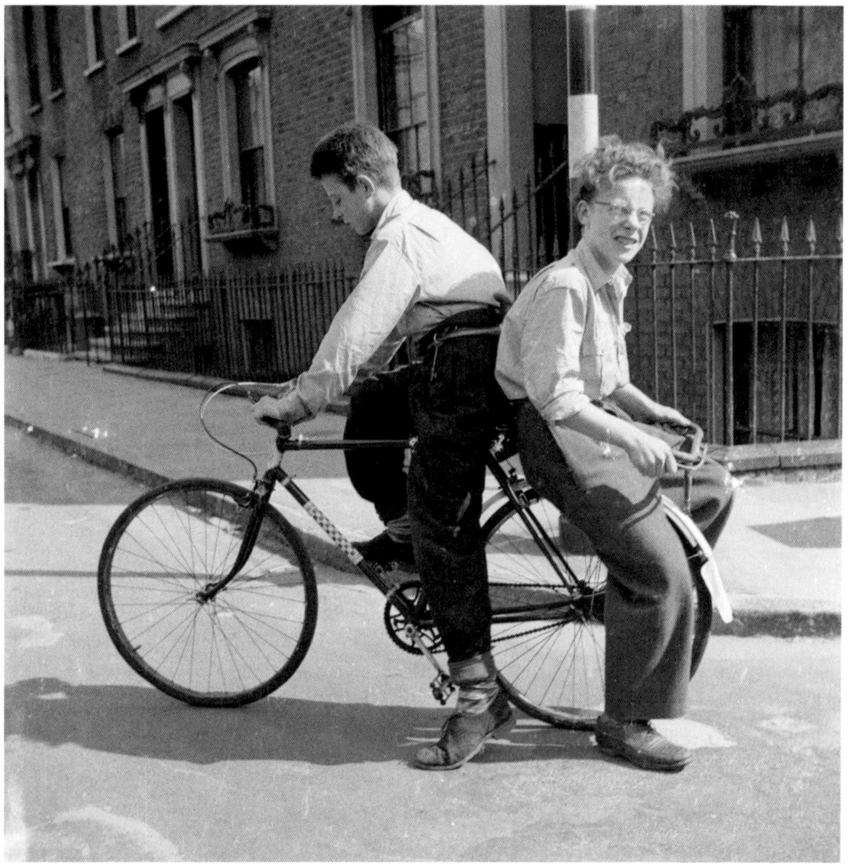

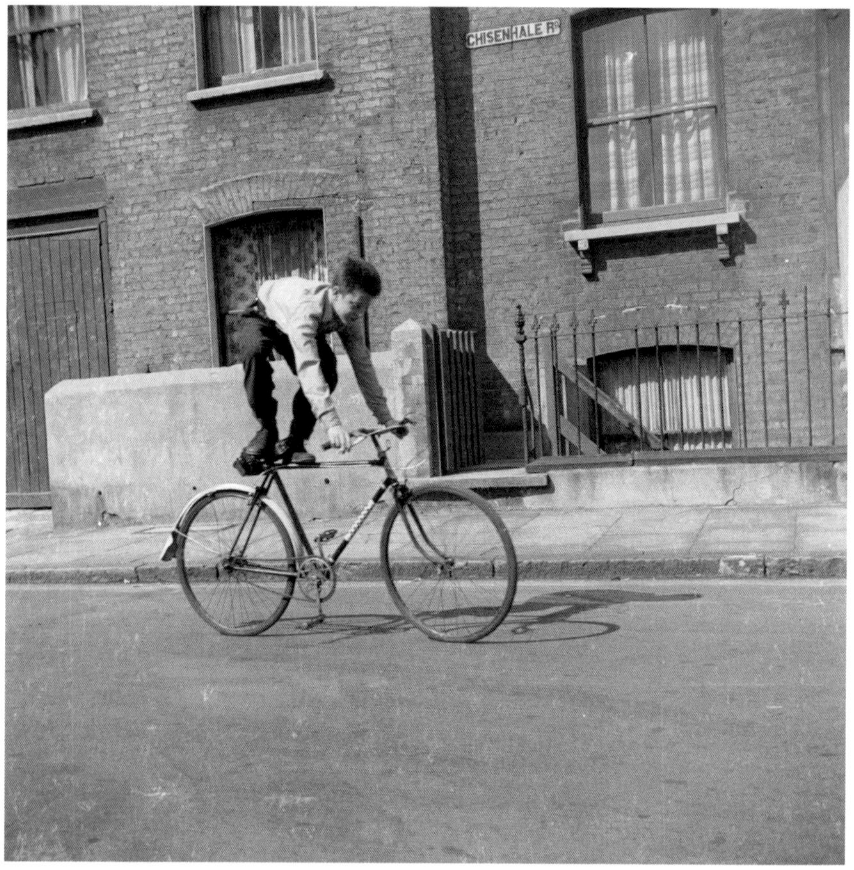

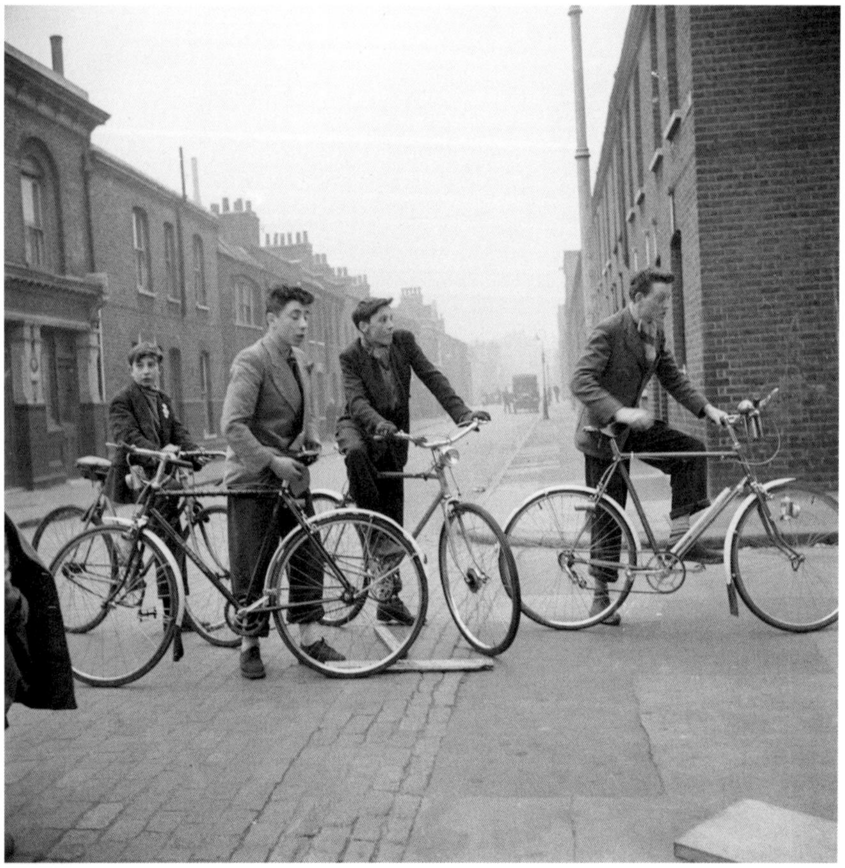

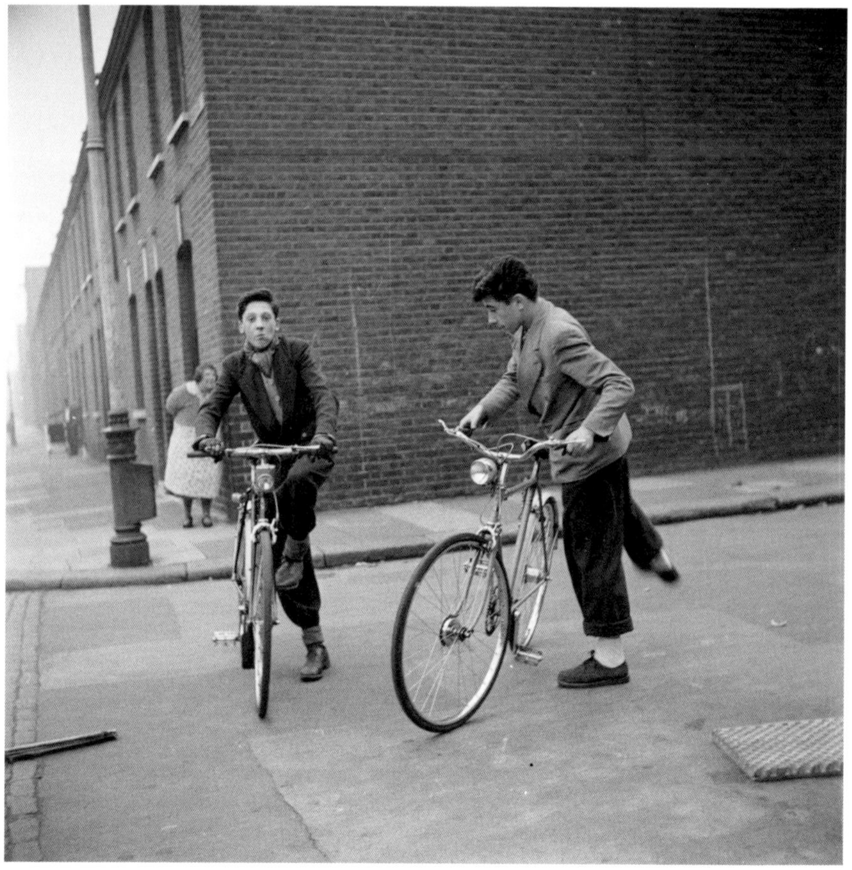

TOP Brian and Leslie Samuels on a bicycle, Chisenhale Road, Bow E3 1950

BOTTOM LEFT AND RIGHT Teenagers on bicycles, Derbyshire Street, Bethnal Green E2

TOP Brian Samuels on a bicycle, Chisenhale Road, Bow E3 1950

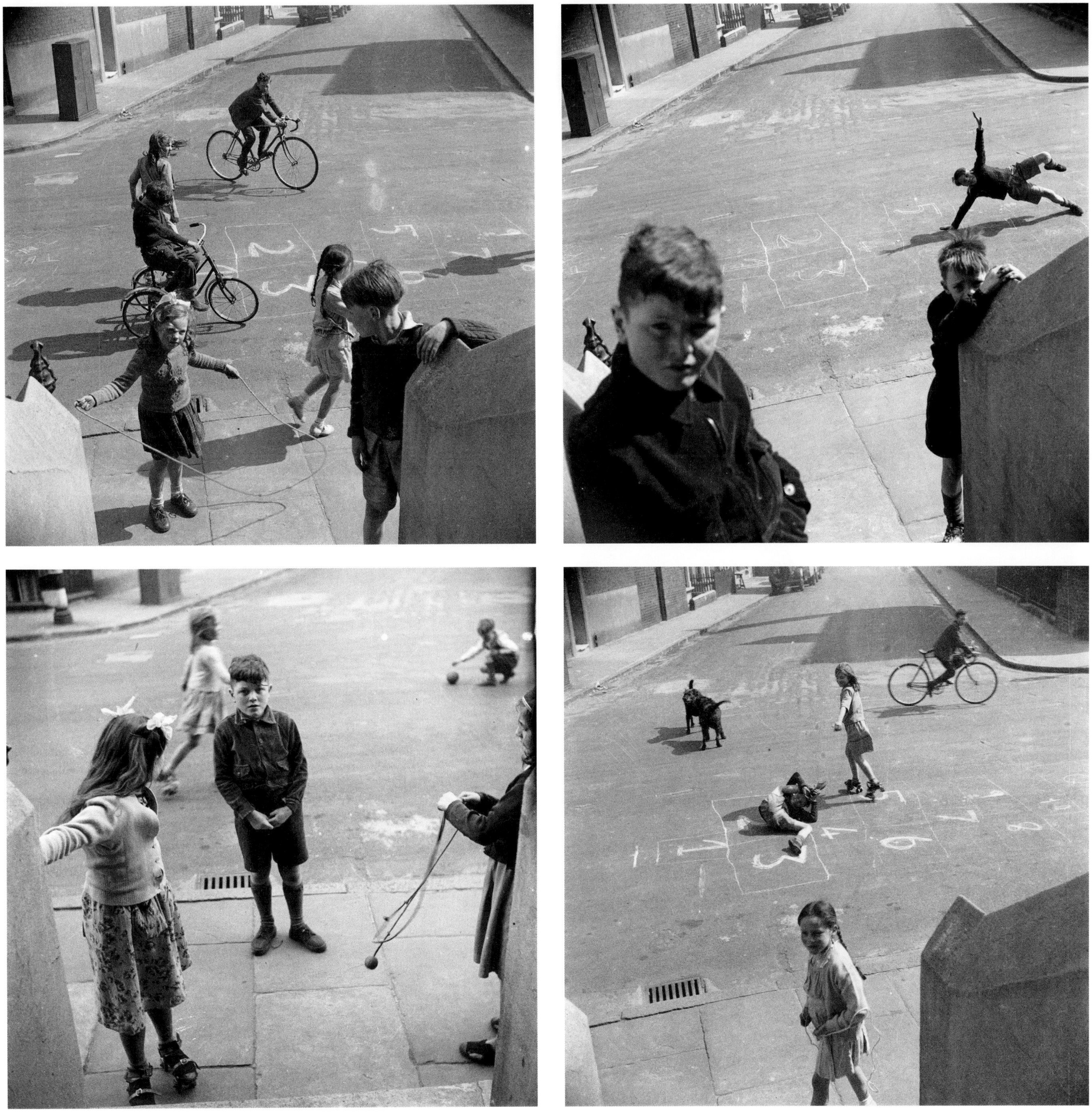

Children playing on Chisenhale Road, Bow E3 1951

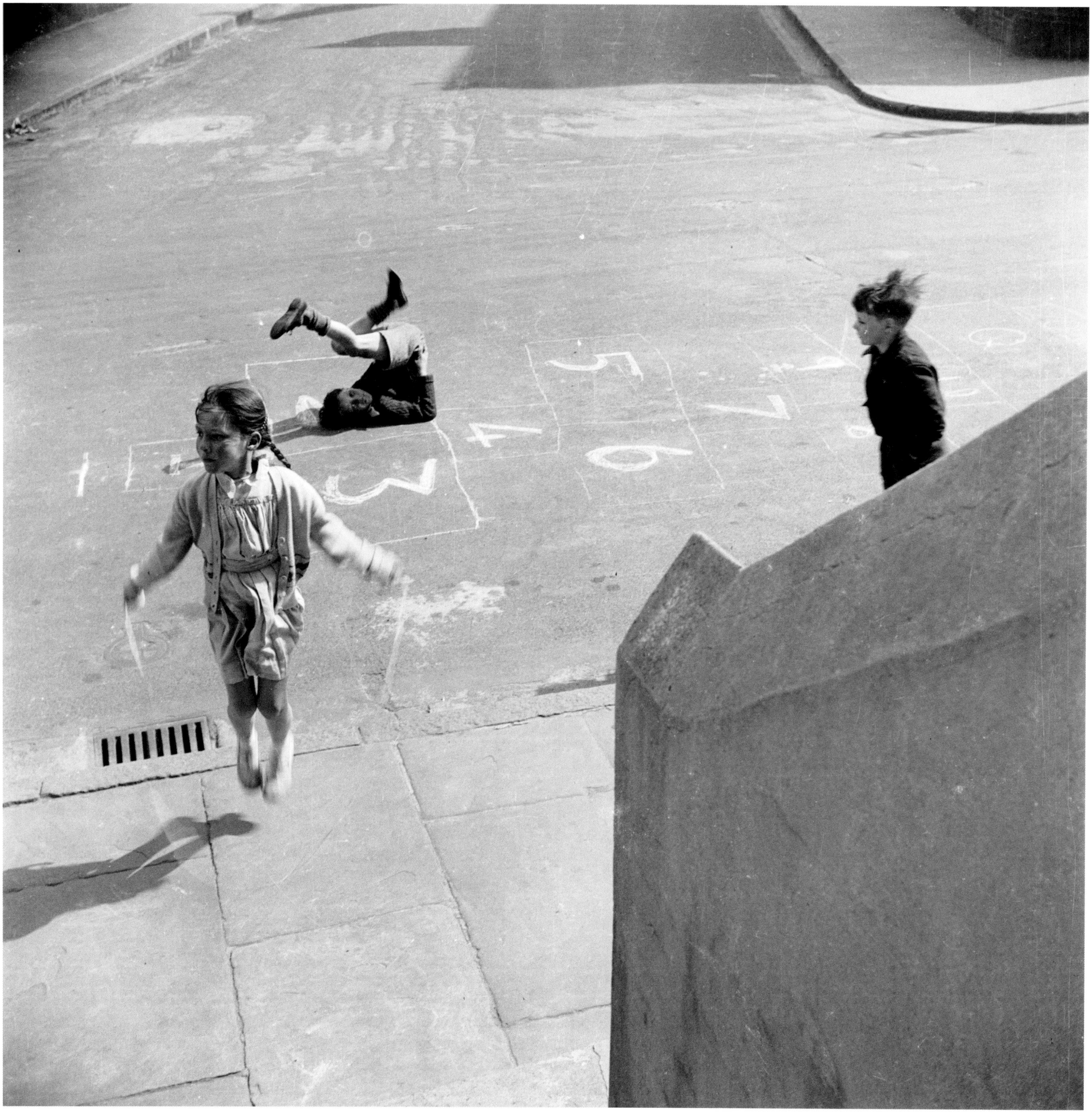

ABOVE Gillian Alexander skipping, Chisenhale Road, Bow E3 1951
OPPOSITE Street party to celebrate the coronation. Hooke House, Gernon Road, Bow E3 1953

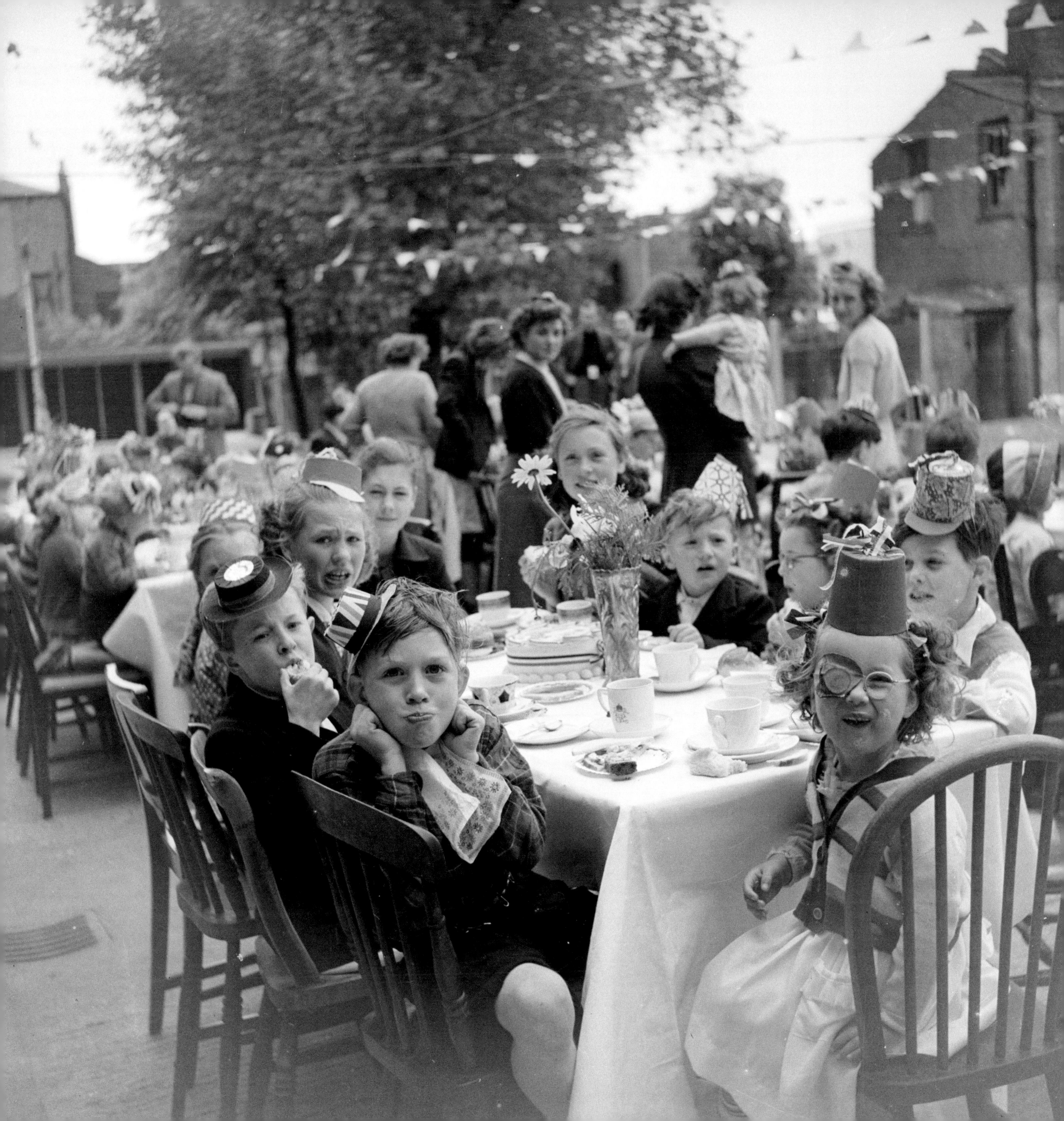

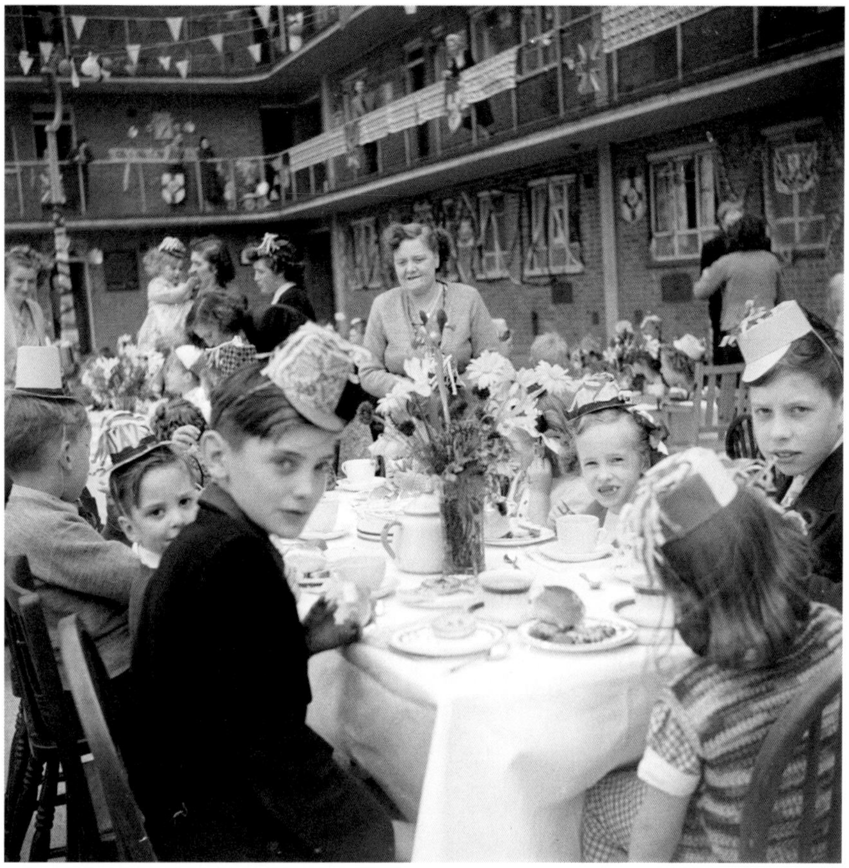

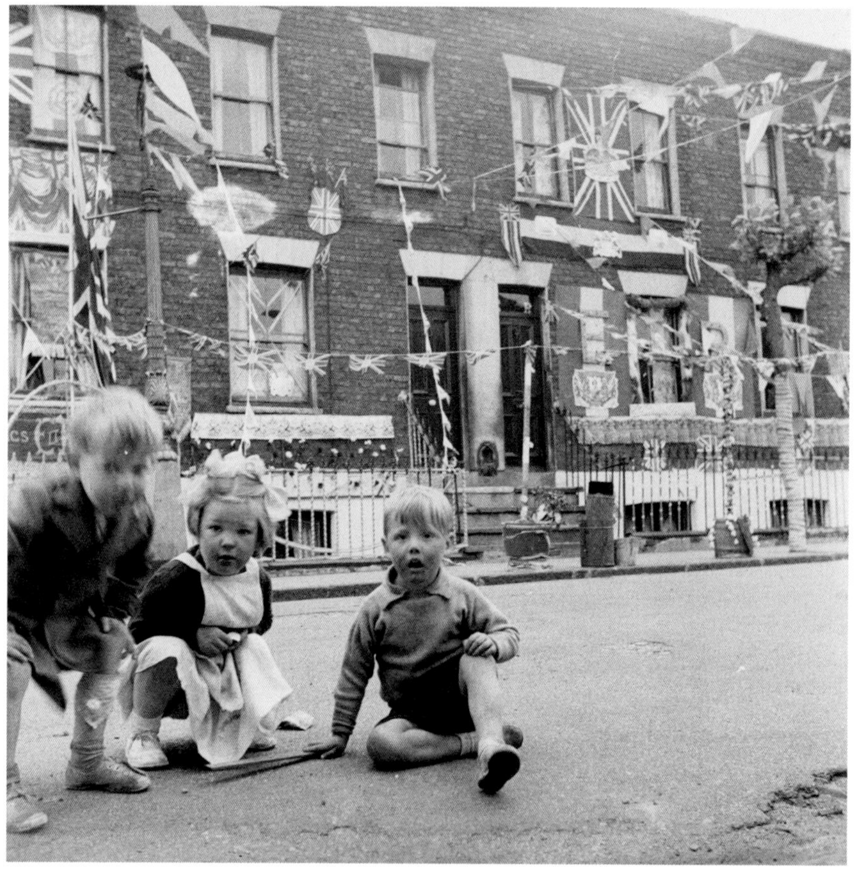

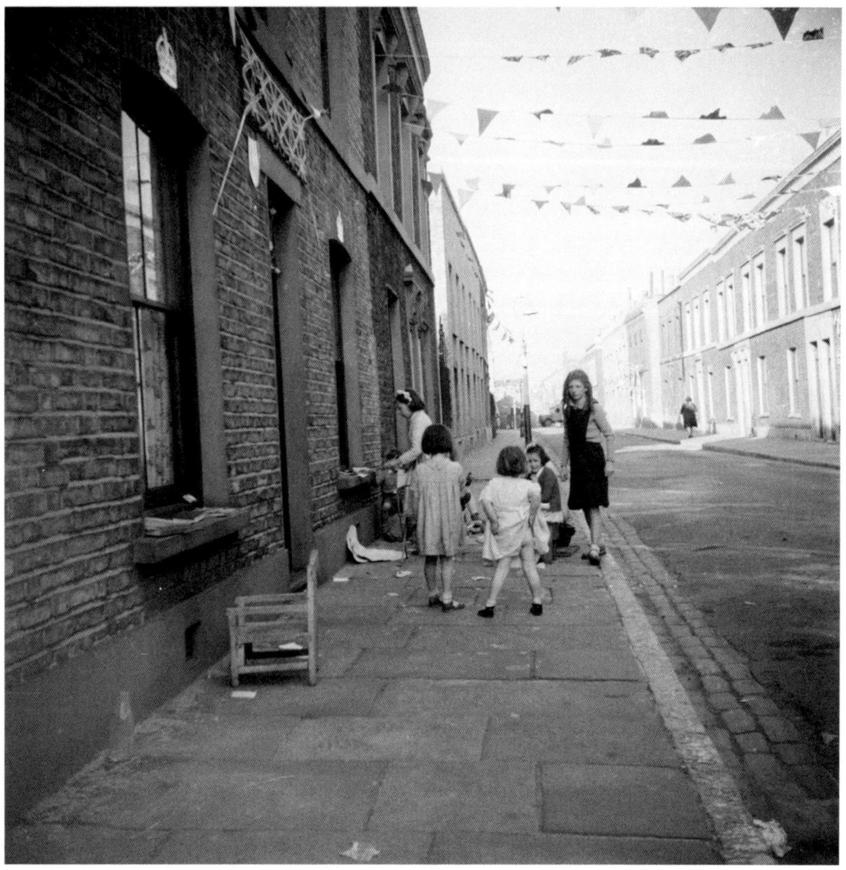

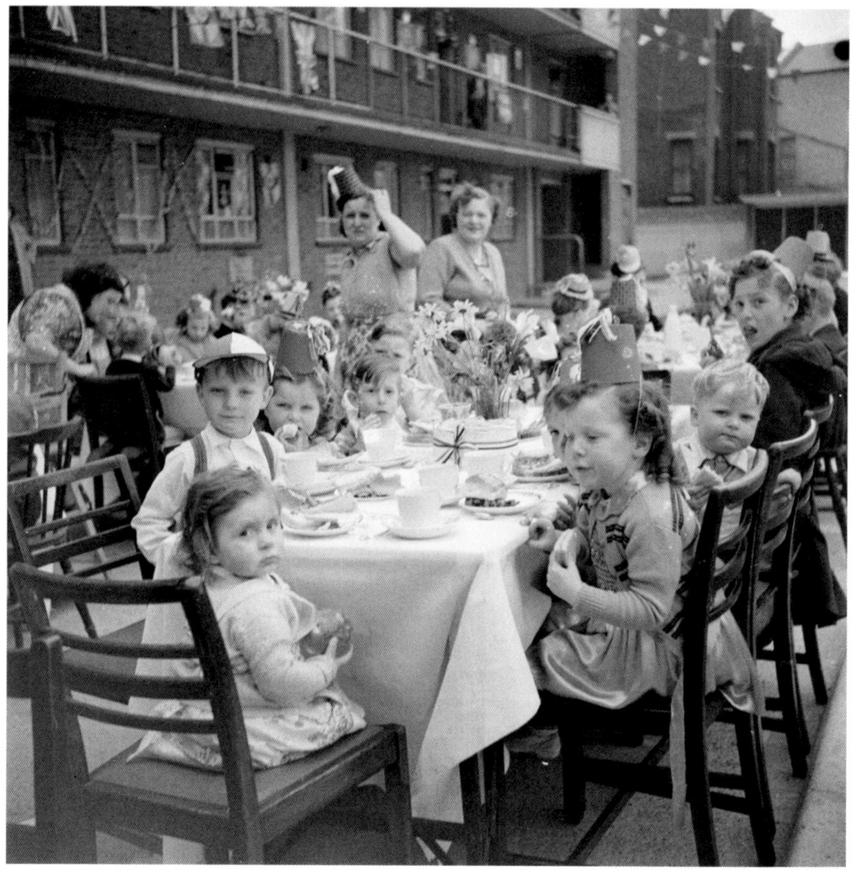

Coronation celebrations 1953

TOP LEFT AND BOTTOM RIGHT Hooke House, Gernon Road, Bow E3

TOP RIGHT Children playing on Chisenhale Road, Bow E3

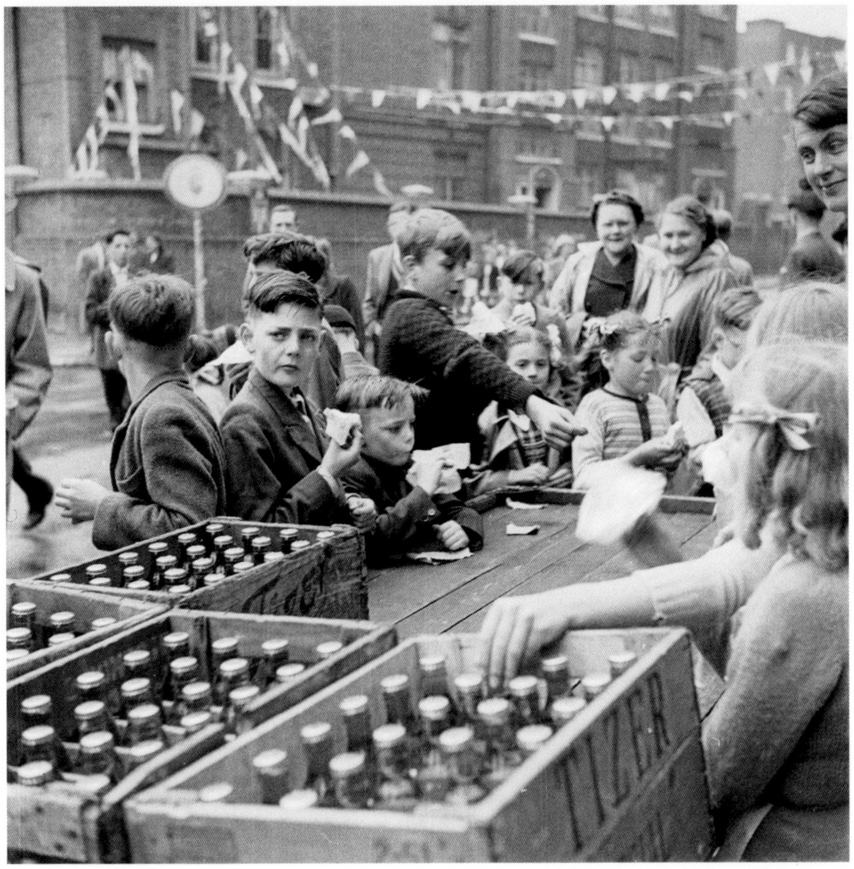

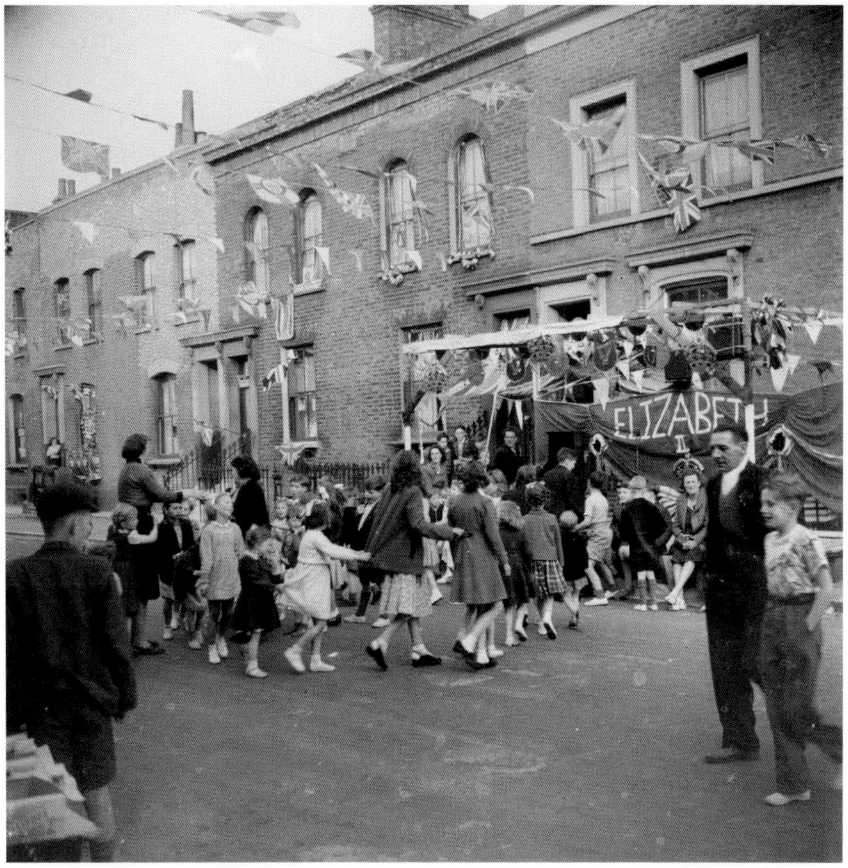

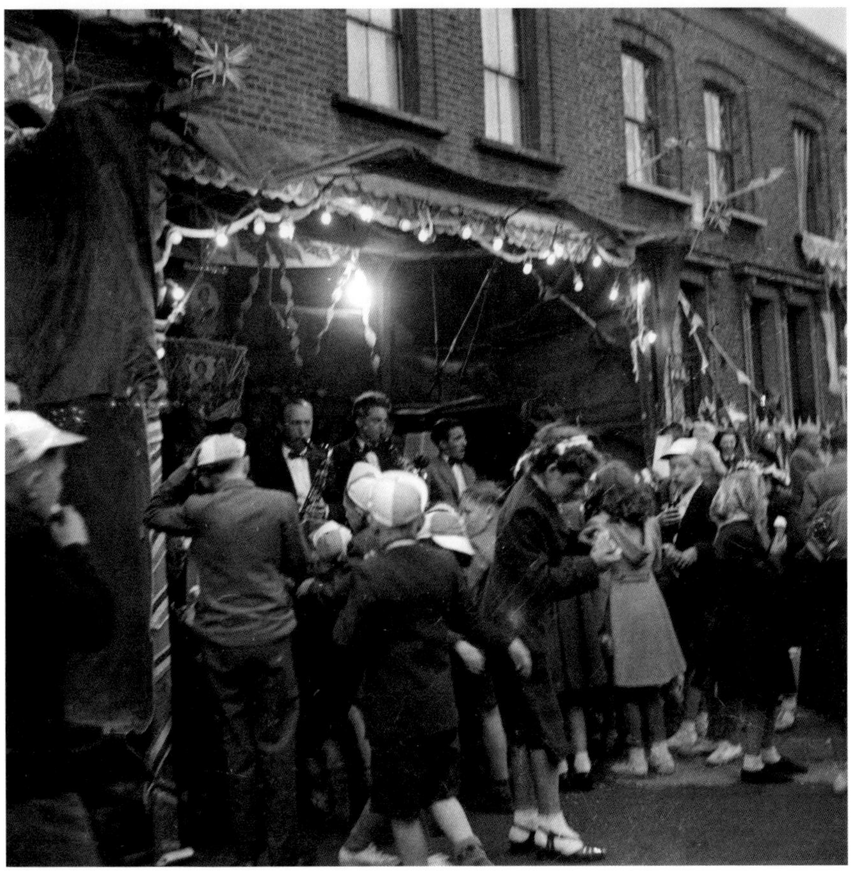

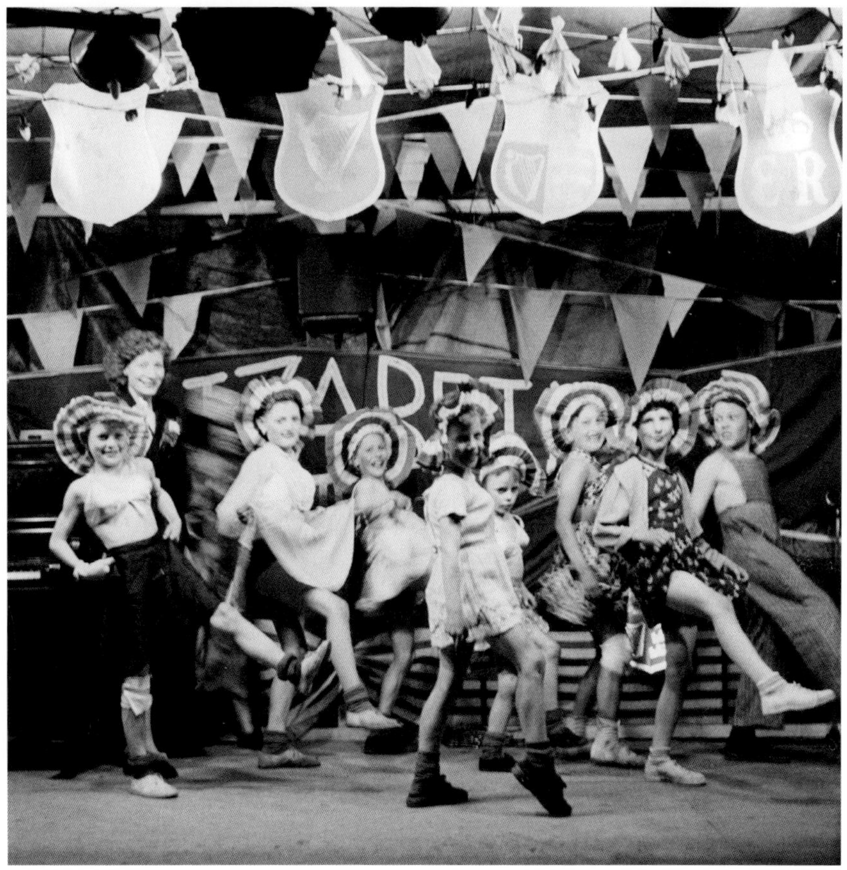

Chisenhale Road, Bow E3

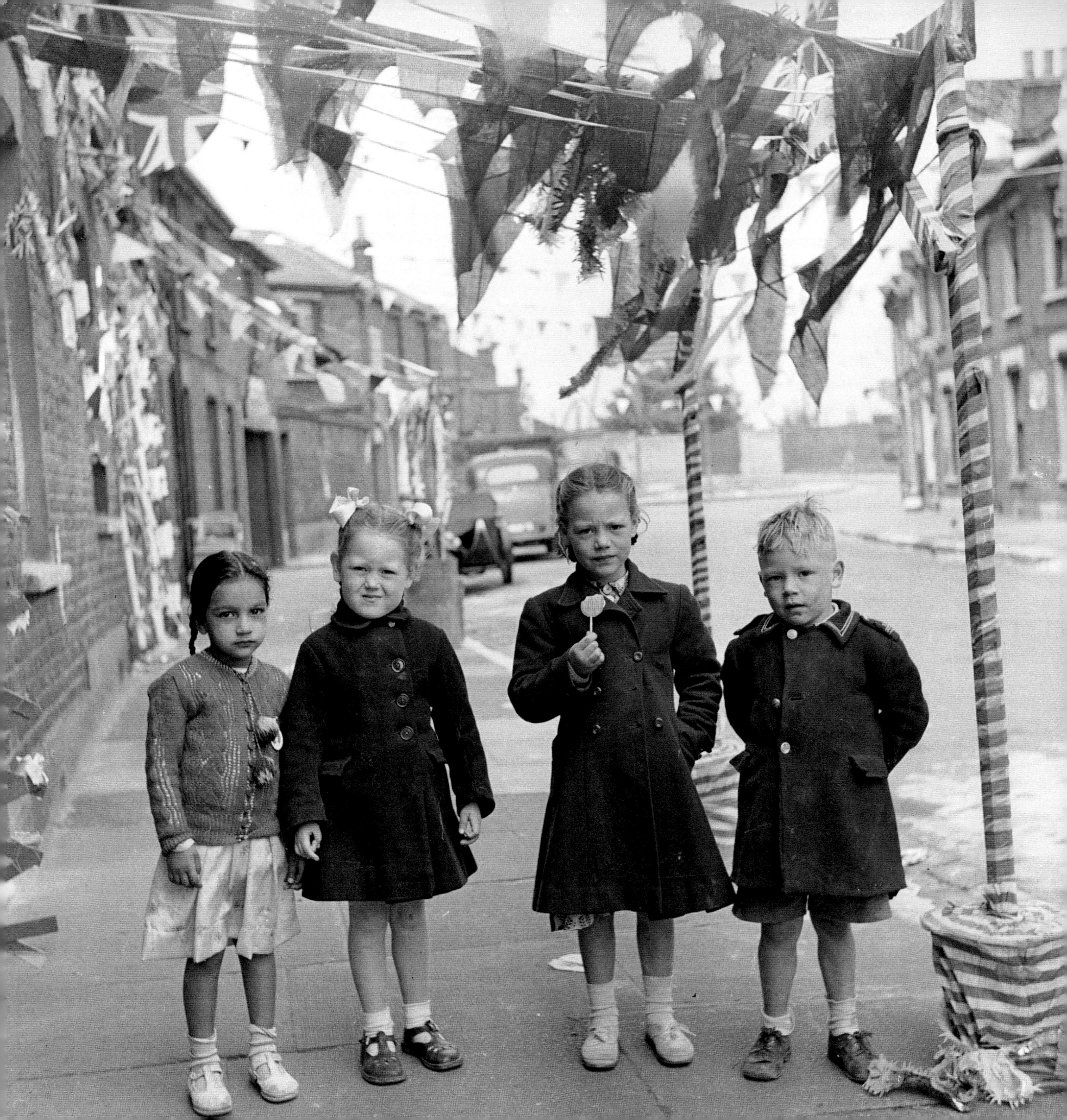

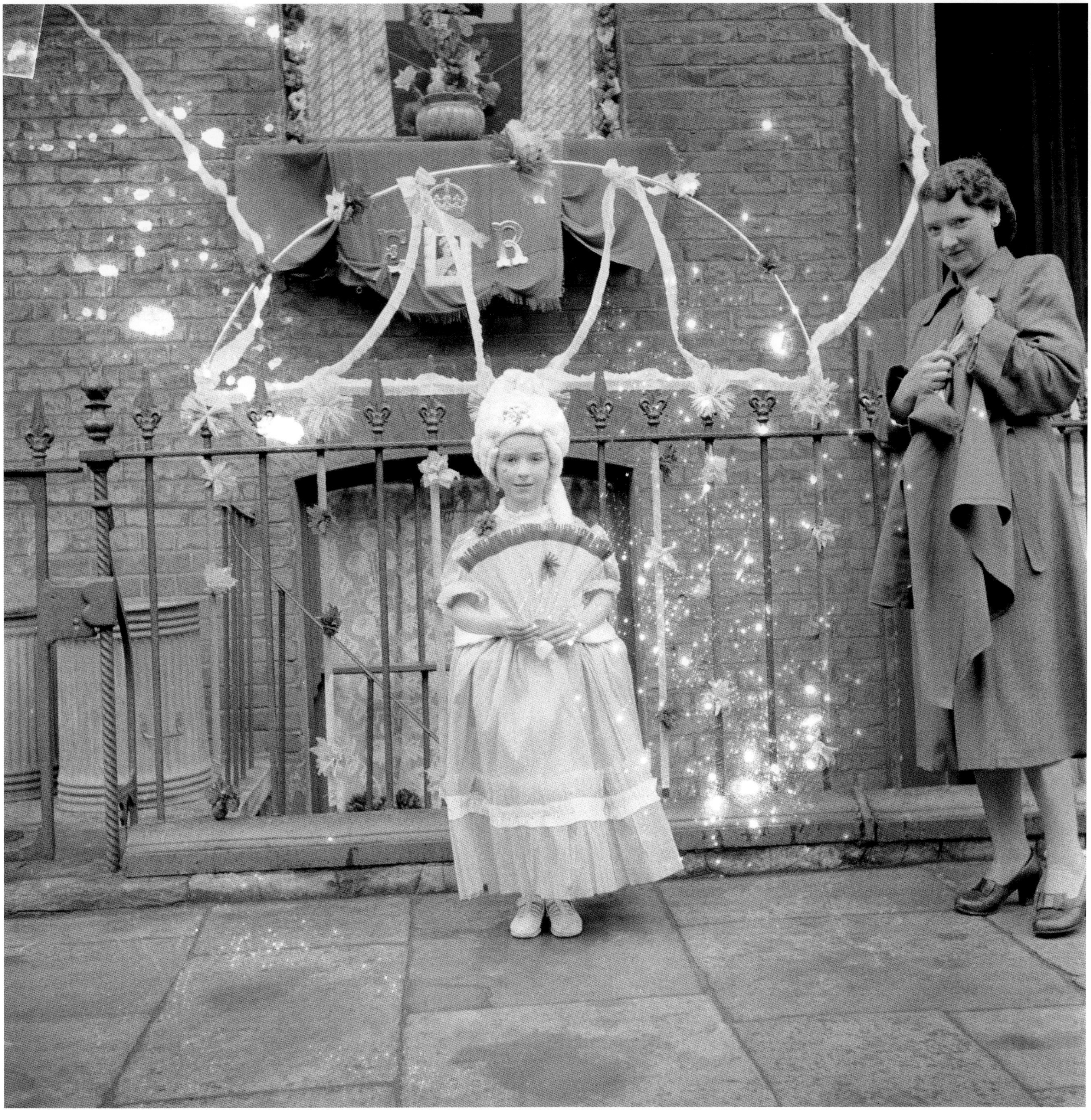

Coronation celebrations 1953

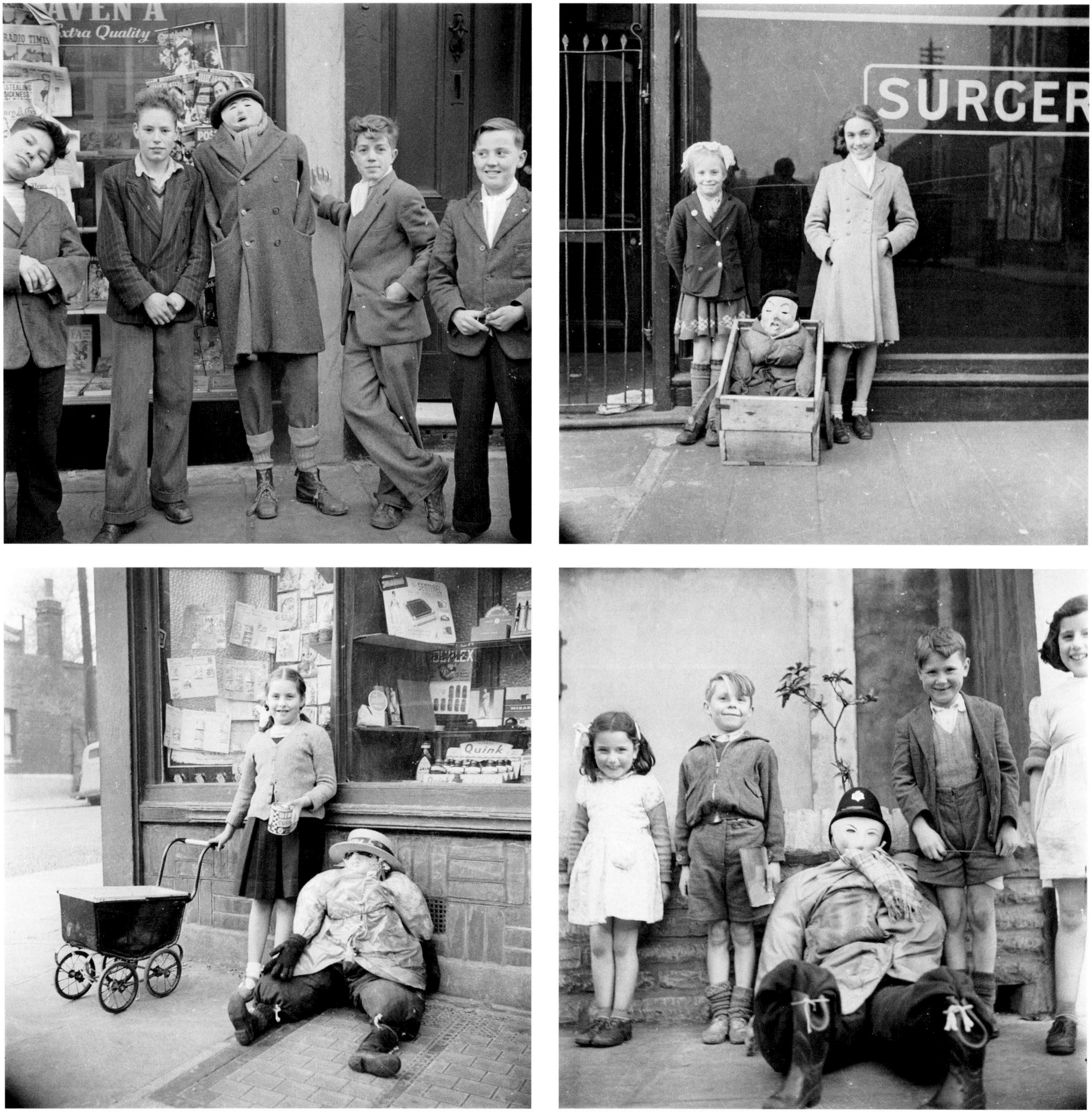

'Penny for the Guy'

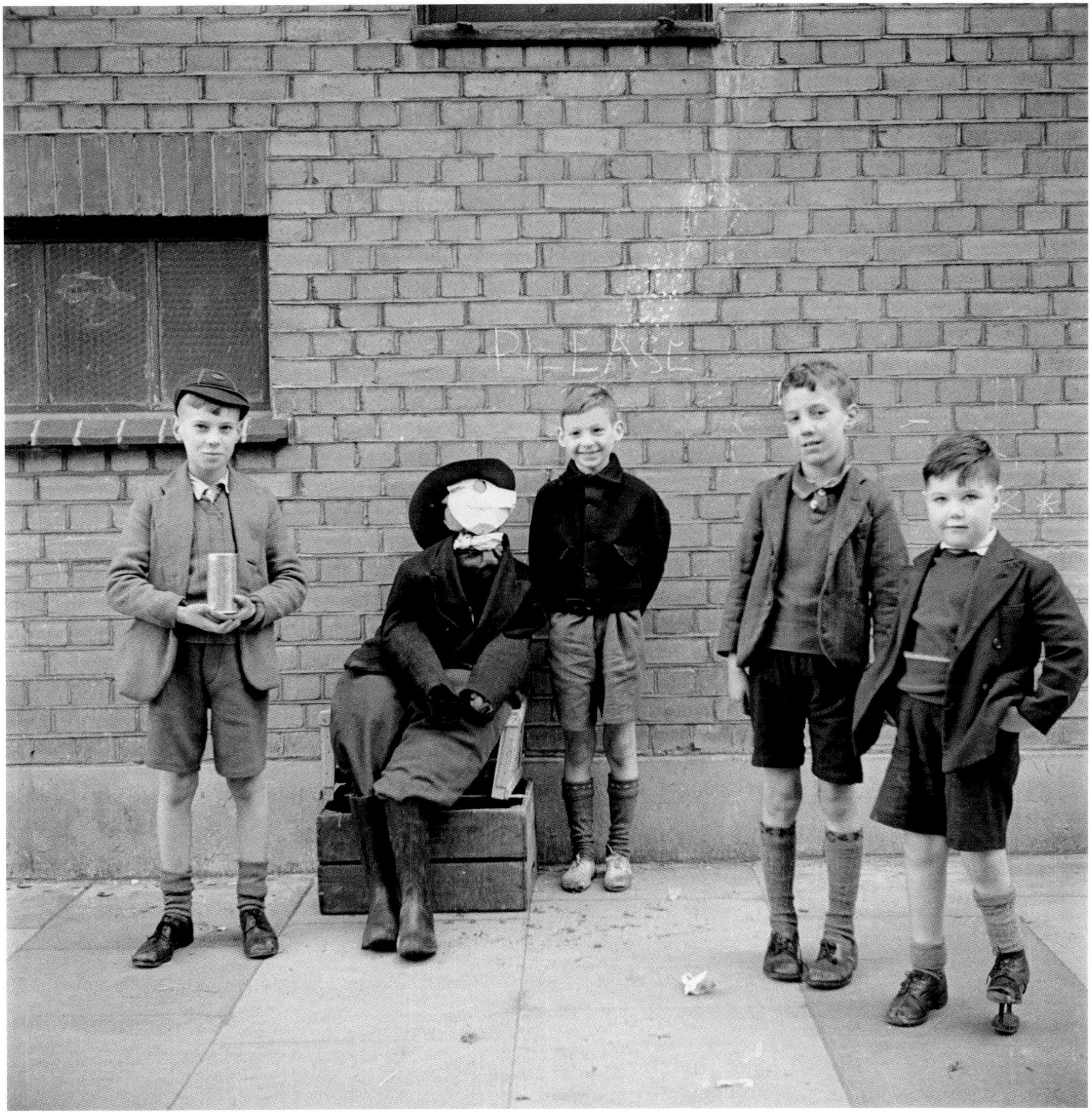
PLEASE

'Our cloth-capped man on his bicycle lives in the more compact geography, working near the living house, trading in the street or living over his small shop in a day to day economy without larder stores and credit accounts.'

Window cleaner outside 46 Chisenhale Road, Bow E3

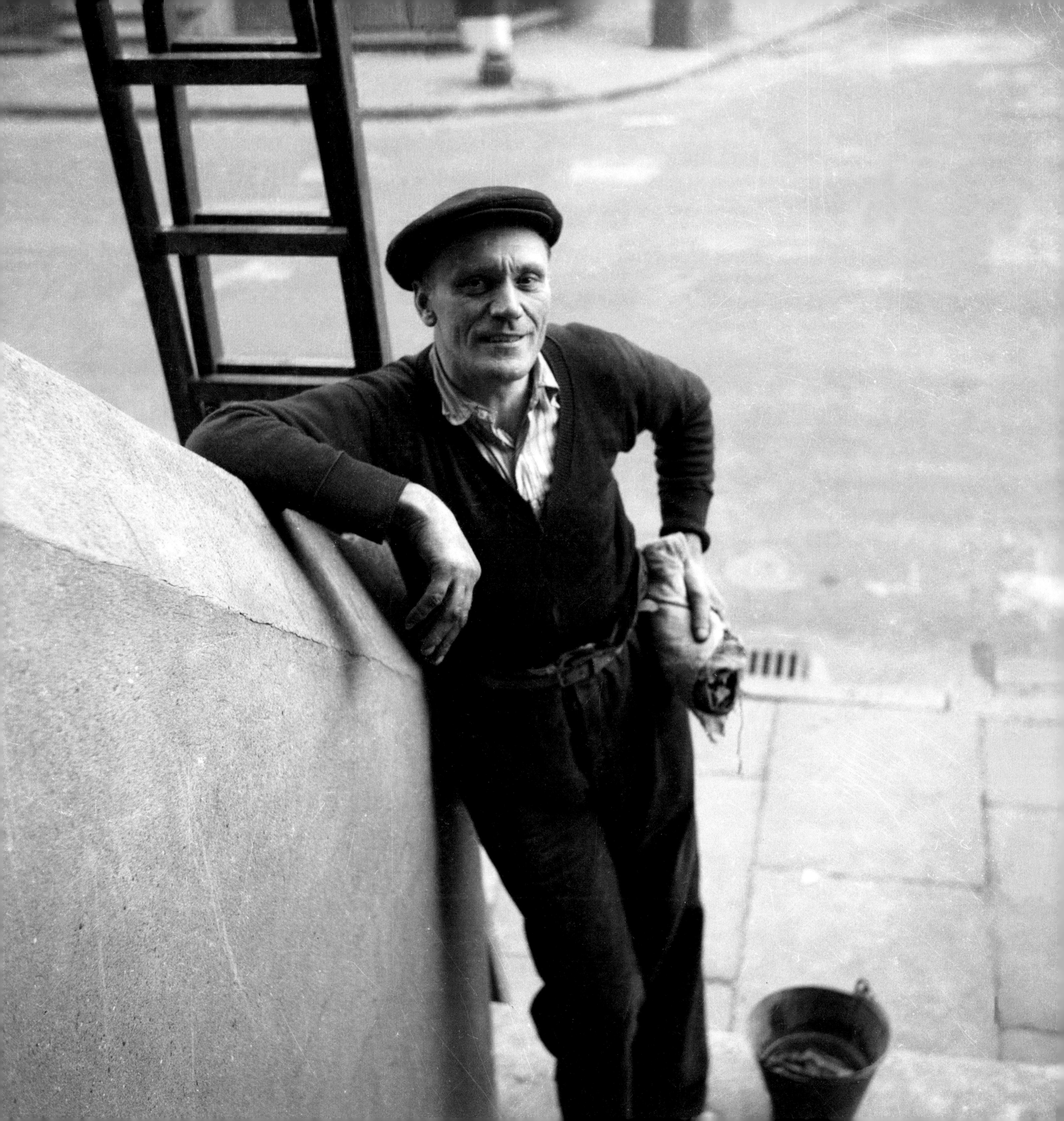

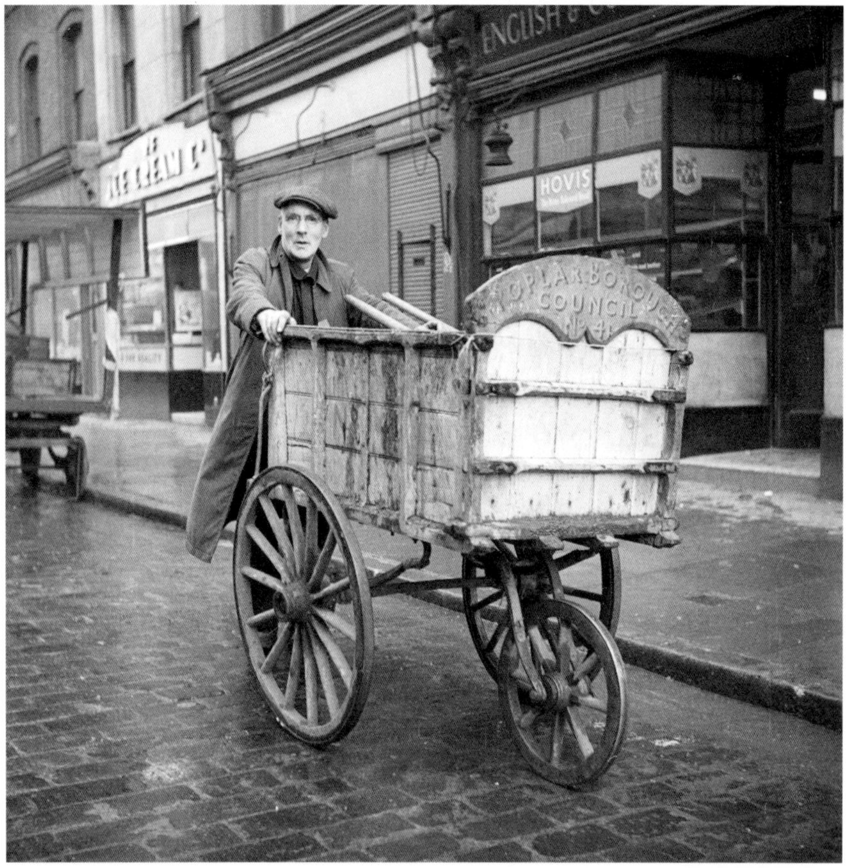

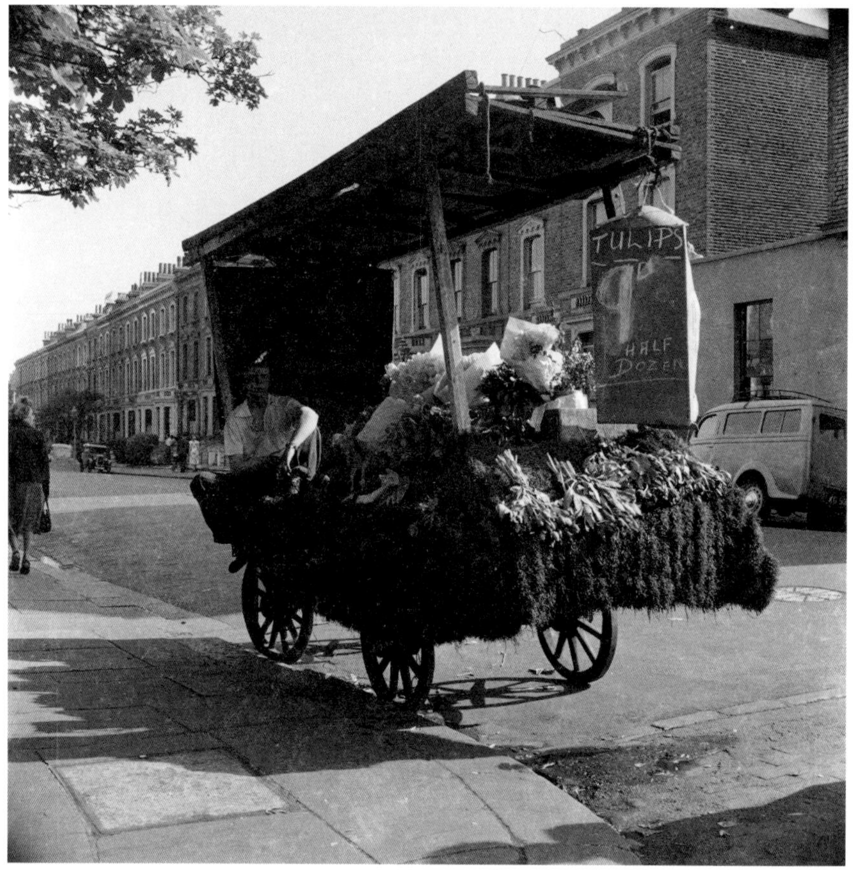

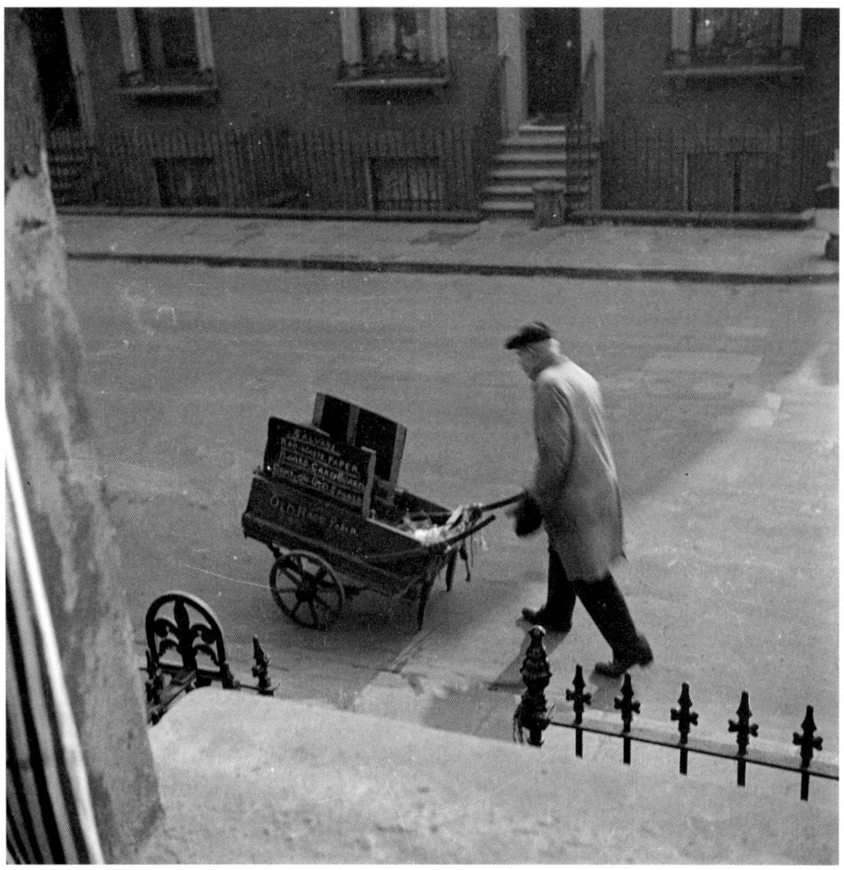

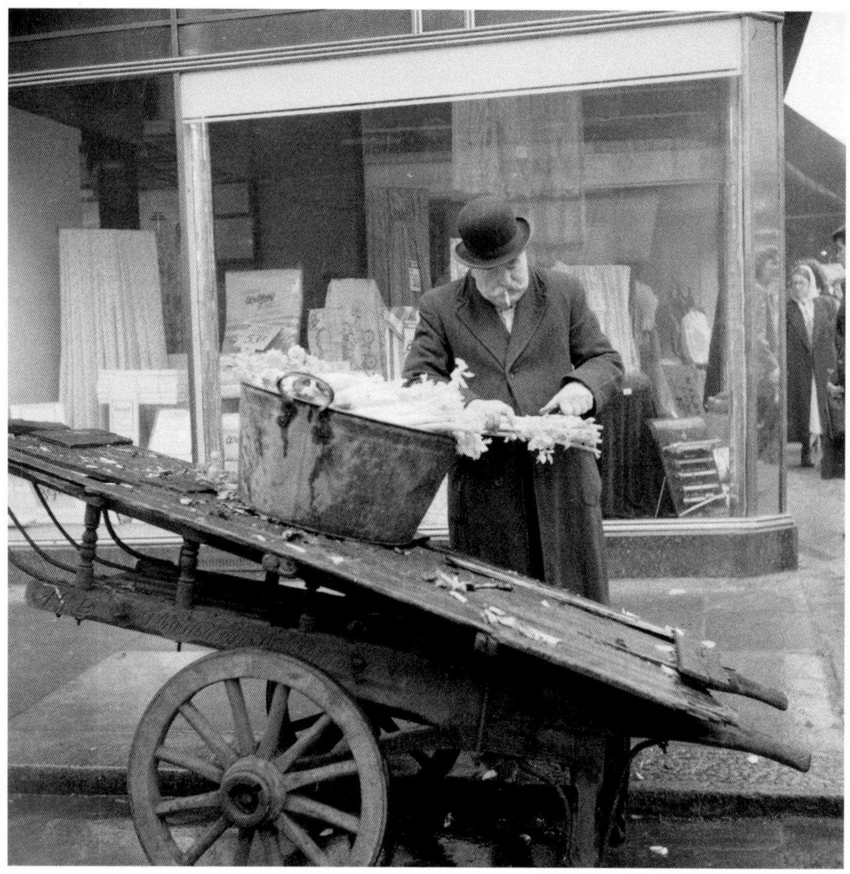

BOTTOM LEFT Rag and paper collector, Chisenhale Road, Bow E3

OPPOSITE *Bert Smith, Knifegrinder in Chisenhale Road*, Bow E3

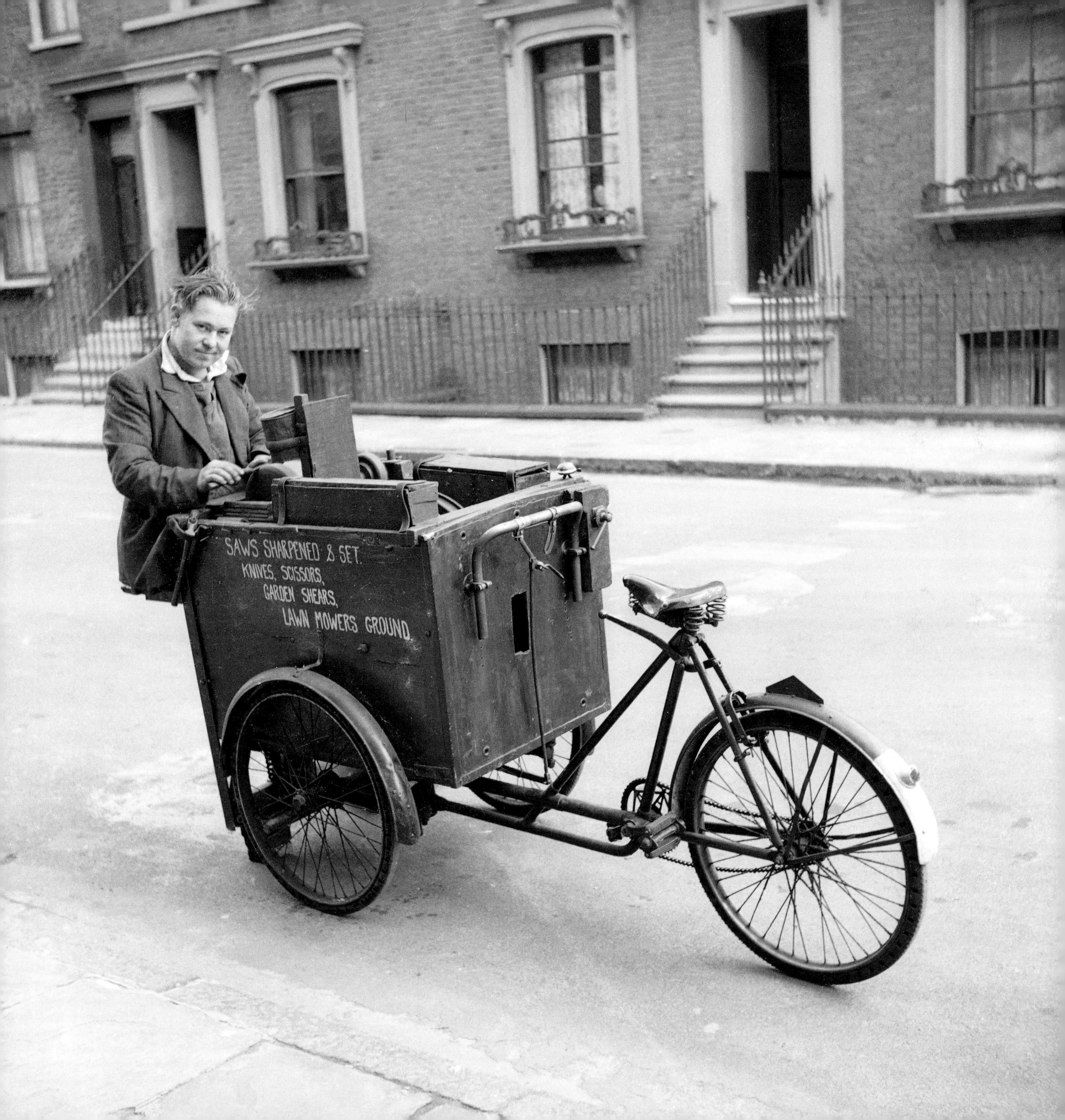
SAWS SHARPENED & SET.
KNIVES, SCISSORS,
GARDEN SHEARS,
LAWN MOWERS GROUND.

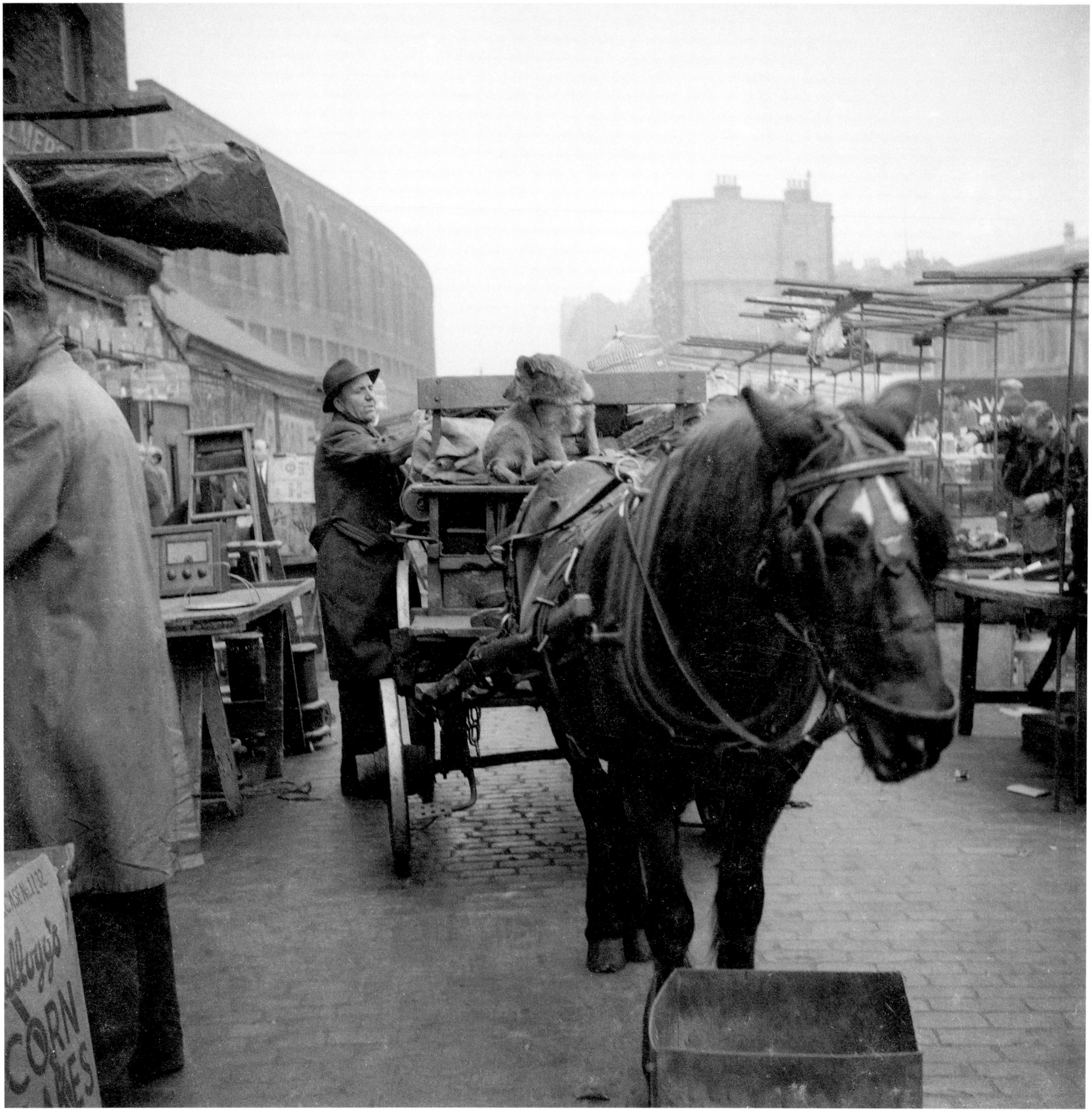
CORN

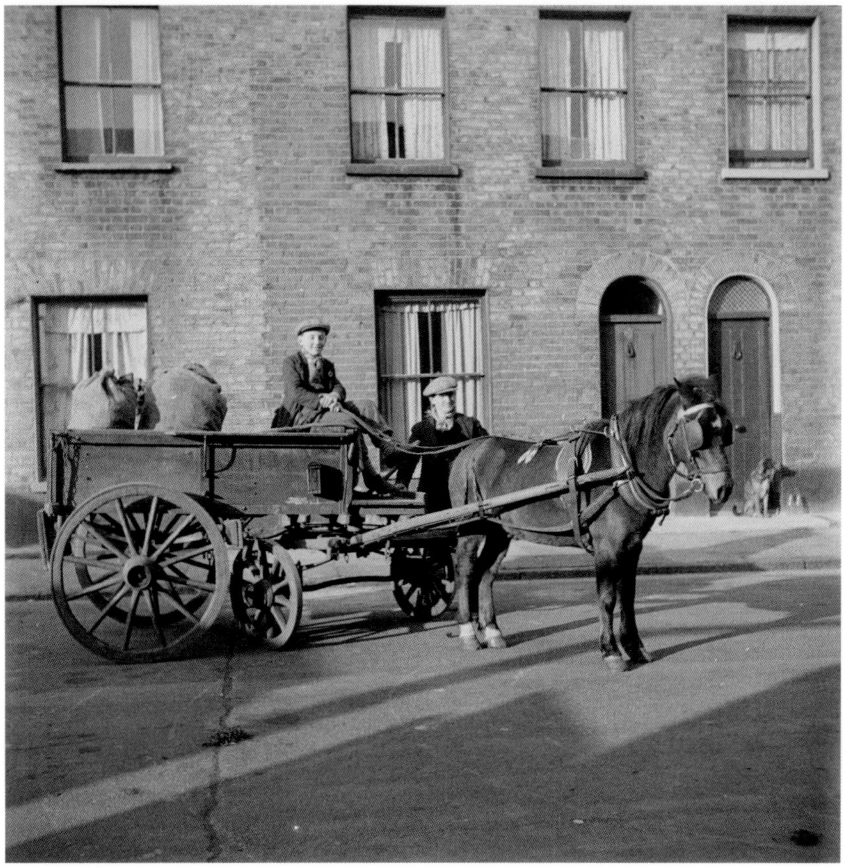

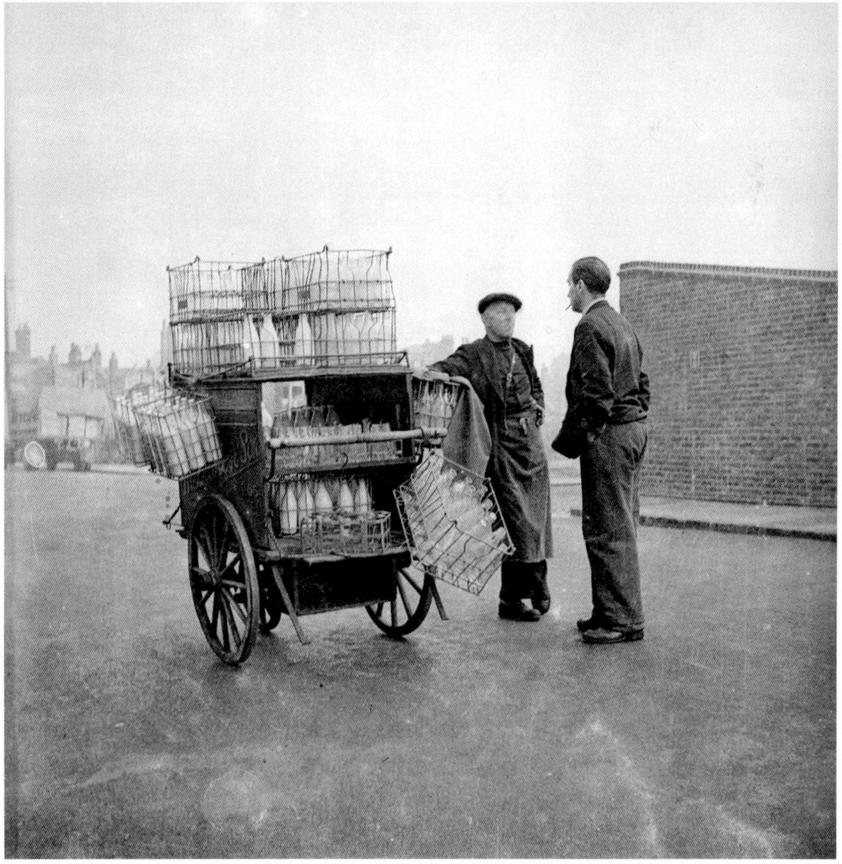

Street merchants

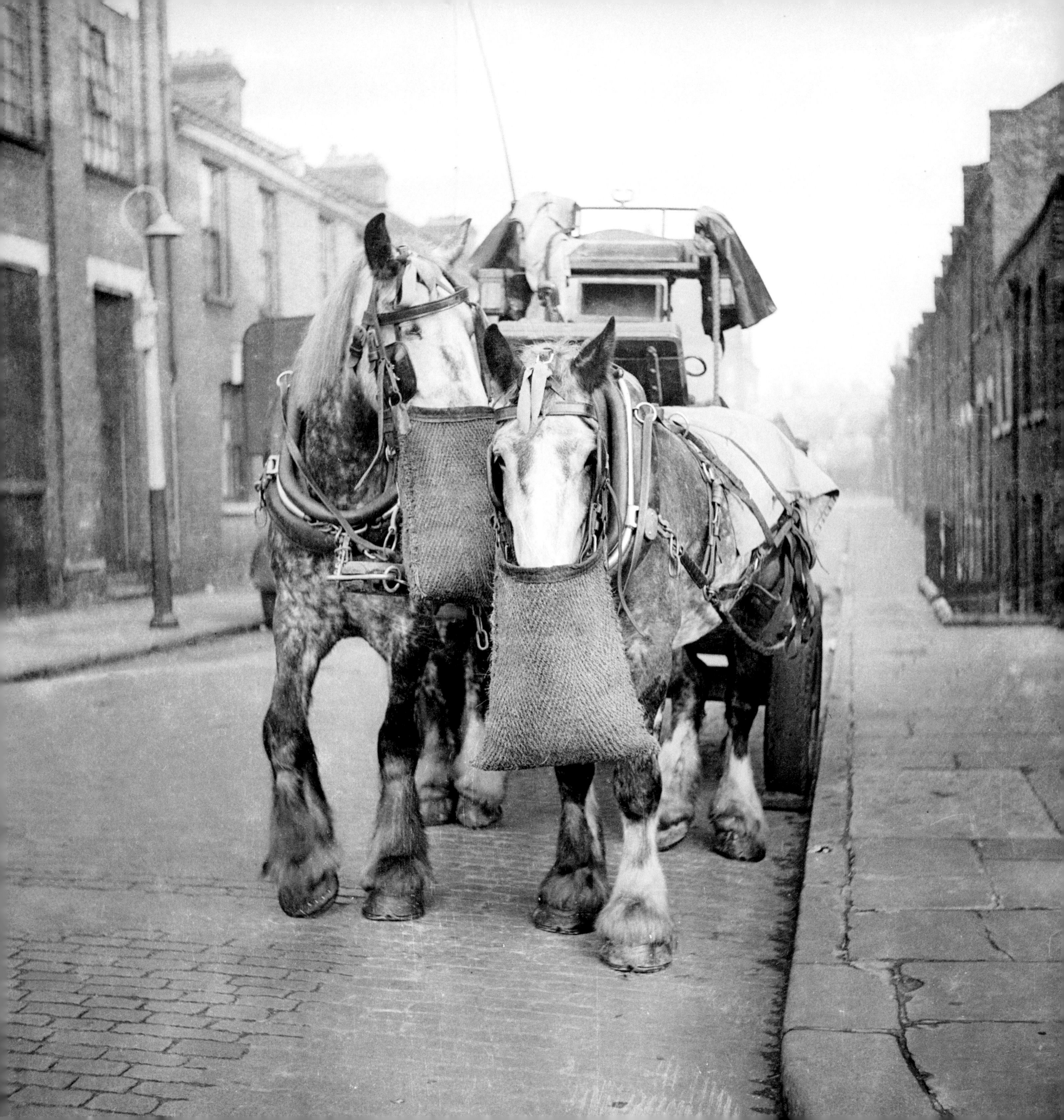

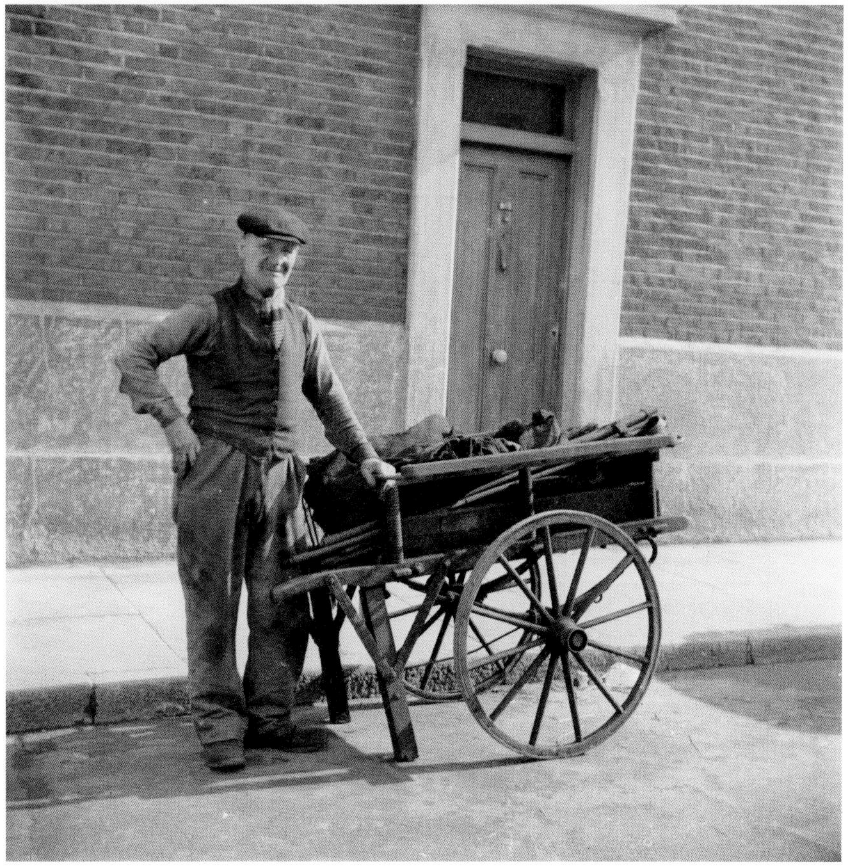

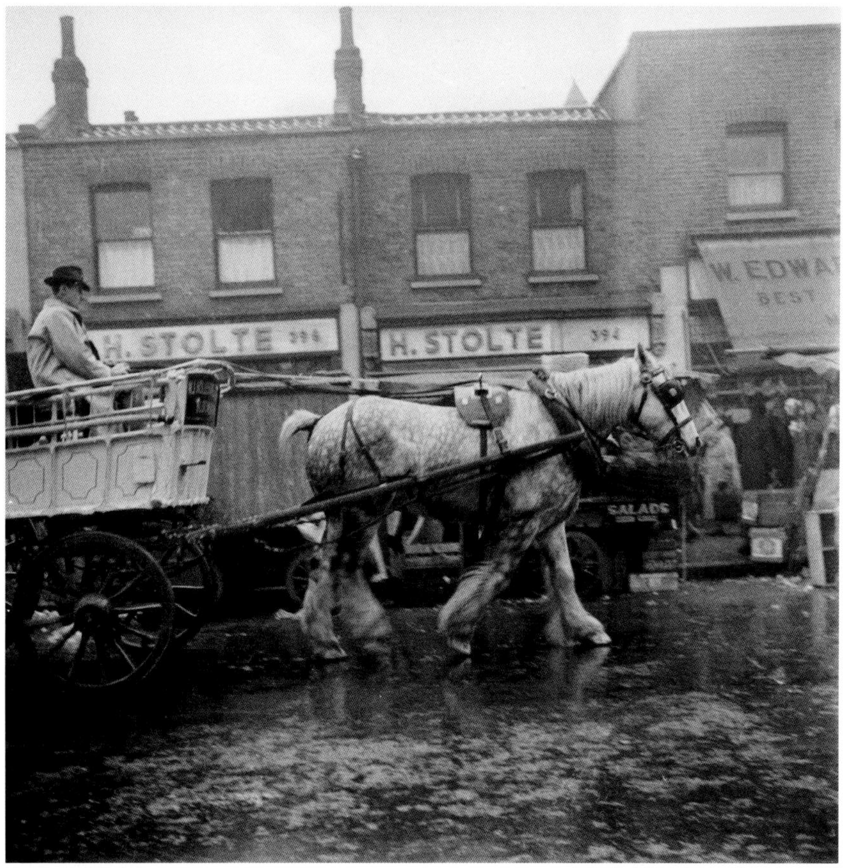

TOP Chimney sweep, Zeland Road, Bow E3
BOTTOM Horse and cart passing Stolte's Bakery Ltd, 394 and 396 Bethnal Green Road, Bethnal Green E2

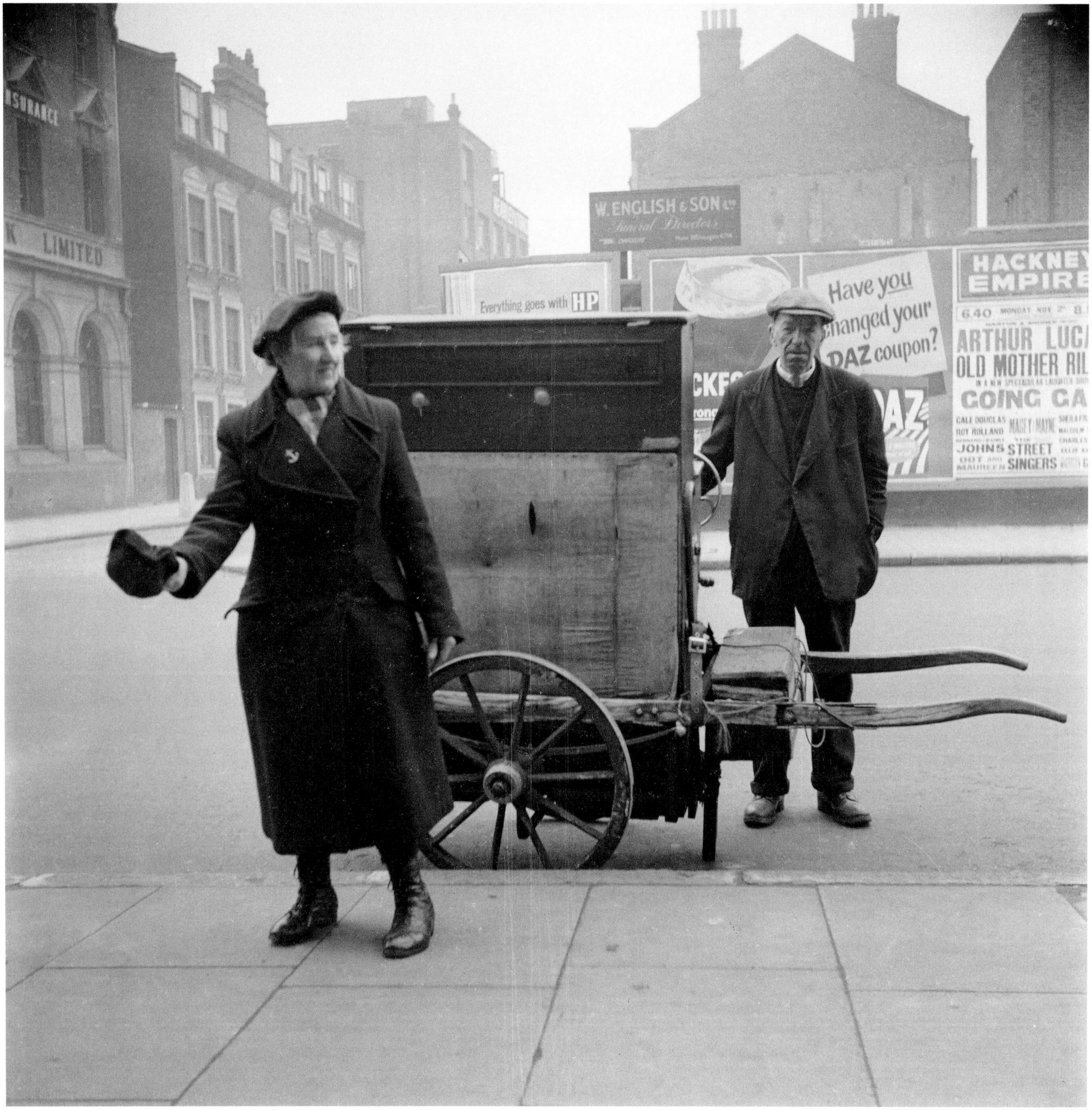

Musical organ, Bethnal Green Road, Bethnal Green E2 1953

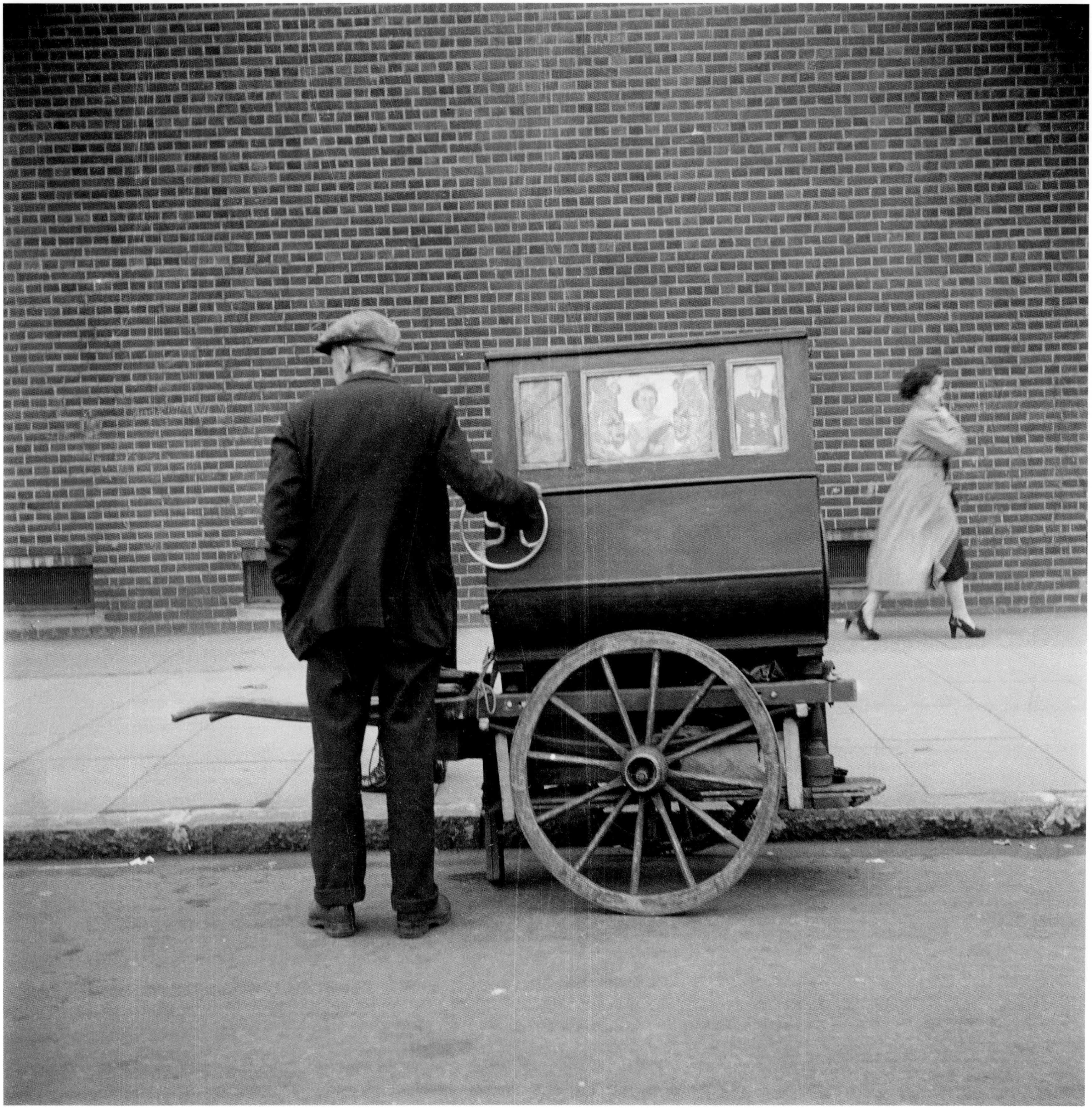

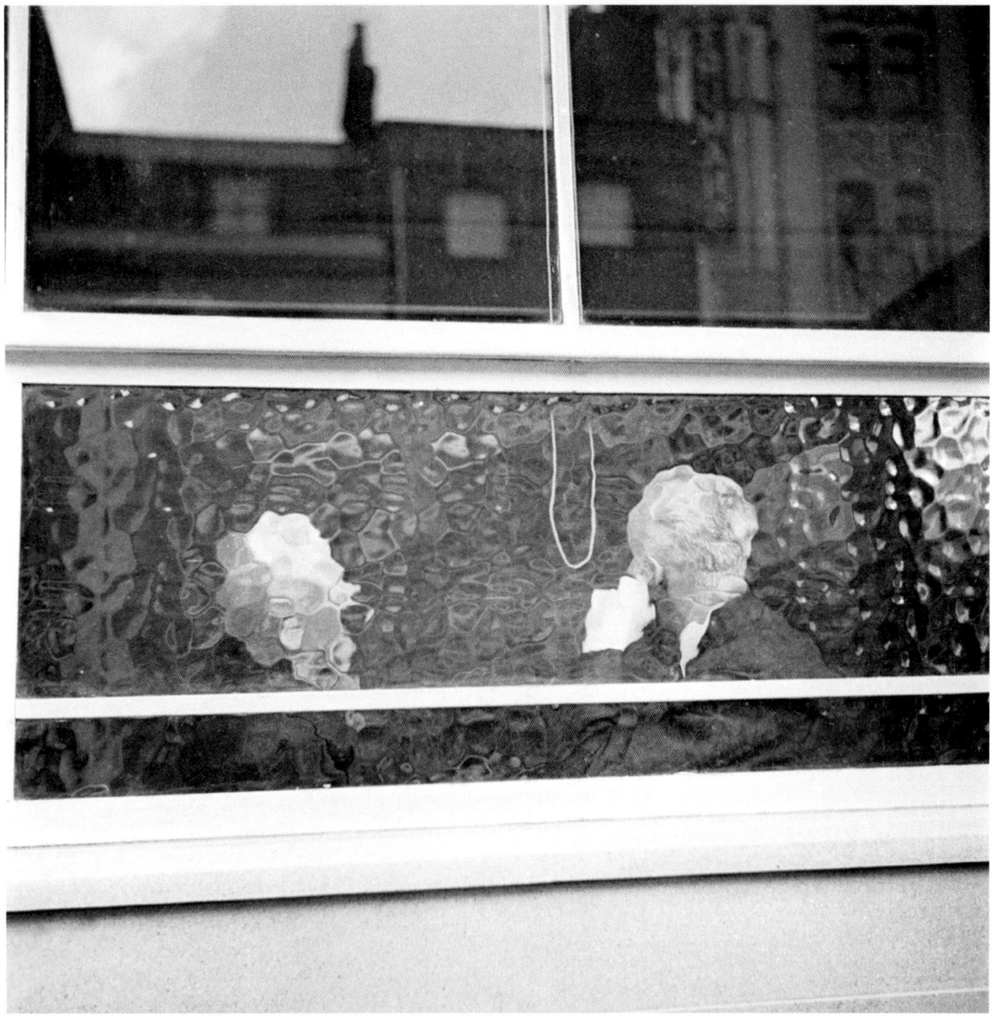

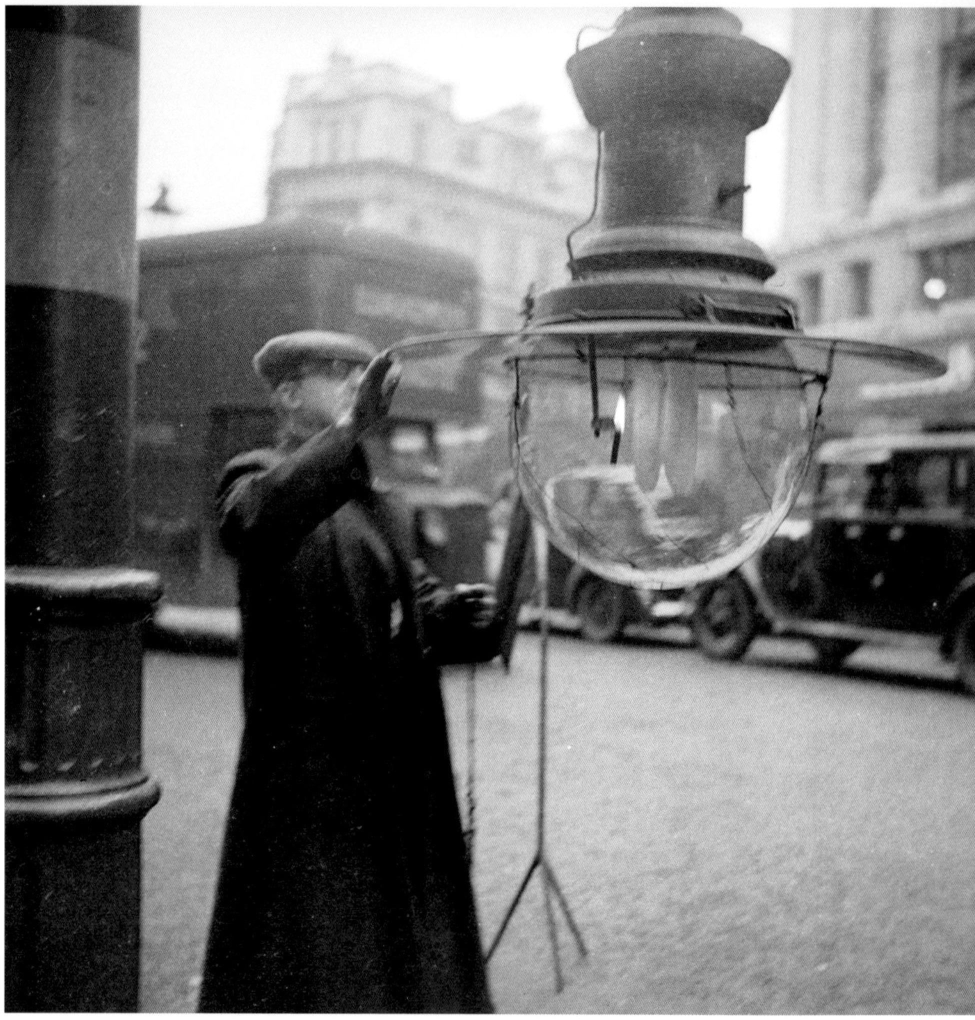

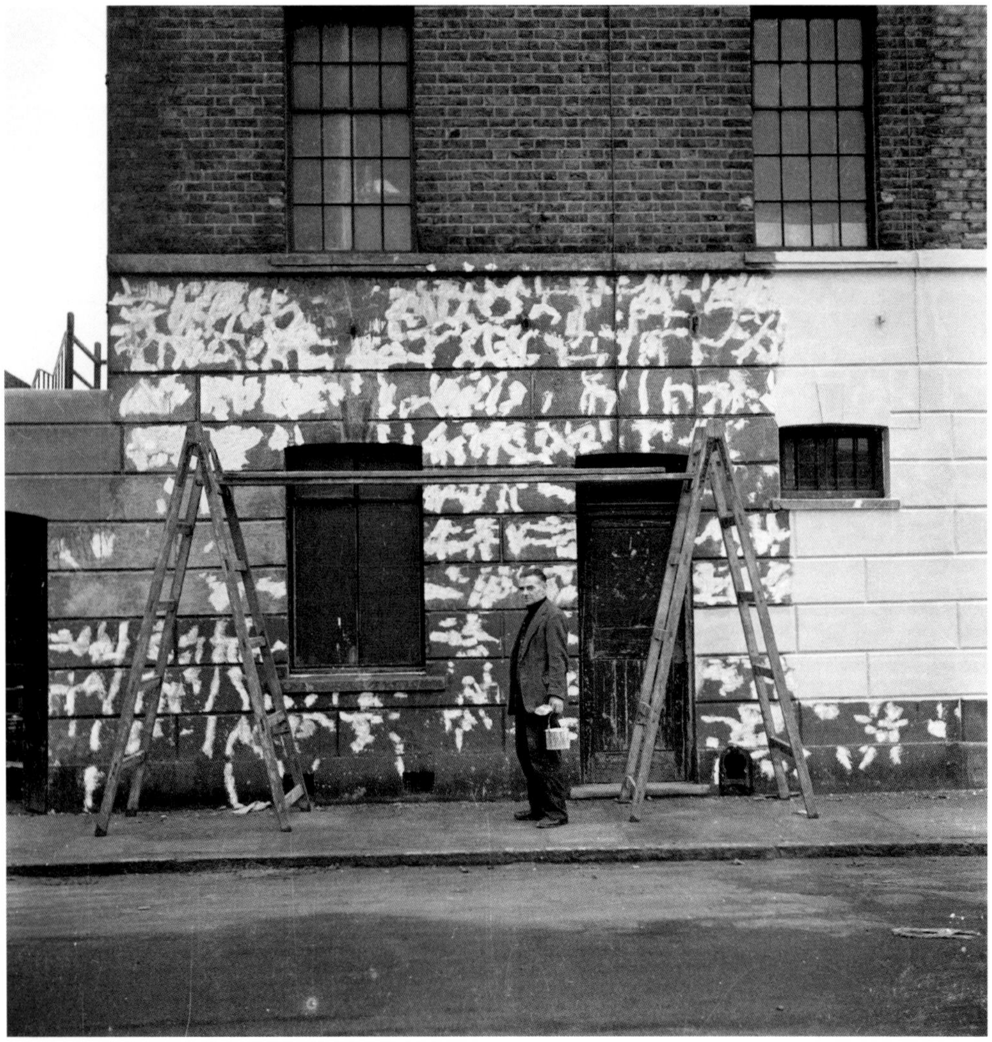

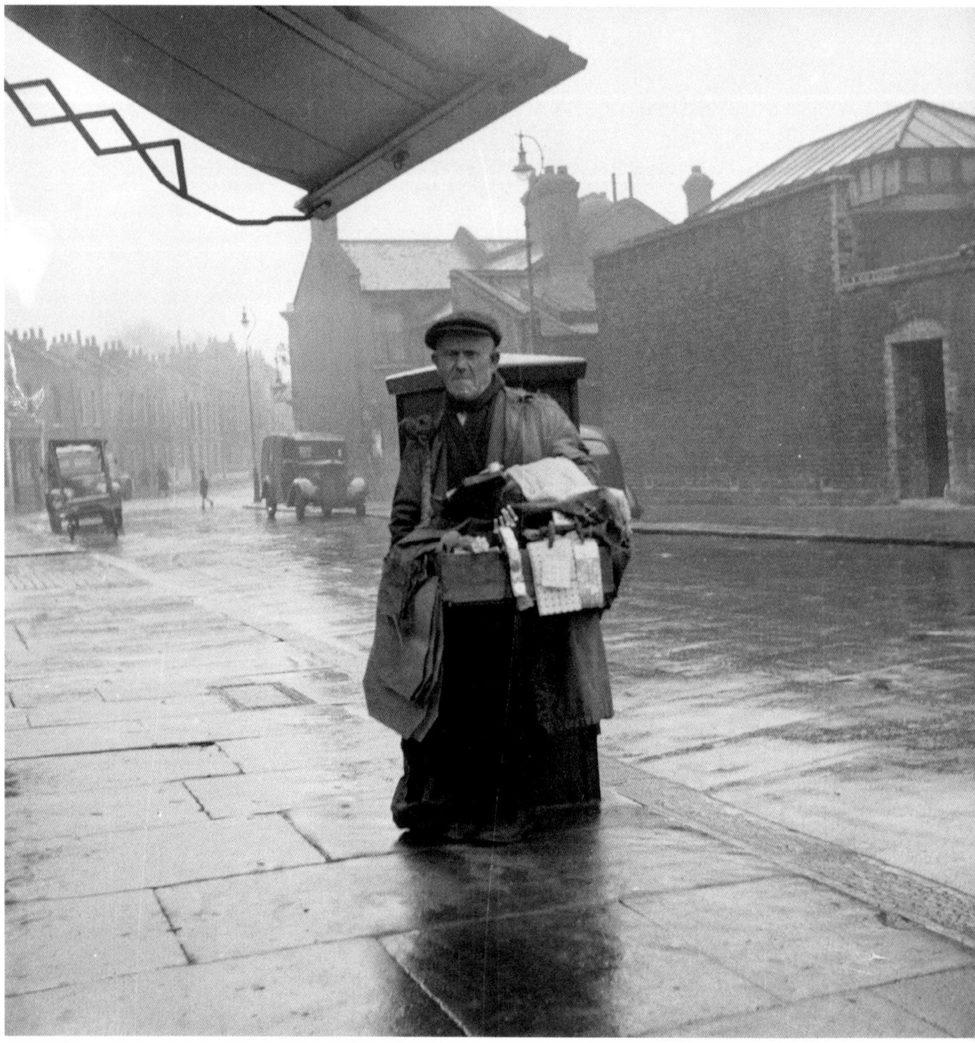

TOP LEFT *Heads Seen through Pub Window, East End*

BOTTOM LEFT *Wall Painting, Stopping Out. Grove Road, Bethnal Green*

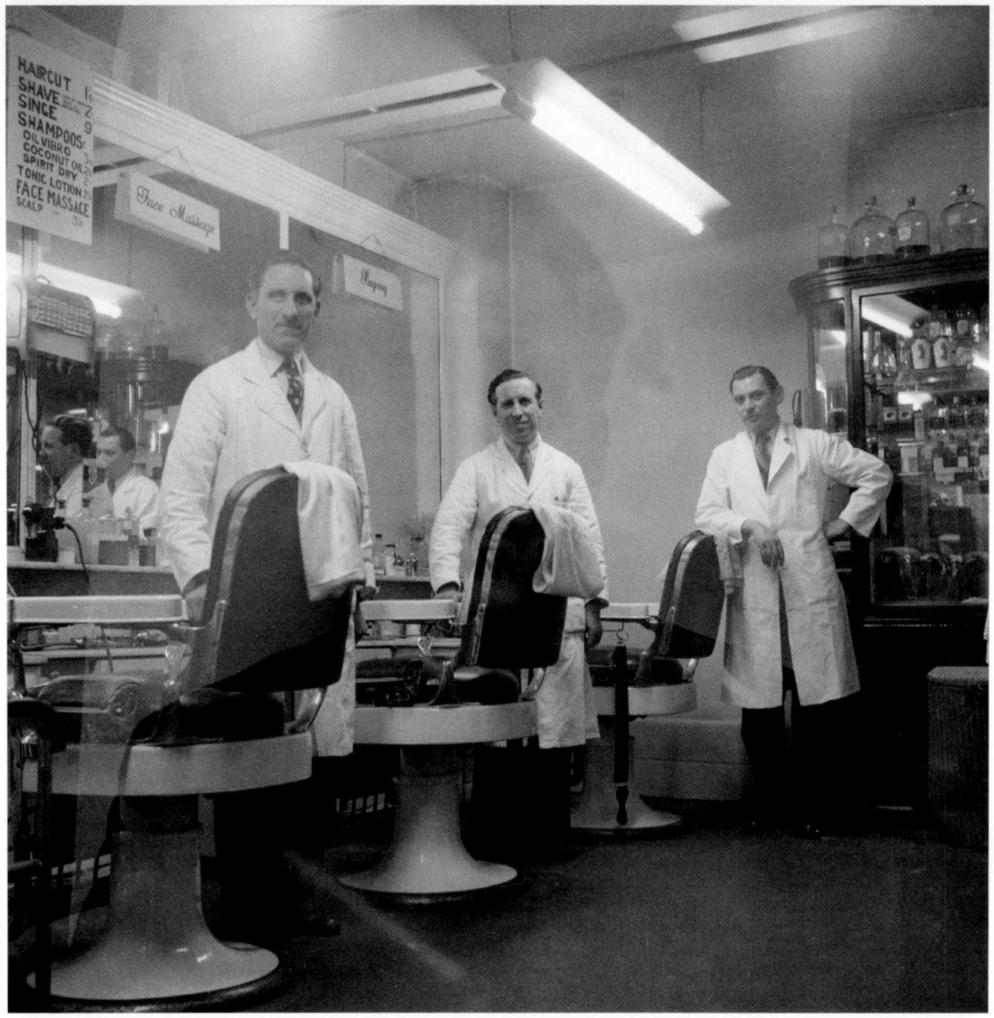

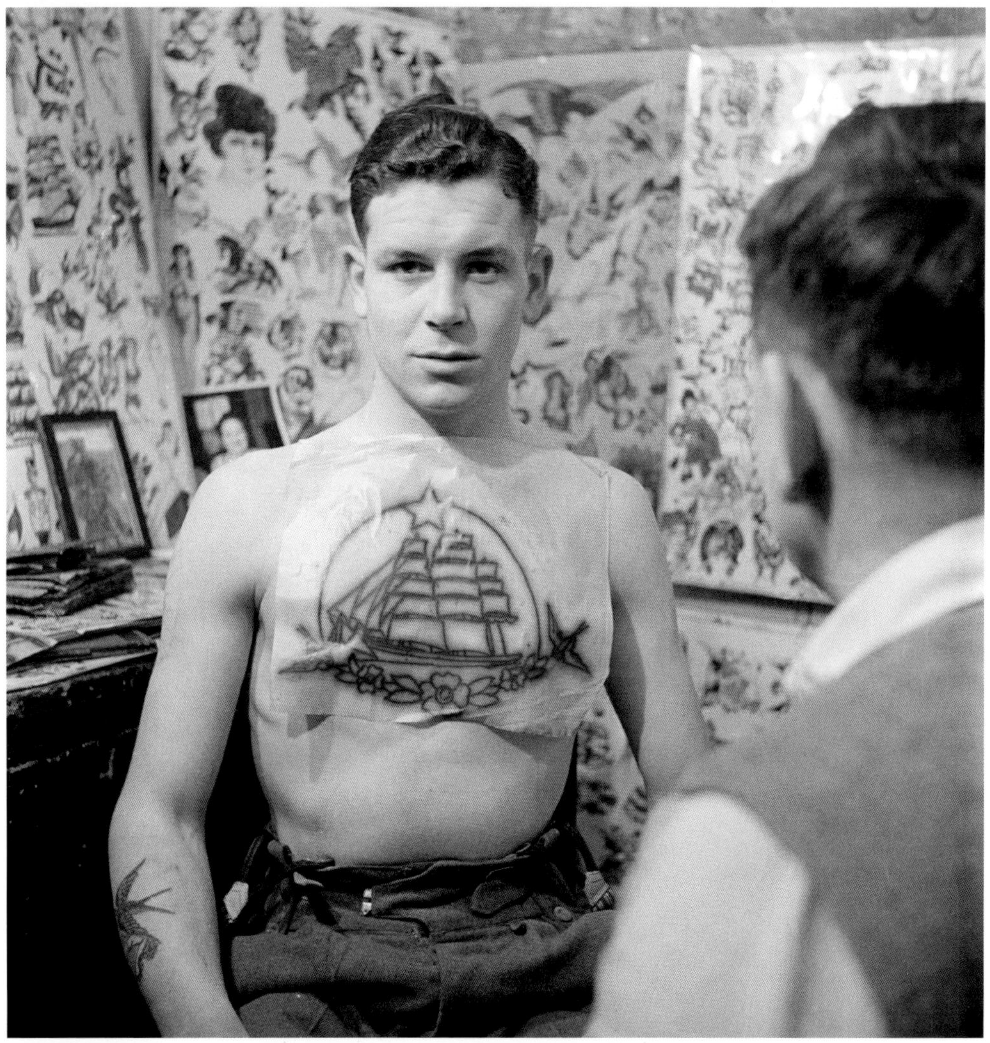

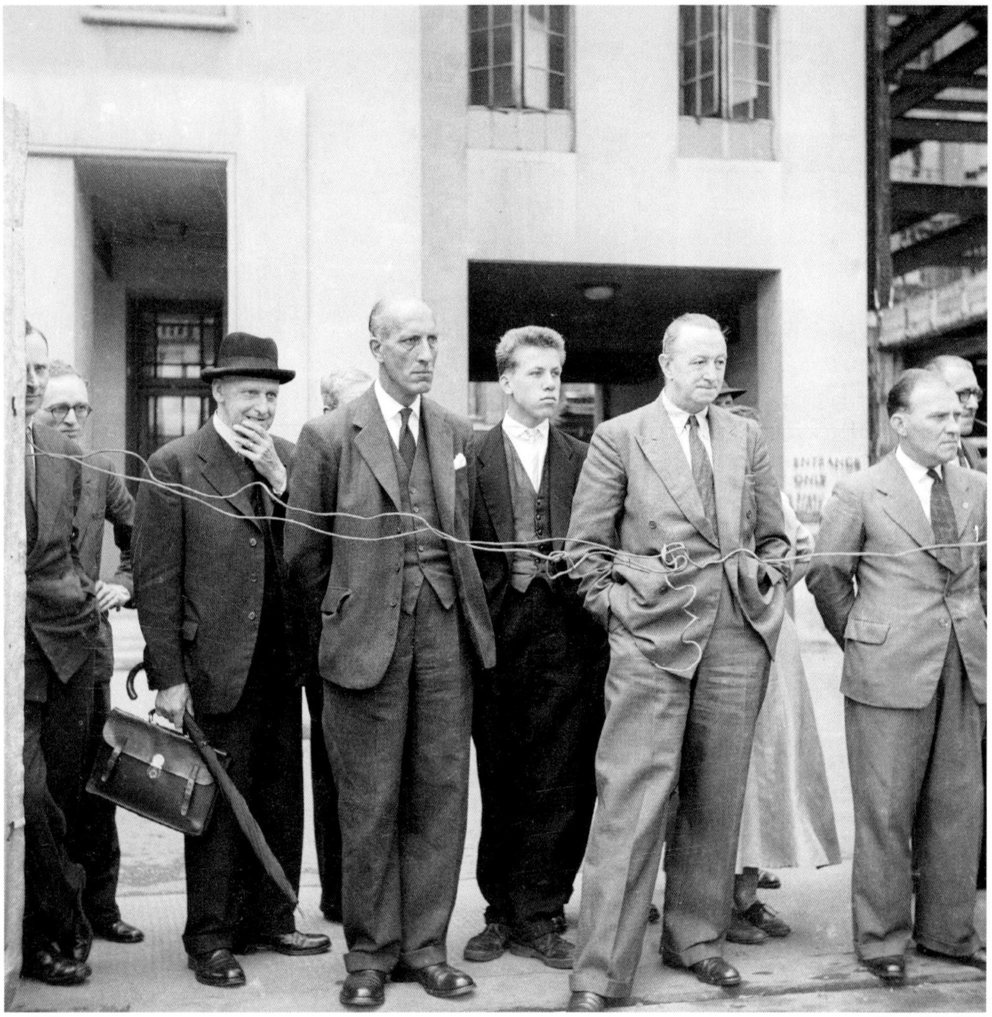

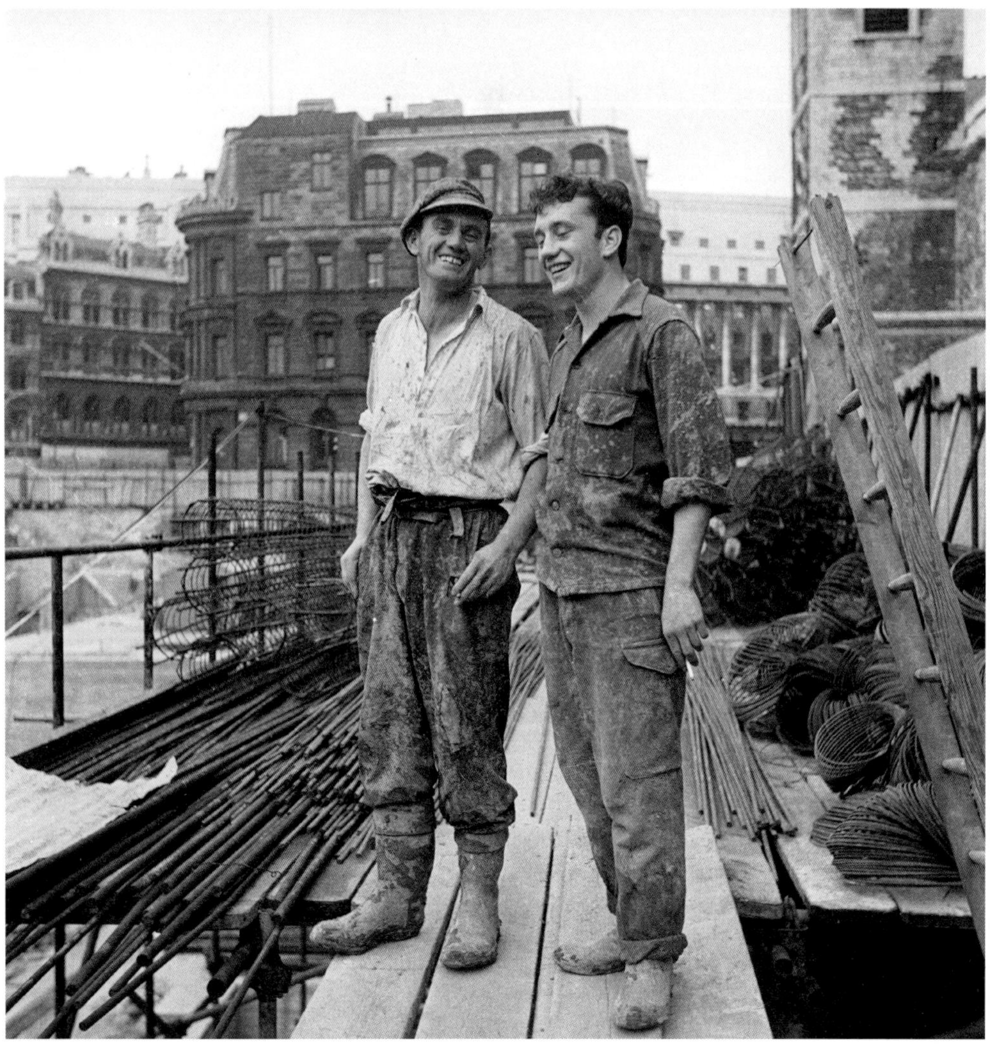

LEFT Businessmen watching the construction of a new building off Cannon Street, City of London EC4

BELOW Workers on a construction site off Cannon Street, City of London EC4

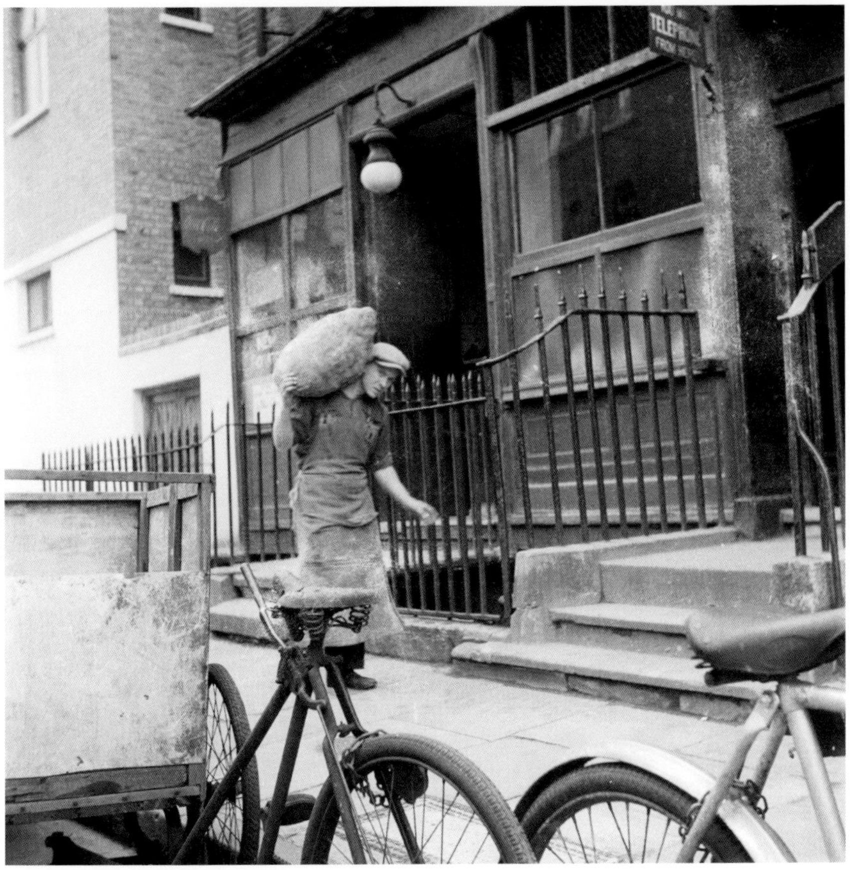

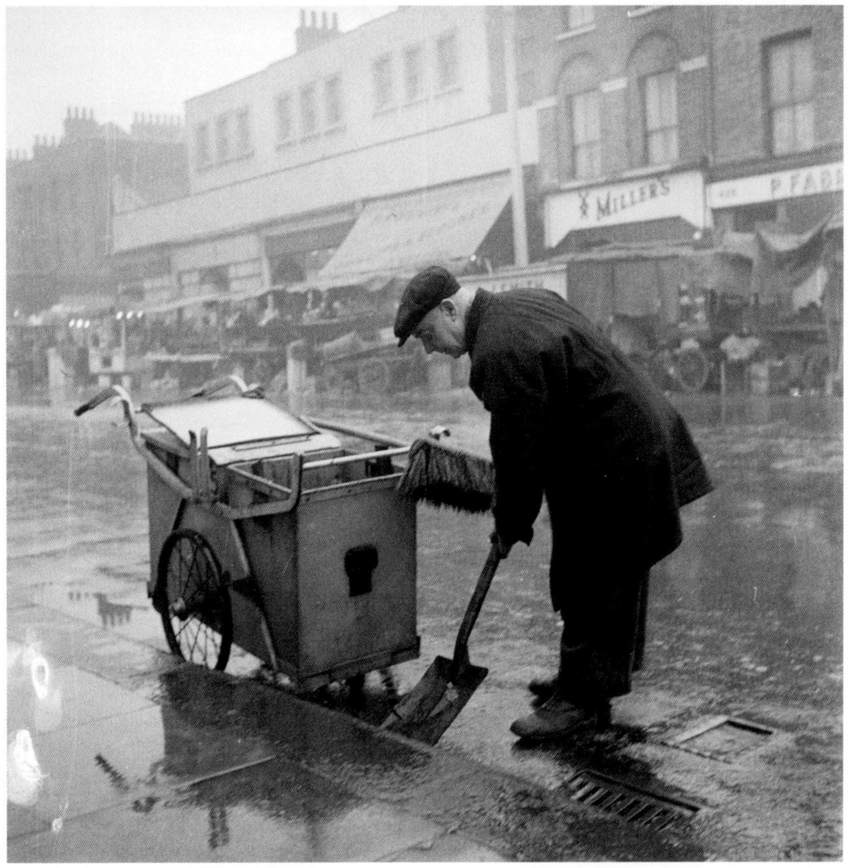

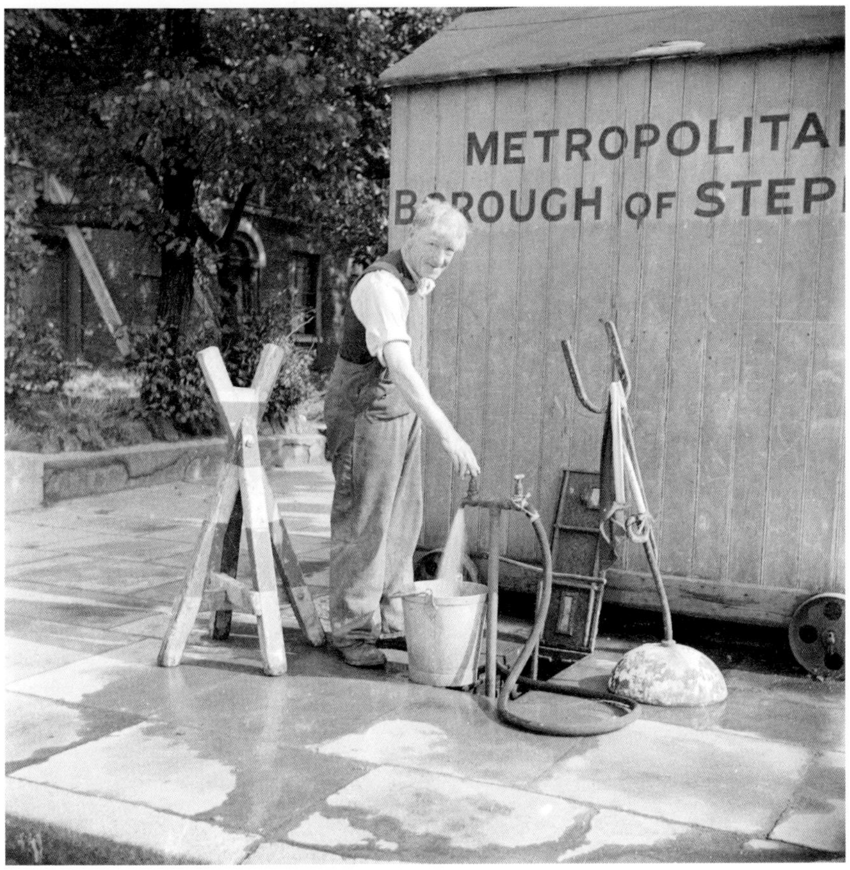

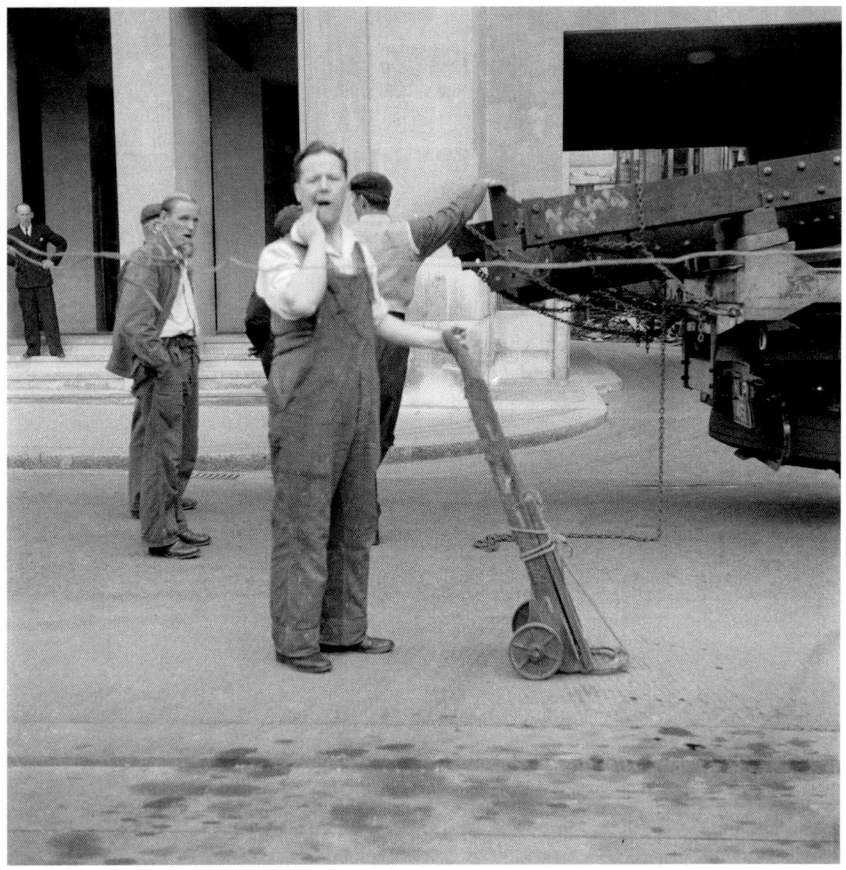

TOP RIGHT Street cleaner, Bethnal Green Road, Bethnal Green E2

BOTTOM RIGHT Delivery man, Cannon Street, City of London EC4

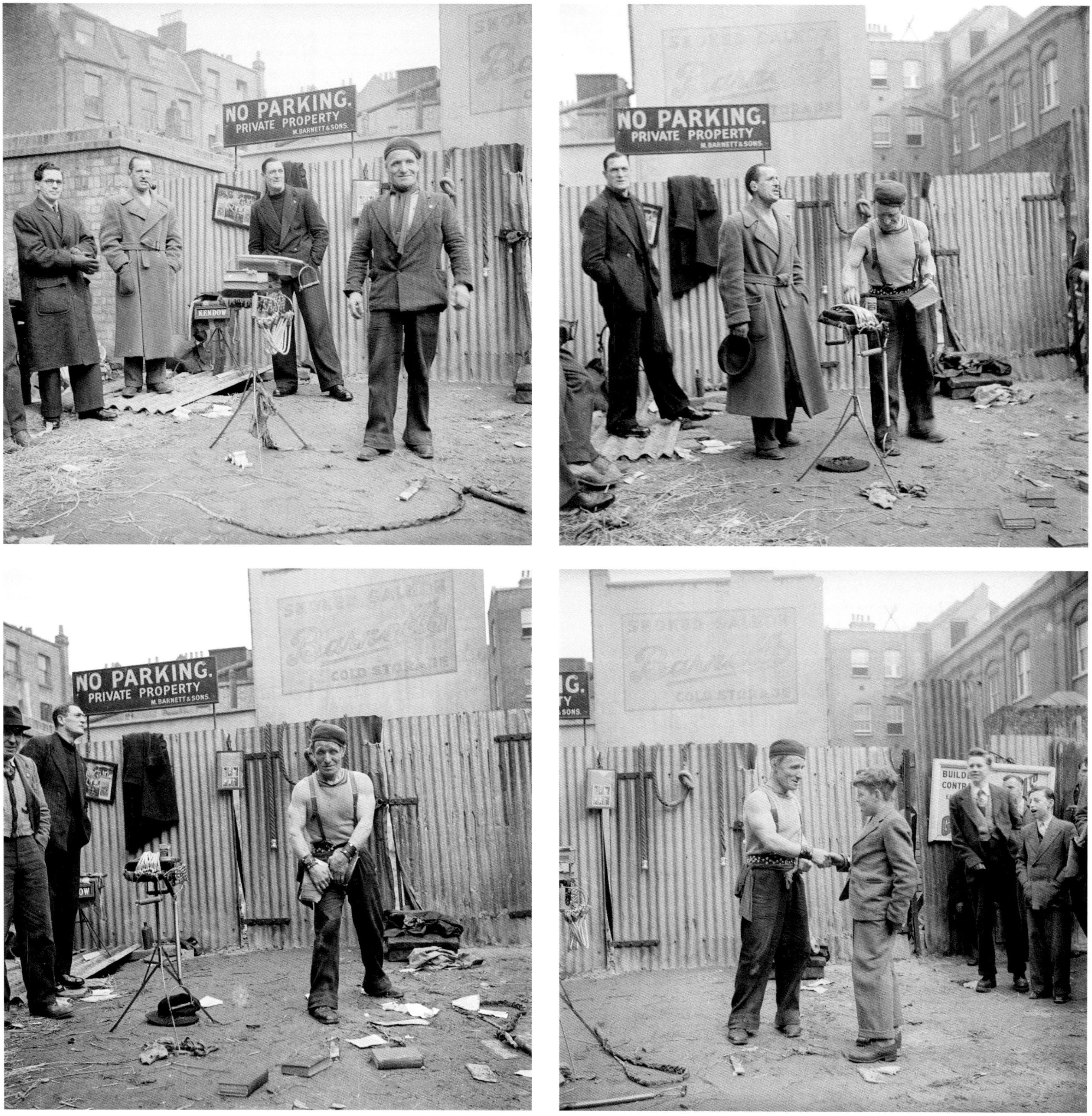

ABOVE *Kendow. Strongman*, off Petticoat Lane, Spitalfields E1 1952

OPPOSITE Crowd gathering around a policeman just off Petticoat Lane, Spitalfields E1 1952

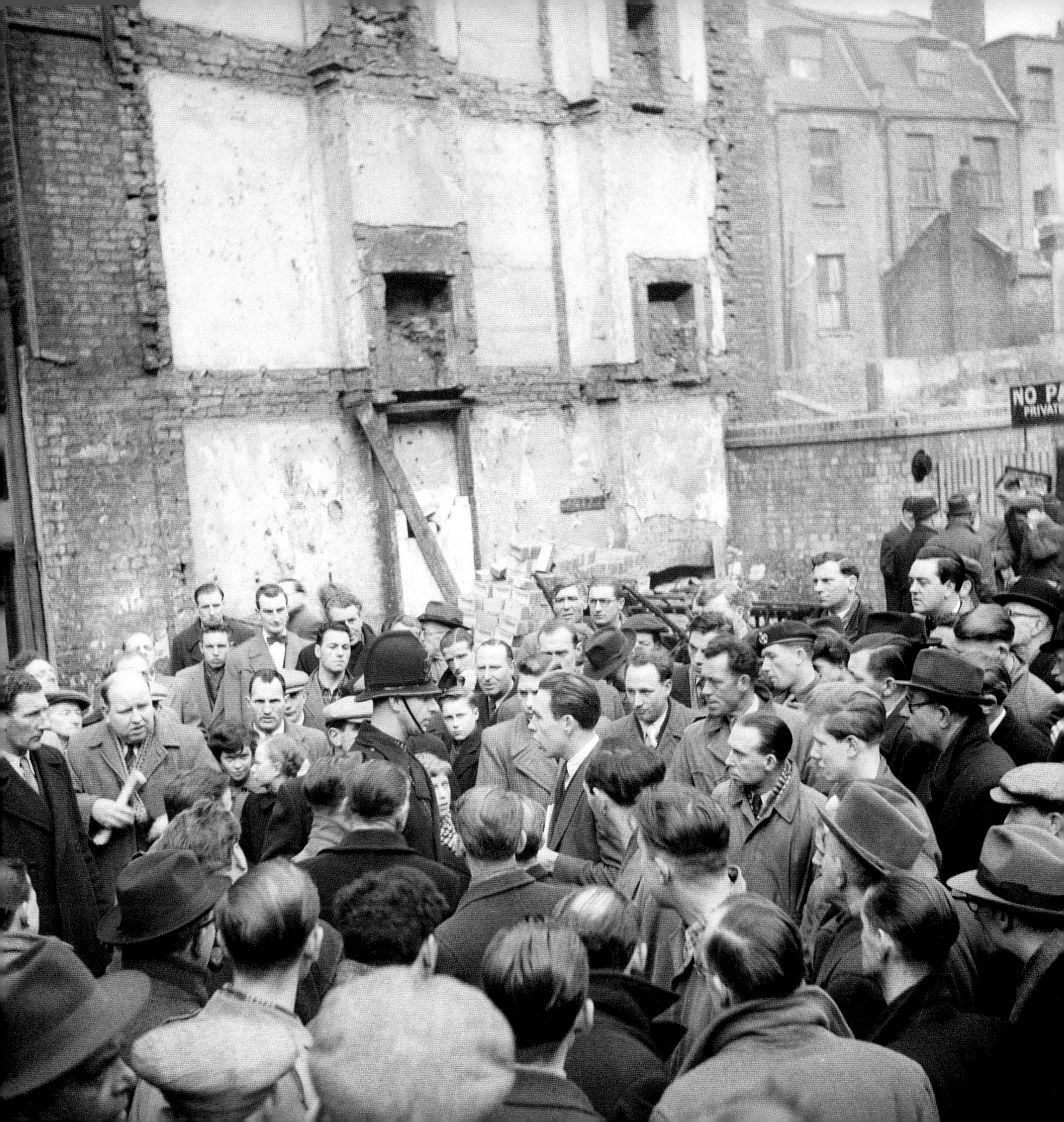
NO PA
PRIVAT

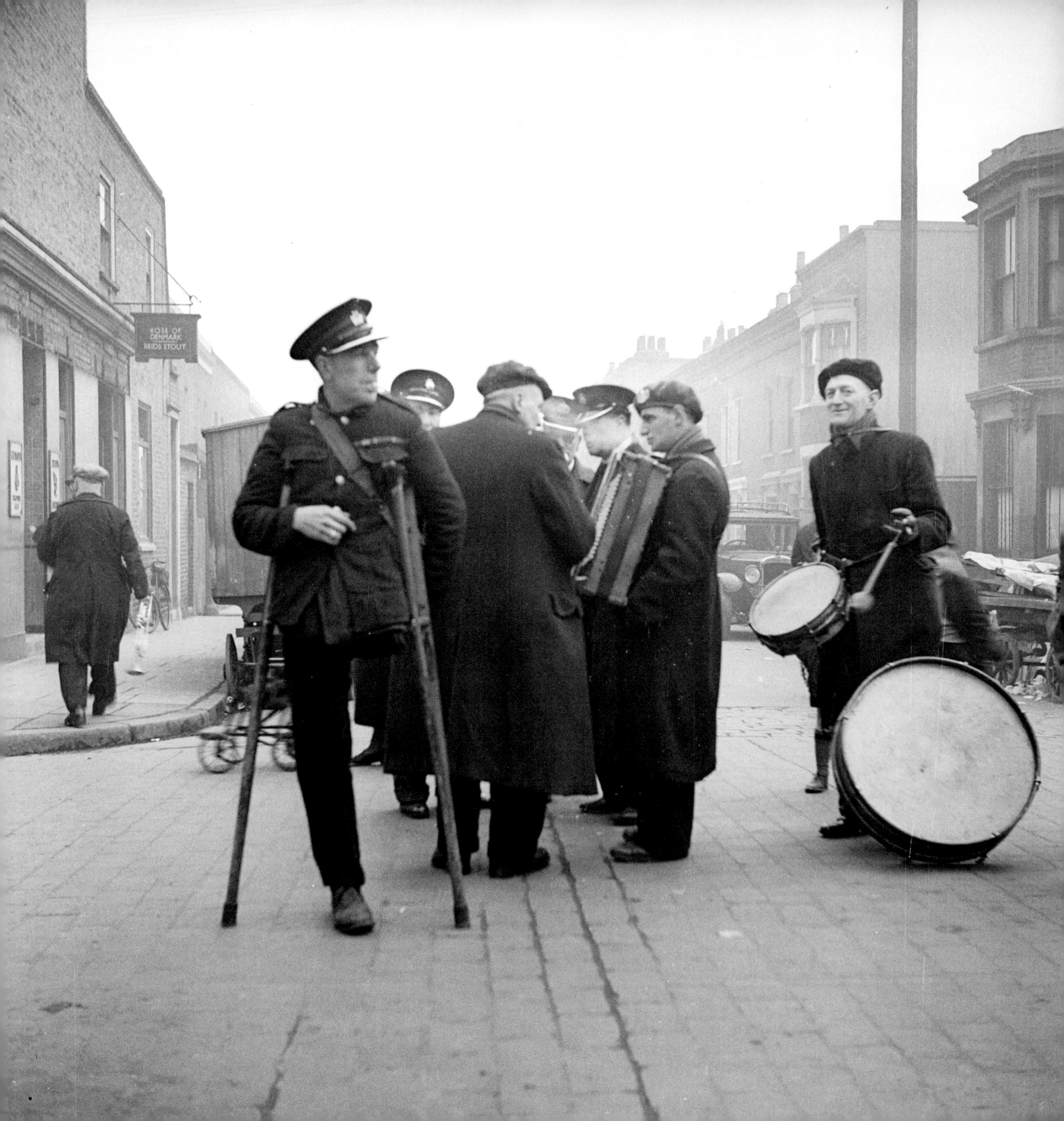
ROSE OF DENMARK
REIDS STOUT

'I wish, looking back, that I had been better technically; that I could have sung the song of every small blotch and blister, of every patch and stain on road and pavement surface, of step and rail and door and window frame. The patched garments, the creaky shoes, the worn bodies, the stout hearts and quirky independent spirit... the sheer capacity to get on with it of the disregarded... the humour and the fatalism of those trapped, possibly by choice in the small tribal liaisons of the back and side streets.'

Corner of Roman Road and Usher Road, Bow E3

CHRONOLOGY

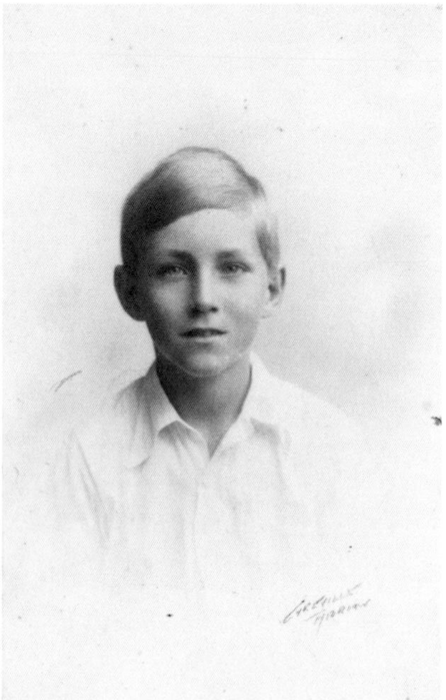
1

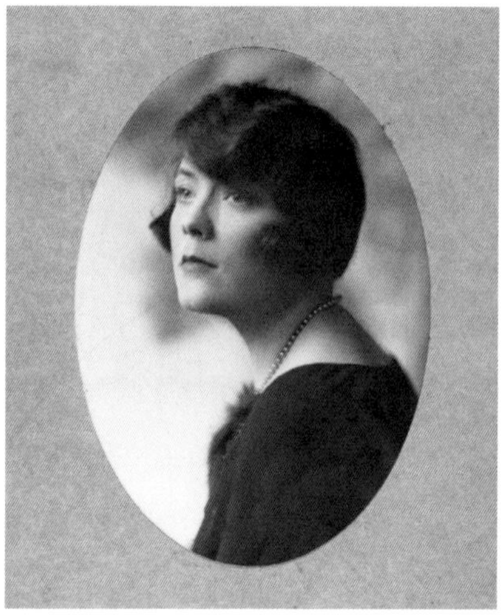
2

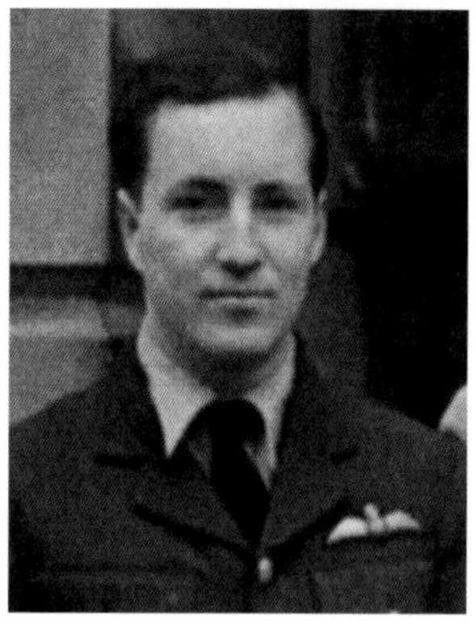
3

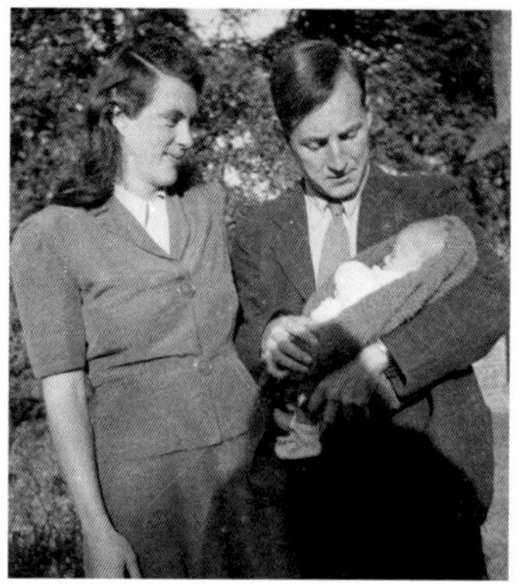
4

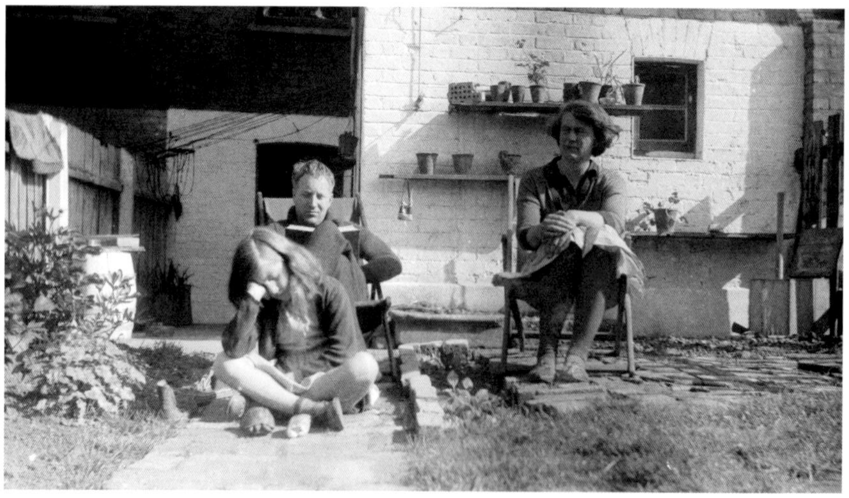
5

1917
Born St John's Wood, London to Kenneth Henderson and Winifred Ellen Lester (Wyn).

1924
Upon the divorce of his parents, moves, along with his older brother Ian, to Wimbledon Common to live with their paternal grandparents (fig.1).

1931
Starts Stowe School, Buckinghamshire but is asked to leave after just three years.

1933
Moves to London and lives with his mother, Wyn Henderson (fig.2), in Gordon Square, Bloomsbury where he meets the Bloomsbury Group.

1935
Studies biology at Chelsea Polytechnic where, dissecting frogs and examining specimens, he develops a keen interest in the microscopic.

1936
Leaves Chelsea Polytechnic early to work at the National Gallery, London as an assistant to Dr Helmut Ruhemann, their full-time picture restorer.

1938
His mother helps Peggy Guggenheim set-up and run the Guggenheim Jeune gallery, Cork Street, London and introduces him to the art world.

Introduced to Marcel Duchamp, who he goes on to help hang a Jean Cocteau exhibition at the Guggenheim Jeune gallery.

Two of his collages are included in an exhibition of collage work at the Guggenheim Jeune gallery, alongside artists such as Pablo Picasso, Georges Braque, Juan Gris, Max Ernst and Yves Tanguy.

1939–45
Serves as a pilot in Coastal Command during the Second World War (fig.3).

1943
Marries Judith Stephen (fig.4), daughter of Karin and Adrian Stephen (brother of Vanessa Bell and Virginia Woolf).

1945
Suffers a nervous breakdown after the war.

Moves to the Bethnal Green, London (fig.5), because of his wife's work on the 'Discover Your Neighbour' project with sociologist J.L. Peterson.

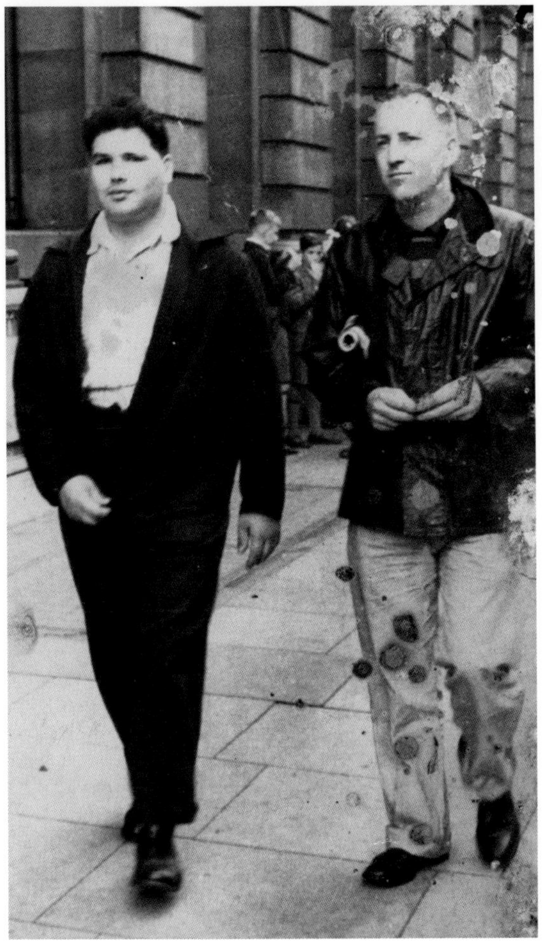

6

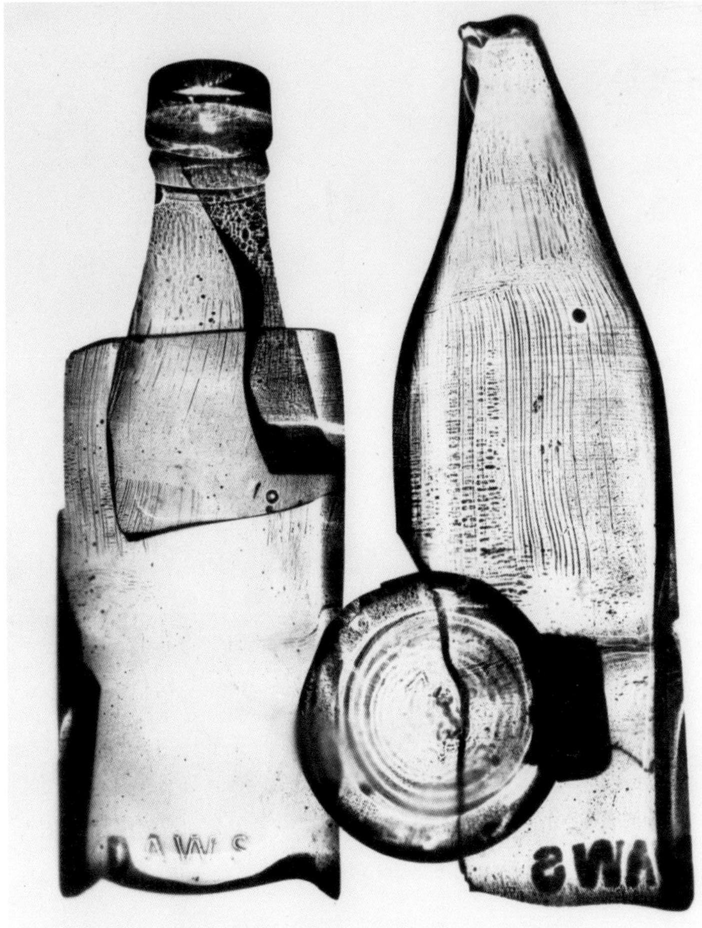

7

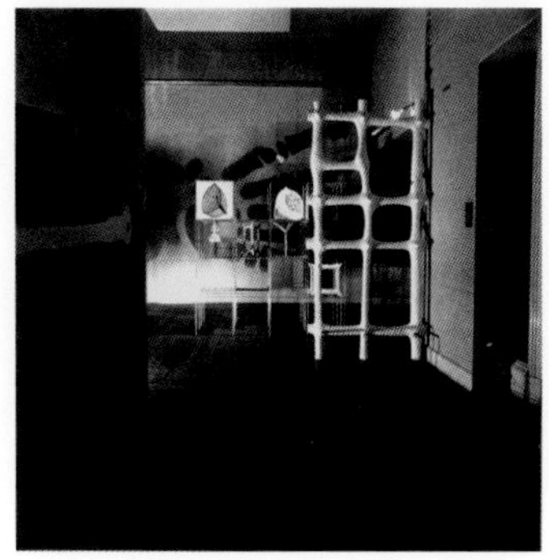

8

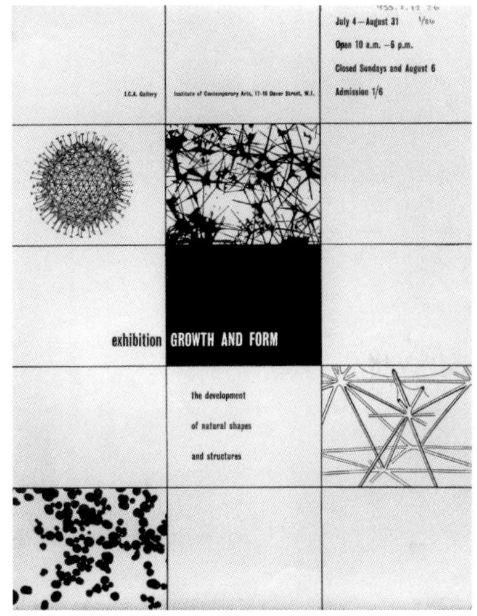

9

Starts at Slade School of Art, London where he becomes friends with fellow students Eduardo Paolozzi (fig.6) and William Turnball.

1947

Visits Paolozzi in Paris and meets Constantin Brâncusi, Alberto Giacometti, Georges Braque, Fernand Léger and Hans Arp.

Borrows a Leica camera from a Mr Humphrey Swingler, to document the Slade School of Art.

Photographs his daughter in Leonard Woolf's garden.

Meets and becomes friends with Richard Hamilton.

1949

Buys a Rolleicord (2¼ in. square negative) and a 5 x 4 plate camera.

Starts to photograph the East End, shooting shop fronts, local markets, children playing, workmen and surfaces, some of which would be used in collages, or on stressed prints.

Paolozzi gives him a photographic enlarger as a gift.

Starts to produce 'Hendograms' or photograms (fig.7).

1951

Visits Viticuso, Italy with Paolozzi where he photographs the town and surrounding area.

Undertakes photographic commissions for *Flair*, *Architectural Review*, *Vogue* (portraits of Cecil Collins), *Melody Maker* and Ronnie Scott.

Starts to produce stressed images using his enlarger and warping or creasing the paper while the image is being developed.

Appointed tutor of Creative Photography at London's Central School of Arts and Crafts.

Takes Henri Cartier-Bresson around the East End for a commission he is undertaking for *Illustrated*.

Photographs the Richard Hamilton exhibition *Growth and Form* at the Institute of Contemporary Arts (I.C.A.) (figs.8–9).

1952

Founds the Independent Group which includes Paolozzi, Turnball and Hamilton, the architects and designers Alison and Peter Smithson, James Stirling, Colin St John Wilson and Edward Wright, and the theorists Lawrence Alloway, Reyner Banham, Toni del Renzio and John McHale.

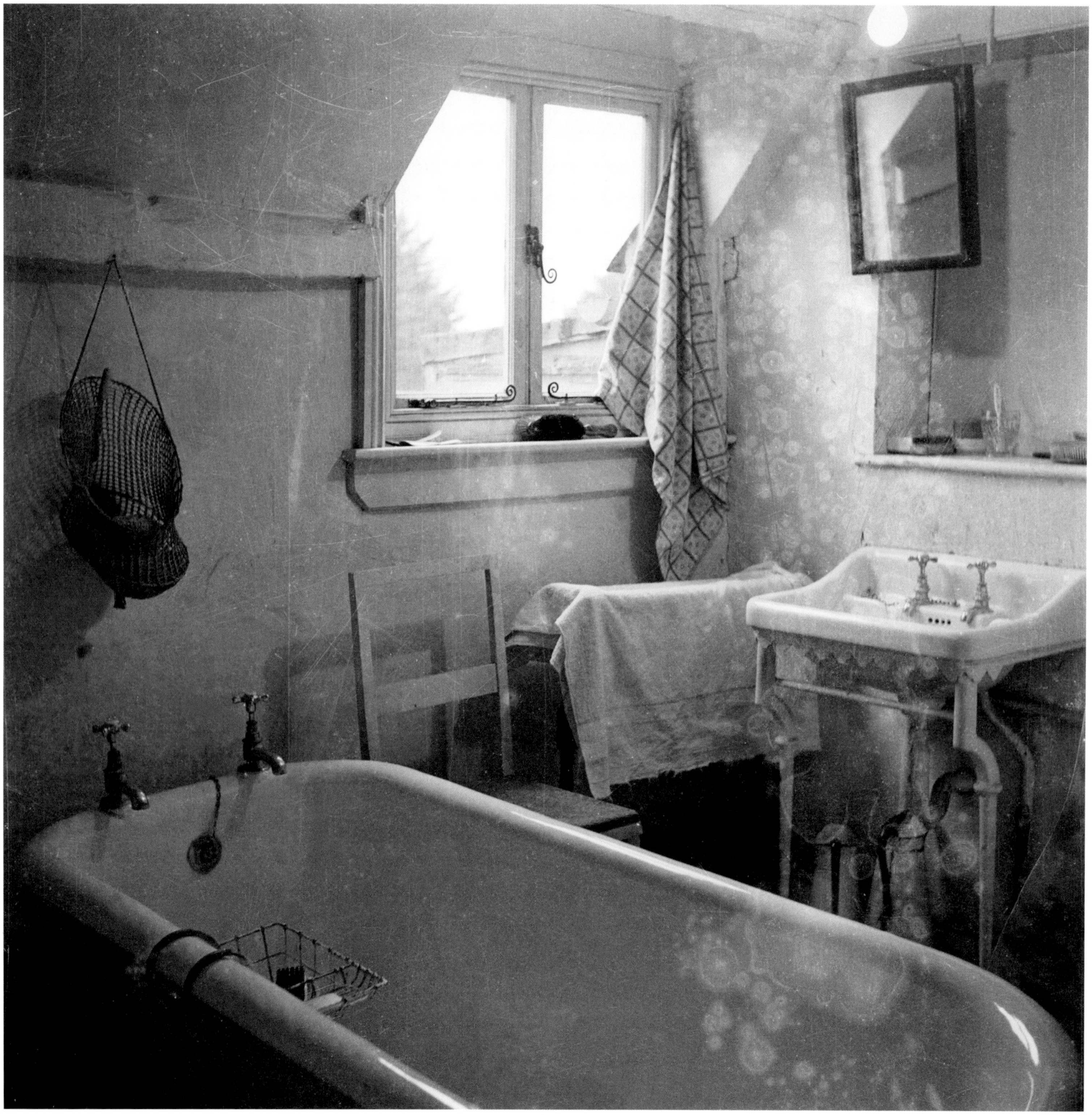

10

‘I started processing my work in “the bathroom” – a room I had persuaded the War Damage crew to install with a bath and sink. It was certainly the only bath with tapped water in the street and an electric water heater.’

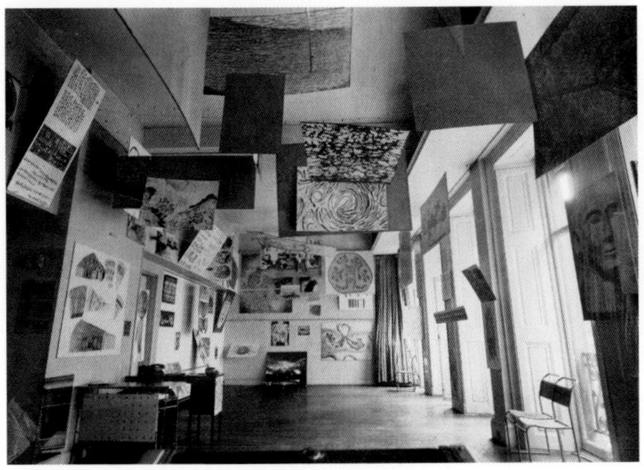

11

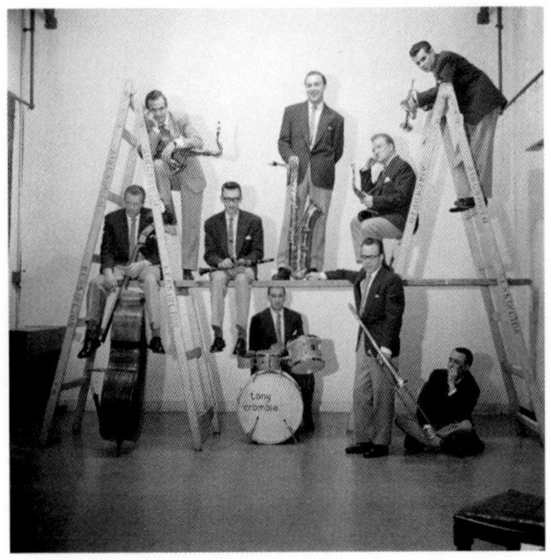

12

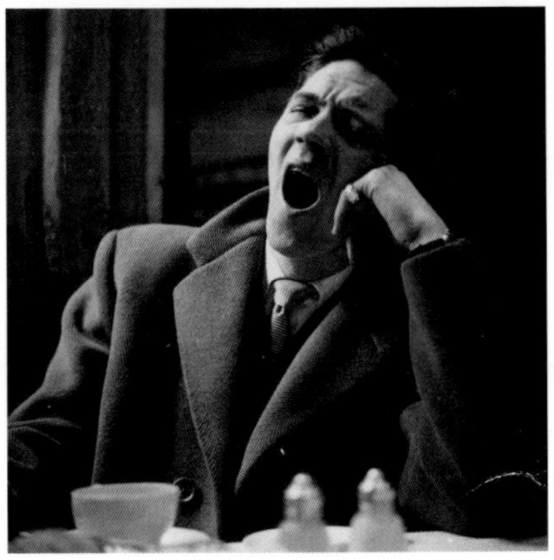

13

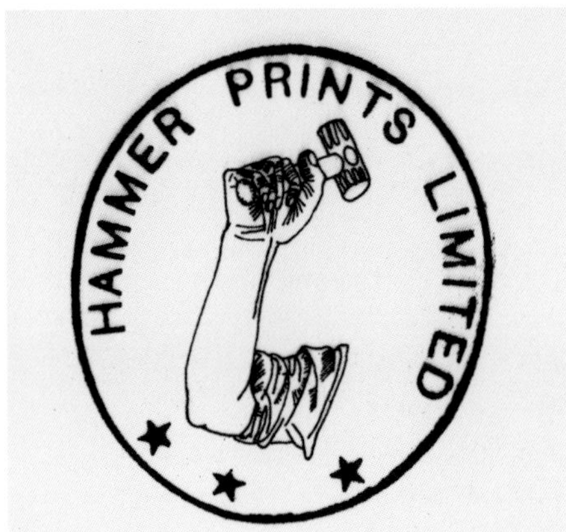

14

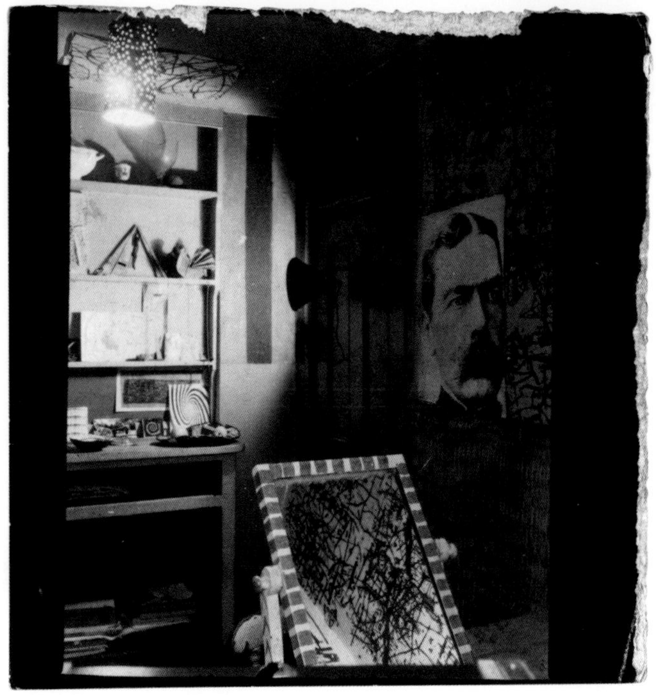

15

1953

Organises the exhibition *Parallel of Life and Art* at the I.C.A. with Paolozzi, Ronald Kenkins and the Smithsons (fig.11).

Seven photographs are displayed in the *Post-War European Photography* exhibition at the Museum of Modern Art (MoMA), New York, including three of the East End.

Photographs the American Jazz concert in aid of Canvey Island Flood Relief Fund.

Photographs Ronnie Scott's band and Jack Parnell (figs.12–13).

Photographs of children playing in Bethnal Green are used in the Smithson's presentation at the CIAM 9 (Congrès Internationaux d'Architecture Moderne) meeting held at Aix-en-Provence.

1954

Henderson family leaves Bethnal Green and moves to Landermere Quay, Essex, where they live in Judith Henderson's family home.

Paolozzi, and his wife Freda, move to Landermere Quay.

The Samuels family, documented by Judith Henderson and now family friends, moves to Landermere Quay.

Exhibition *Photo-Images* in the Members Room of the I.C.A.

Sets up Hammer Prints Ltd, a textile design company with Paolozzi (figs.14–15).

1956

Exhibition *This is Tomorrow* – a collaboration with Paolozzi and the Smithsons opens at the Whitechapel Art Gallery, London (figs.16–17).

1957

Starts teaching at Colchester School of Arts, Essex.

1960

Solo exhibition *Nigel Henderson* held at the School of Architecture, Cambridge University.

1961

Solo exhibition *Nigel Henderson Recent Work* at I.C.A. in London.

1965

Becomes Head of Photography at Norwich School of Art, Norfolk.

1972

Judith Henderson dies.

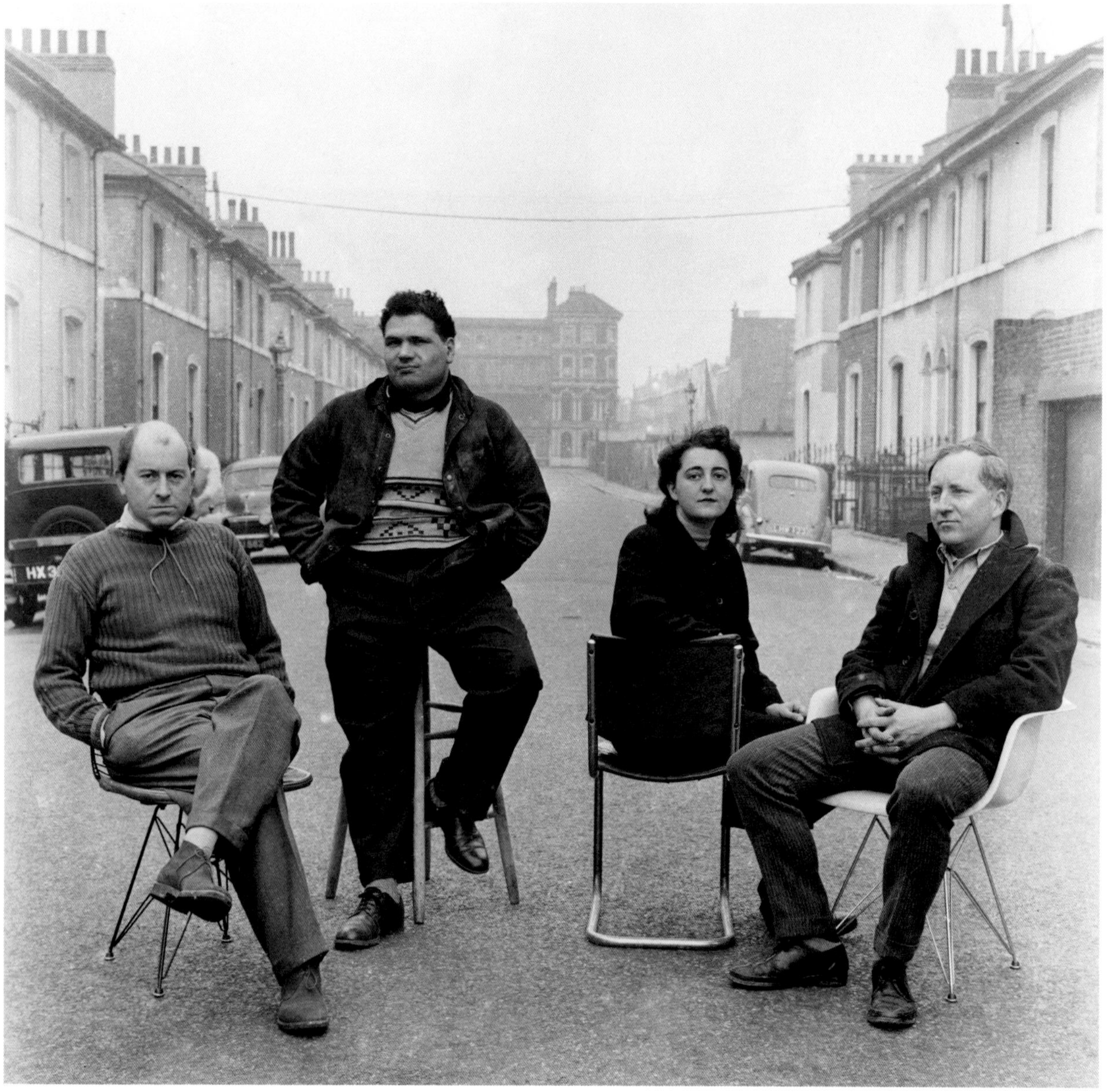

16

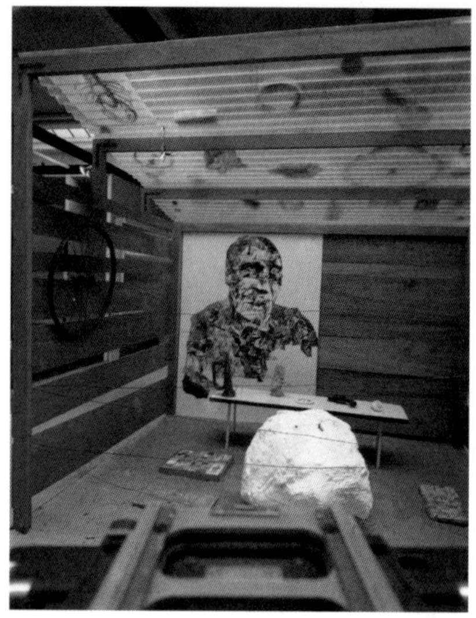

17

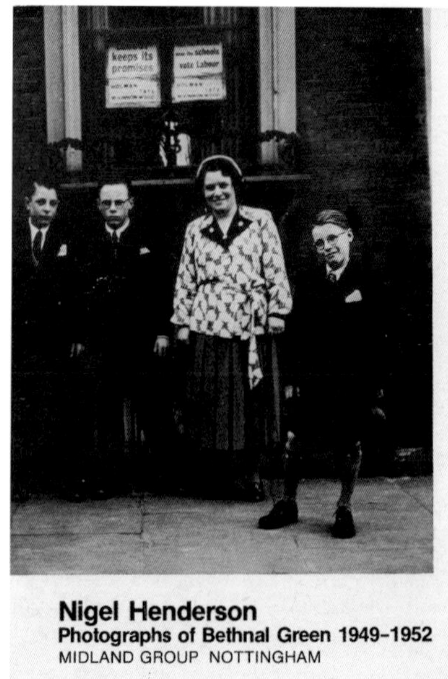

18

1977

Retrospective exhibition *Nigel Henderson: Photographs, Collages, Paintings* at Kettle's Yard, Cambridge.

Exhibition *Nigel Henderson: Paintings, Collages and Photographs* at Anthony d'Offay Gallery, London, which includes seventeen images of the East End of London.

1978

First and only exhibition based around photographs of the East End, *Nigel Henderson, Photographs of Bethnal Green 1949–1952*, at Midland Group Gallery, Nottingham (fig.18).

1982

Exhibition *Nigel Henderson*, including new works at Norwich School of Art, which subsequently travels to Sheffield and Southampton.

1983

Exhibition *Nigel Henderson – Head Shots: Self-Portraits and Imagined Landscapes 1960–1983* at Serpentine Gallery, London.

1985

Nigel Henderson dies in Thorpe-le-Soken, Essex.

1989

Exhibition *Nigel Henderson 1917–1986 Collages* at Birch & Conran, London.

1990

Group exhibition *The Independent Group: Postwar Britain and the Aesthetics of Plenty* at I.C.A., London

2001

Exhibition *Nigel Henderson: Parallel of Life and Art* at Gainsborough's House, Suffolk which subsequently travels to Sheffield, Edinburgh and London.

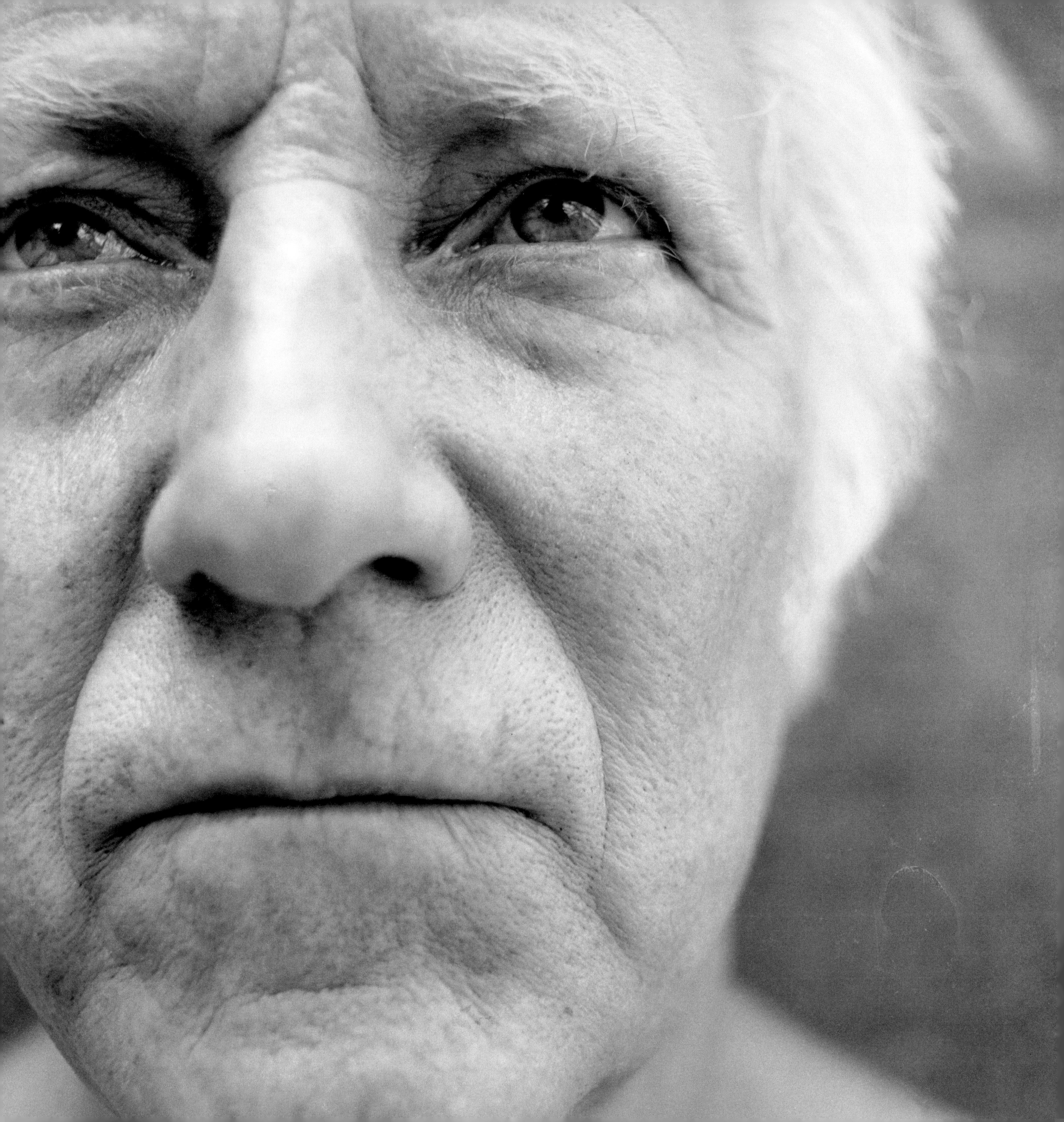

FURTHER READING

Michelle Cotton, *Nigel Henderson & Eduardo Paolozzi: Hammer Prints Ltd. 1954–1975*, 2nd edn, Colchester 2013

Nigel Henderson: Photographs, Collages & Paintings, exh. cat., Anthony d'Offay Gallery, London 1977

Nigel Henderson, Photographs of Bethnal Green 1949–1952, exh. cat., Midland Group, Nottingham 1978

Nigel Henderson: Head-lands, Self-portraits and Imagined Landscapes 1960–83, exh. cat., Serpentine Gallery, London 1983

Ben Highmore, 'Hopscotch Modernism: On everyday life and the blurring of art and social science', *Modernist Culture*, vol. 2, no. 1, May 2010, pp.70–79

Claude Lichtenstein and Thomas Schregenberger (eds.), *As Found: The Discovery of the Ordinary*, Zurich 2001

David Robbins (ed.), *The Independent Group: Postwar Britain and the Aesthetics of Plenty*, Cambridge, Massachusetts and London 1990

Victoria Walsh, *Nigel Henderson: Parallel of Life and Art*, London 2001

SOURCES OF QUOTES

Pages 7 and 11
Nigel Henderson, *Photographs of Bethnal Green 1949–1952*, exh. cat., Midland Group, Nottingham 1978, pp.1 and 3 respectively. ('Memories of London 1949' was originally published in T. Crosby (ed.), *Uppercase*, no. 3, London 1961.)

Page 20
'Notes on the Street': Nigel Henderson, in a letter to Mr Pearson dated 29 June 1956 (TGA 9211/2/30). Mr Pearson was an editor of 244 Magazine, School of Architecture, University of Manchester.

Page 34
Undated manuscript, Henderson Estate.

Pages 52 and 88
First draft of a prose poem on London written in 1949 for his friend Paolozzi. MS Henderson Collection (TGA 9211/4/3).

Page 70 (first quote)
Nigel Henderson and Chris Mullen, *Nigel Henderson*, exh. cat., Norwich School of Art 1982, p.27

Pages 70 (second quote), 105 and 108
Nigel Henderson, *Photographs of Bethnal Green 1949–1952*, exh. cat,, Midland Group, Nottingham 1978, pp.3, 55 and 5 respectively.

THE CONTRIBUTORS

Clive Coward

Clive Coward is Manager of Tate Images, the commercial picture library of Tate. He has previously managed British Museum Images and worked within the historical collections of the Wellcome Trust and Royal Geographical Society. He has a MA in English from the University of Sussex (1996–7) and a BA in Ancient History and Social Anthropology from University College London (1992–5).

Andrew Wilson

Andrew Wilson is Senior Curator of Modern and Contemporary British Art and Archives at Tate. Over the past twenty-five years his research has focused on post-war art and culture, often with a specific emphasis on wider countercultures. He is the author of *Richard Hamilton: Swingeing London 67 (f)* (Afterall 2011), and his essays have been published widely in books and exhibition catalogues. In 2016 he curated the major exhibition *Conceptual Art in Britain 1964–1979* at Tate Britain and edited the accompanying catalogue. He also co-curated the retrospective exhibition *David Hockney* at Tate Britain in 2017. He is a founding fellow of the London Institute of Pataphysics.

ACKNOWLEDGEMENTS

This publication would not have been possible without the help and support of many people. Firstly, my thanks go to the Henderson family – Jo, Ned and Stephen Henderson – for allowing us to produce this book, and for their continued support throughout. I would also like to thank Tate Archive and Tate Photography for their assistance; Rosie Ram, Henderson Archivist, for providing additional help with the quotes; and the Heritage Lottery Fund, for making the digitisation project possible.

I am grateful to Andrew Wilson for kindly writing the introduction; the staff at the Library and Archive in Bishopsgate Institute who provided access to their collection; and to Martin Parr for his enthusiastic response to the book.

Thanks to Peter Dawson of Grade Design for making the book look so wonderful, and at Tate Enterprises: Bill Jones, Jacky Klein, Elizabeth Lovatt, Emma O'Neill, Emma Poulter, John Stachiewicz, Jonas Vanbuel and Laura Wright, all of whom played a part in commissioning, producing or supporting this publication. In particular, thank you to my colleagues at Tate Images: Louise Burley, Chris Sutherns, William Swainger and David Thompson for their patience and support.

Finally, I would like to thank Gillian Pritchard and Peter La Monica for their enthusiasm and encouragement throughout this project.

CREDITS

Every effort has been made to trace the copyright holders of the images reproduced in this book. The publisher would like to apologise for any omissions or errors and, on notification, would be happy to make corrections in future reprints of this title.

All of the images reproduced in this book are © Nigel Henderson Estate / Tate Archive, unless otherwise stated.

Nigel Henderson's collection was generously presented to Tate Archive in two parts – first in 1992 by Janet Henderson and the Henderson family (TGA 9211), and then in 2010 by Jo, Ned and Stephen Henderson and the Henderson families (TGA 201011/3/1). The vast majority of images in this book come from the latter gift.

Each item in the Henderson collection has its own Tate Archive (TGA) number. The numbers for the images reproduced in this book are provided in the following list. The majority of images are from the TGA 201011/3/1 collection, where the first number relates to the contact sheet and negative roll and is followed by the individual negative number. Those that begin with an * are from the TGA 9211 collection.

The Tate Archive numbers can be used to search online at: http://www.tate.org.uk. The numbers in brackets refer to the digital images which can be searched or licensed via the Tate Images website at http://www.tate-images.com. The image references are listed in order of appearance, working clockwise from the top left.

Front cover 146/2 (MB2870)
Back cover 92/9 (MB2234)
*9/6/66 (MA7605)
122/1 (MB2582)

Page
2 131/6 (MB2695)
6 44/1 (MB1773)
8 143/6 (MB2838)
10 *8/1/9/2VMA7282)
12 P79309
P79310
13 Library of Congress Prints and Photographs Division
14 T07109 © ADAGP, Paris and DACS, London 2017
P77161 © ADAGP, Paris and DACS, London 2017
15 144/3 (MB2847)
146/6 (MB2874)
117/12 (MB2533)
128/11 (MB2664)
144/2 (MB2846)
44/1 (MB1773)
17 *5/2/93 (MA7220) © The estate of Nigel Henderson & © reserved
18 T12444 © Trustees of the Paolozzi Foundation, Licensed by DACS 2016 / © Nigel Henderson Estate / Tate Archive
21 92/11 (MB2236)
22 92/12 (MB2237)
92/6 (MB2231)
23 92/10 (MB2235)
24 92/8 (MB2233)
25 93/5 (MB2242)
92/5 (MB2230)
92/9 (MB2234)
92/3 (MB2228)
26 94/1 (MB2250)
27 93/4 (MB2241)
28 99/4 (MB2310)
*9/6/123 (MA7663)
94/7 (MB2256)
93/2 (MB2239)
29 93/3 (MB2240)
93/1 (MB2238)
93/12 (MB2249)
128/7 (MB2660)
30 119/1 (MB2546)
31 6/8 (MB1383)
128/10 (MB2663)
32 137/1 (MB2762)
102/1 (MB2343)
102/2 (MB2344)
33 137/4 (MB2765)
7/3 (MB1390)
*9/6/74 (MA7613)
138/6 (MB2779)
35 130/7 (MB2684)
36 80/8 (MB2104)
37 143/3 (MB2835)
38 130/10 (MB2687)

39 128/12 (MB2665)
57/10 (MB1932)
124/3 (MB2608)
143/7 (MB2839)
40 142/11 (MB2831)
133/4 (MB2717)
139/11 (MB2796)
124/9 (MB2614)
41 81/4/1/MB2108
146/4 (MB2872)
42 55/7 (MB1905)
43 56/7 (MB1917)
44 133/12 (MB2725)
45 142/1 (MB2821)
44/3 (MB1775)
46 140/11 (MB2808)
124/8 (MB2613)
146/2 (MB2870)
142/10 (MB2830)
47 146/8 (MB2876)
48 120/11 (MB2568)
49 *9/6/13 (MA7558)
50 126/12 (MB2641)
85/3 (MB2149)
51 127/8 (MB2649)
53 5/1 (MB1364)
54 125/6 (MB2623)
138/10 (MB2783)
50/11 (MB1852)
7/2 (MB1389)
55 *9/6/60 (MA7599)
45/6 (MB1788)
130/5 (MB2682)
56 125/4 (MB2621)
45/11 (MB1793)
57 6/1 (MB1376)
58 *9/6/66 (MB7605)
140/10 (MB2807)
147/5 (MB2885)
133/3 (MB2716)
59 124/12 (MB2617)
124/7 (MB2612)
60 114/12 (MB2497)
113/9 (MB2482)
115/1 (MB2498)
122/3 (MB2584)
61 117/6 (MB2527)
62 113/6 (MB2479)
63 115/2 (MB2499)
119/6 (MB2551)
116/1 (MB2510)
115/3 (MB2500)
64 112/12 (MB2473)
65 112/11 (MB2472)
*6/20 (MA7565)
116/9 (MB2518)
116/12 (MB2521)
66 113/4 (MB2477)
67 114/4 (MB2489)
68 114/8 (MB2493)
115/8 (MB2505)
122/10 (MB2591)
115/9 (MB2506)
69 114/5 (MB2490)
71 *9/6/16 (MA7561)
72 55/9 (MB1907)
73 132/8 (MB2709)
44/4 (MB1776)
74 117/8 (MB2529)
117/9 (MB2530)
117/7 (MB2528)
57/7 (MB1929)
75 44/5 (MB1777)
76 137/8 (MB2769)
77 136/1 (MB2750)
142/2 (MB2822)
78 107/1 (MB2403)
105/7 (MB2385)
106/5 (MB2395)
106/9 (MB2399)
79 117/12 (MB2533)
146/6 (MB2874)

128/11 (MB2664)
*9/6/39 (MA7584)
80 144/3 (MB2847)
81 90/1 (MB2206)
82 90/4 (MB2209)
88/3 (MB2184)
90/5 (MB2210)
80/7 (MB2103)
83 87/1 (MB2170)
81/2 (MB2106)
87/6 (MB2175)
146/3(MB2871)
84 82/8 (MB2124)
85 85/9 (MB2155)
86 54/1 (MB1887)
*9/6/48 (MB7587)
54/2 (MB1888)
*9/6/51 (MB7590)
87 54/5 (MB1891)
89 53/4 (MB1879)
90 121/2 (MB2571)
122/11 (MB2592)
121/4 (MB2573)
121/10 (MB2579)
91 123/10 (MB2603)
92 114/7 (MB2492)
93 110/6 (MB2444)
123/11 (MB2604)
94 *9/6/28 (MA7573)
95 122/1(MB2582)
109/6 (MB2432)
96 122/2 (MB2583)
97 122/7 (MB2588)
98 *9/6/14/1 (MA7559)
95/8 (MB2269)
137/9 (MB2770)
6/9 (MB1384)
99 45/3 (MB1785)
53/6 (MB1881)
100 129/9 (MB2674)
119/12 (MB2557)
101 145/9 (MB2865)
121/11 (MB2580)
46/6 (MB1799)
121/5 (MB2574)
102 52/3 (MB1866)
51/7 (MB1860)
52/2 (MB1865)
51/5 (MB1858)
103 52/6 (MB1869)
104 *9/6/84 (MA7623)
106 FIG.1: Studio portrait of Nigel Henderson as a boy. J. H. Greville (Marlow, UK) c.1920s. Black and white photograph 15 x 10. *8/1/1 (MA7251)

FIG.2: Studio portrait of Wyn Henderson. Knightsbridge Studios (London, UK) c.1920s. Black and white photograph 16.5 x 11.5 *8/2/7 (MA7407)

FIG.3: Nigel and Judith Henderson on their wedding day. Unknown photographer 1943. Black and white photograph, dimensions unknown. Tate Archive

FIG.4: Nigel and Judith Henderson holding a baby – probably Drusilla (also known as Jo) or Justin. Unknown photographer c.1944–46. Black and white photograph 9.5 x 5. *8/1/5 (MA7256) © reserved

FIG.5: Nigel, Judith and Drusilla (Jo) Henderson in the garden of 46 Chisenahle Road, Bethnal Green. Unknown photographer c.1952. Black and white photograph 8 x 13. *8/1/11 (MA7285) © reserved

107 FIG.6: Nigel Henderson and Eduardo Paolozzi. Unknown photographer c.1947. Black and white photograph 9.5 x 5. *8/1/6 (MA7257) © reserved

FIG.7: Photogram of a milk bottle. Nigel Henderson 1949–51. Black and white photograph 16.3 x 12. *10/4 (MA8178)

FIG.8: Installation shot of the *Growth and Form* exhibition at the I.C.A. Nigel Henderson 1951. Black and white photograph, dimensions unknown. *9/5/12 (MO0310)

FIG.9: *Growth and Form* poster. Unknown artist 1951. Print on paper 97.3 x 52.1. (MO0412) © I.C.A. /held at Tate Archive

108 FIG.10: Bathroom interior. Nigel Henderson 1949–53. Black and white photograph 5.5 x 5.5. *9/6/101 (MA7640)

109 FIG.11: Installation view of *Parallel of Life and Art* exhibition. Nigel Henderson 1953. Black and white photograph 11.5 x 16. *5/2/83 (MA7210)

FIG.12: Jazz musicians including Jimmy Deuchar, Ken Wray, Ronnie Scott, Tony Crombie, Lennie Bush, Peter King, Derek Humble and Benny Green. Nigel Henderson c.1949–56. Black and white photograph 5.5 x 5.5. 158/2 (MB2980)

FIG.13: Jack Parnell in a restaurant. Nigel Henderson c.1949–56. Black and white photograph 5.5 x 5.5. 176/5 (MB3188)

FIG.14: Hammer Prints Ltd logo c.1954–61. 6/1/1 (MO1068)

FIG.15: Interior of Henderson's house at 46 Chisenhale Road. Nigel Henderson c.1949–54. Black and white photograph 10 x 10. *9/6/124 (MA7664)

110 FIG.16: Nigel Henderson, Eduardo Paolozzi, Alison and Peter Smithson. Unknown photographer c.1949–56. Black and white photograph 12 x 9. 73/4 (MB2074)

FIG.17: An installation shot of the Patio and Pavilion installation from *This is Tomorrow* exhibition at the Whitechapel Art Gallery. Nigel Henderson 1956. Black and white photograph, dimensions unknown. (MO0159)

FIG.18: Front cover of *Nigel Henderson, Photographs of Bethnal Green 1949–1952*, exh. cat., Midland Group, Nottingham 1978

111 Nigel Henderson head shot. Nigel Henderson, date unknown. Black and white photograph 5.5 x 5.5. *8/1/19/52 (MA7363) © reserved

120 Nigel Henderson's hand. Nigel Henderson, date unknown. Black and white photograph 5.5 x 5.5.*8/1/19/58 (MA7369) © reserved

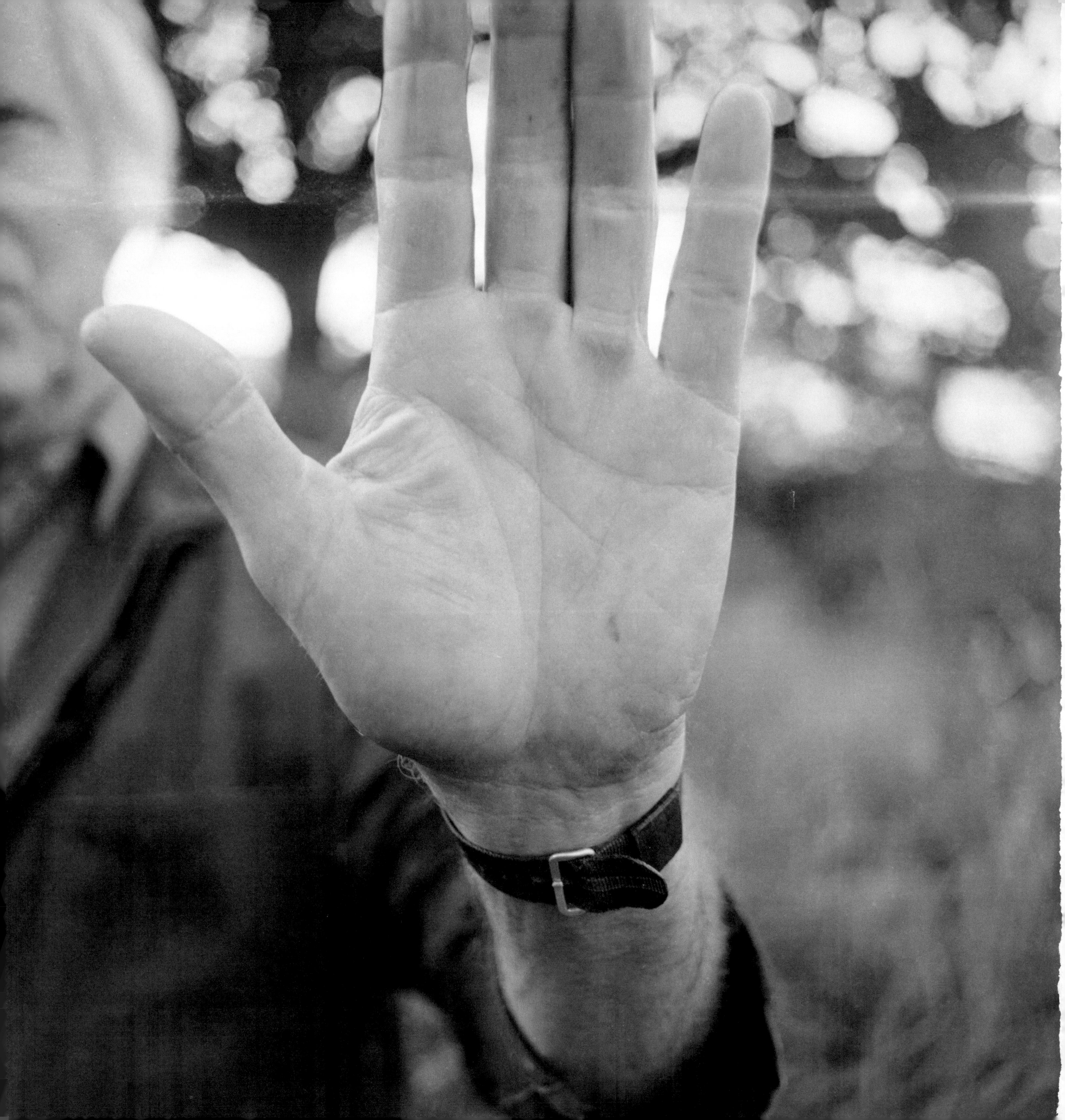

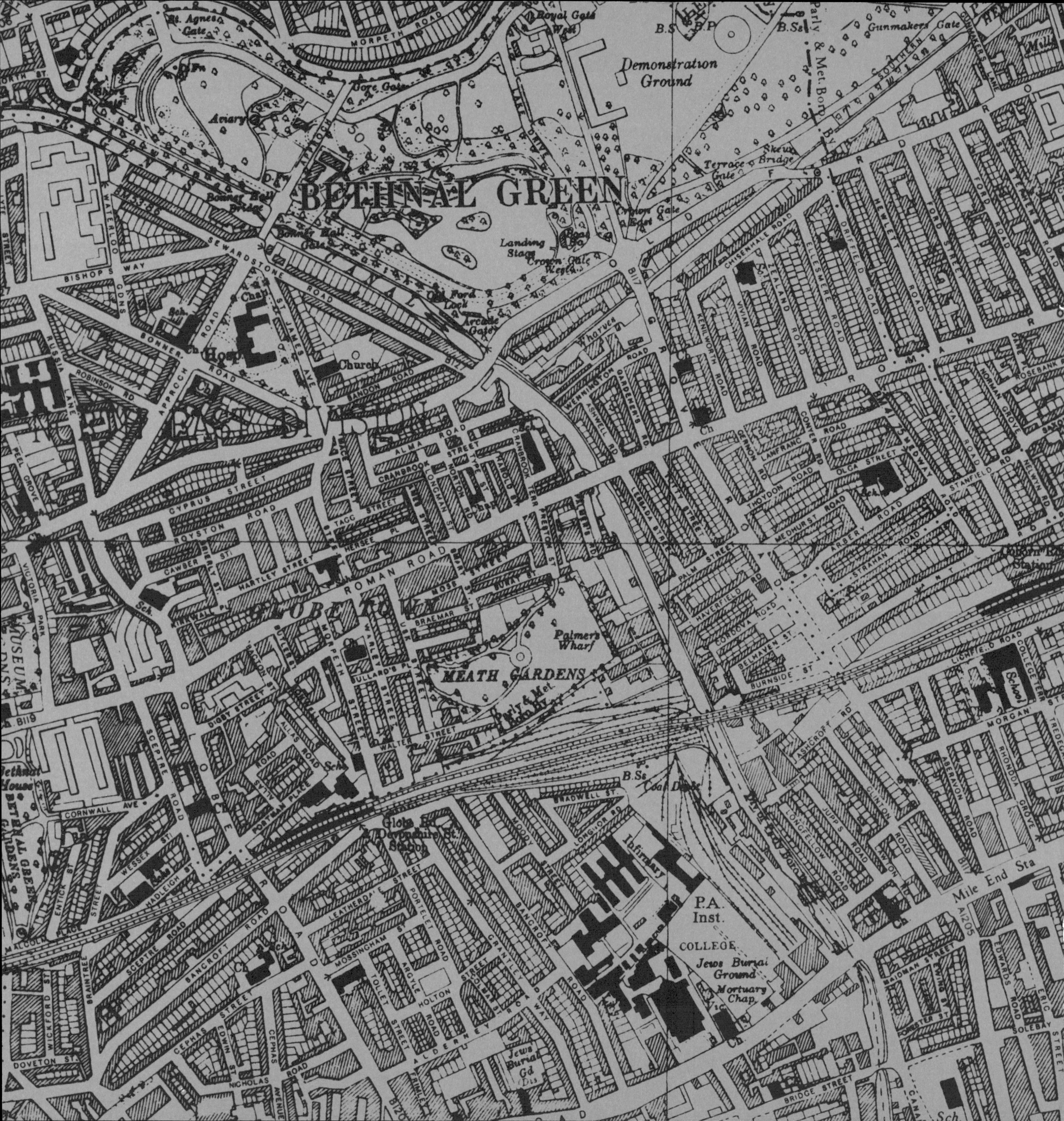
BETHNAL GREEN
EAST DIVISION
GLOBE TOWN
MEATH GARDENS
Demonstration Ground
St. Agnes Gate
Royal Gate West
Gunmakers Gate
Gore Gate
Aviary
Bonner Hall Bridge
Bonner Hall Gate
Terrace Gate
Skew Bridge
Crown Gate East
Crown Gate West
Landing Stage
Old Ford Lock
Arcade Gate
Wharves
Palmers Wharf
MORPETH ROAD
SEWARDSTONE ROAD
BISHOPS WAY
BONNER ROAD
APPROACH ROAD
ST. JAMES AVE
BANDON ROAD
ALMA ROAD
CYPRUS STREET
ROYSTON ROAD
ROMAN ROAD
HARTLEY STREET
CAWBER ST
VICTORIA PARK
PEEL GROVE
RUSSIA LANE
ROBINSON RD
WATERLOO GDNS
Church
Hosp.
Chap.
Sch.
WENNINGTON ROAD
GARDENERS RD
ASHWELL RD
CHISENHALE ROAD
KENILWORTH ROAD
VIVIAN ROAD
ZEALAND ROAD
ELLESMERE ROAD
DRIFFIELD ROAD
HEWLETT ROAD
FORD ROAD
NORMAN GROVE
ROSEBANK RD
LYAL ROAD
CONYER ROAD
LAMFRANC RD
OLGA STREET
MEDWAY ROAD
STANFIELD RD
THOYDON ROAD
MEDHURST ST
ARBERY ROAD
STRAHAN ROAD
PALM STREET
HAVERFIELD RD
CORDOVA ROAD
BELMAVEN ST
BURNSIDE ST
LICHFIELD ROAD
COLLEGE TERR
School
MORGAN ST
TREDEGAR
ASHCROFT RD
ABERAVON ROAD
RHONDDA GROVE
LONGFELLOW ROAD
JUPPS ROAD
CLINTON ROAD
Mile End Sta
P.A. Inst.
COLLEGE
Jews Burial Ground
Mortuary Chap.
Infirmary
BRADWELL ST
LONGNOR RD
MOODY STREET
BANCROFT ROAD
Coal Depot
B.Ss
Globe Rd. Devonshire St. Station
PORTMAN PLACE
CORNWALL AVE
WESSEX ST
HADLEIGH ST
SCEPTRE ROAD
GLOBE ROAD
DIGBY STREET
ALLAS ROAD
WALTER STREET
BULLARD'S PL
MORPETH STREET
BRAEMAR ST
LEATHERDALE STREET
PORTELET ROAD
MOSSINGHAM ST
TOLLET STREET
ARGYLE ROAD
HOLTON ROAD
ALDERNEY ROAD
Jews Burial Gd
CEPHAS STREET
EDWIN ST
NICHOLAS ROAD
DOVETON ST
WICKFORD ST
BRAINTREE ST
MALCOLM PLACE
ENTICK ST
BANCROFT ROAD
BRIDGE STREET
MAIDMAN STREET
EWING ST
EDWARDS ROAD
ERIC STREET
SOLEBAY STREET
FORSTER ST
Bethnal House
BETHNAL GREEN GARDENS
MUSEUM
Parly & Met. Boro. Bdy.